American Quilts, Quilting, and Patchwork

An
Early American Society
Book

American Quilts, Quilting, and Patchwork

Adelaide Hechtlinger

stackpole books

AMERICAN QUILTS, QUILTING, AND PATCHWORK

Copyright © 1974 by
Adelaide Hechtlinger

Published by
STACKPOLE BOOKS
Cameron and Kelker Streets
Harrisburg, Pa. 17105

Printed in U.S.A.

Library of Congress Cataloging in Publication Data

Hechtlinger, Adelaide.
    American quilts, quilting, and patchwork.

    1. Quilting--United States. 2. Patchwork--United
States. I. Title.
TT835.H38   746.9'7   74-13398
ISBN 0-8117-0092-5

Contents

PART II — QUILT BASICS

PART III — QUILTS TODAY

PART IV — QUILTS ON DISPLAY

ACKNOWLEDGMENTS

RESOURCE MATERIAL

INDEX

Introduction

THE PIECED QUILT, often mentioned in American literature, is part of our American heritage. Mrs. Wiggs of Cabbage Patch fame said that when one was piecing quilts, one was "keepin' the peace and doin' away with the scraps."

Quilting, Grandma's work of necessity, has become today's folk hobby. People all over the country are talking quilts and seeing exhibitions of them. Stores feature handmade quilts, and nearly every needlework department offers a collection of easily finished quilt kits. Skill and previous experience are of little importance.

However, there still are many women who would prefer to design as well as sew their own quilts. For these women this book will have special meaning since it contains quilt and quilting patterns that can be used to make a quilt "from scratch."

The book also describes items other than quilts that are quilted or made of patchwork. Some of these designs are shown here for the first time. For the collector the book contains many pictures of museum quilts and tips on the collecting of quilts, both old and new.

It is the author's hope that this book will add to the knowledge of women already quilting and will interest additional women in taking up this fascinating hobby.

Part 1
QUILTS PAST

Chapter 1

Terms Used in Quilting

Album Quilt: A quilt made up of elaborately designed blocks, each created and carefully stitched by a different woman. In years past when such a quilt was finished, it usually was presented as a gift.

All Quilted Quilt: A quilt made of top and bottom with filler between. The top and bottom are large pieces of fabric. If the cloth is plain or white, an elaborate design is drawn on top and quilted. When printed material is used, the quilting usually follows the pattern of the cloth.

All White Quilt: *See* Counterpane.

Appliqué: Sometimes called a laid-out quilt because pieces in the design are cut from various materials, laid on a plain background, and secured in place with a fine hemming stitch or buttonhole stitch.

Back: Entire widths of yard goods, stitched together to make a single piece the size of the top of the quilt.

Backing: *See* Back.

Binding: Finishing off raw edges of an otherwise complete quilt. This can be done by: (1) turning the edges of the top back over the lining, and sewing them down with hemming stitches, or (2) turning the narrow edge of the bottom layer over the top layer and hemming it, or (3) binding the three layers together with bias tape.

Block: A single bit of material or two or more pieces joined to make a pattern. Quilts are usually divided into sections to make the sewing less cumbersome; there may be four or more of these parts or blocks. The block can be a square, a rectangle, or a hexagon. It is sometimes called a patch in a pieced quilt. The only quilt not divided into blocks is the comforter.

Blocking: This is simply ironing the quilt or its parts before and after its setting. (*See* Setting.)

Border: Band surrounding the quilt proper which might be of plain material, or pieced, or appliquéd. The border is not found on all quilts.

Comforter: A quilt of one-color material, three to four inches thick. It consists of three layers: cover, lining, and back. The three are quilt-stitched together in a simple or elaborate design.

Corner Block: The block used in a border to turn a corner.

Cotton Batting: This is batting used for lining and can be of cotton made for quilting or of polyester or some other synthetic material.

Counterpane: A white bedcover made of two layers of material, without an inner filling. The design motif is raised in relief by padding with cotton after the quilting is completed.

Coverlet: A quilt used on bed primarily for warmth, not large enough to cover the pillows.

Crazy Quilt: A quilt made of random design of pieces of material varying in size and color.

Fill: The cotton or wool wadding placed between the top and the back.

Filler: *See* Fill.

Four Block Quilt: Four large blocks make up this quilt. There may be a border around the four blocks.

Friendship Quilt: *See* Album Quilt. This quilt is made as a gift for a specific person.

Hexagon Quilt: A pieced quilt made by cutting a right triangle from each corner of a square, leaving a figure with six equal sides.

Italian-Style Quilting: Also known as Cord Quilting. A purely decorative form of quilting in which two layers are used—a muslin backing and a top. The design is stamped or punched onto the under muslin, which is securely tacked to the top fabric. The design is outlined from the wrong side with a double row of small running stitches, worked through both layers, about ⅛" to ¼" apart. A cord or length of thick wool is threaded from the back through the muslin, thus throwing the outline of the design into relief. The lining or padding of the entire quilt added after the work is finished.

Lattice Strip: A strip used between blocks to set off the blocks. The lattice is usually about three inches wide and can be pieced.

Marking: Tracing the quilting design on the top.

Marriage Quilt: The bride-to-be usually had a "baker's dozen" quilts that she herself made. The thirteenth, or the Marriage Quilt, was often the most elaborate one and had such symbols as cupids, doves, love knots, and hearts; it was used as a spread on the marriage bed. This quilt could be made only after a girl was engaged.

In some sections of the country it was believed to be bad luck for a bride to work on her own Marriage Quilt; so friends would make special blocks signed individually in India ink or embroidery, and all the blocks were then made into a quilt for the bride. This quilt is also known as the Bride's Quilt in some localities.

Medallion Quilt: A quilt that may be pieced or appliquéd, with a central motif that tells a story, no matter how simple.

Nine Patch Quilt: A quilt made up of nine blocks usually arranged in a square of three horizontal blocks and three vertical blocks.

Patch: Either a single piece of cloth or two or more pieces joined to form a pattern.

Patchwork: A pieced quilt, with the pieces cut in squares, triangles, or diamonds and sewed together to form a design in a larger block.

Pieced Quilt: *See* Patchwork.

Presentation Quilt: Same as Album Quilt and often given to the minister or another leader in the community.

Puff: Usually a New England quilt three or four inches thick; a local name for a tacked quilt.

Putting In: Act of fastening to the quilting frames the edges of the back and top, between which the fill has been evenly spread.

Quilt Bottom: Any soft, loosely woven material used as the bottom layer of the quilt.

Quilt Top: The top layer of the quilt; it should be of any fabric that is smooth, soft, and colorfast, with little or no shrinkage when washed.

Quilting Frame: Rack upon which the three layers of the quilt are stretched to facilitate the stitching operation.

Quilting Hoop: A piece of equipment used to hold a small portion of the quilt taut while the design is being sewn in. Used instead of the quilting frame.

Quilting Stitch: The stitch through cover, lining, and back that serves to hold the three parts of the quilt together. It is both functional and decorative.

Rolling: Revolving the two end bars of a quilting frame to wind and store the quilted portions, thus leaving the unquilted part centered on the frame.

Sash Work: *See* Lattice Strip.

Set: The material as well as the method used for setting the blocks together.

Setting: After the blocks are appliquéd or pieced, they are sewn together to form the quilt's design as a whole. This is known as setting the quilt.

Shadow Quilting: This is a variation of Italian or Cord Quilting. A thin transparent material such as silk or organdy is used, and the wool used for padding is brightly colored so that it shows through the upper layer and gives a "shadow" effect. The work can be pressed when it is finished by covering it with a cloth and using the tip of the iron on the areas between the corded lines. A well-padded ironing cloth or small pad will make it easier to make the quilting stand out.

Stuffing: *See* Fill.

Tacking: Fastening the three layers together by means of single stitches knotted or tied at regular intervals of three or four inches; used when filling is very thick.

Tacking Out: Removing the quilting from the frames.

Template: A pattern used as a guide in shaping something accurately. In quilt-making the template is the pattern used for cutting out the various parts of the block. It usually was made formerly of a heavy paper of tin; today it is made of plastic.

Throw: A coverlet.

Tied: *See* Tacking.

Top: Completed patchwork—blocks, set, and border used as the top of the three layers of a quilt.

Trapunto Quilting: This form of quilting is done through two layers—the top fabric and a layer of muslin. It is most commonly used for cushions. The design is drawn on the muslin before it is tacked securely to the top layer. The design is a single outline, stitched from the back through the two layers. Cotton wadding is then drawn through the muslin from the back. The scarcity of cotton suitable for this delicate work makes trapunto rather rare.

Trapunto was popular in the New England colonies at the same time as linsey-woolsey coverlets. The designs usually were feather wreaths, princes' plumes, roping, cornucopias, baskets of flowers and leaves. Trapunto required an excellent needlewoman since its stitches were more noticeable than in other styles. On a white spread the stitches were extremely small and precise.

Up and Down Method: This is a method of quilting in which each stitch is made in two separate movements—upward and downward—and not in one movement as is usually done.

Wadding: *See* Fill.

Winter Quilts: Quilts that are very heavy and warm, usually tacked or tied instead of quilted.

Chapter 2

A Short History of Quilts in America

QUILTS IN COLONIAL America resembled those of the lands from which the quilters had come. Wealthy and socially prominent settlers in the South made quilts of the English type until the Revolutionary War, when everything English was frowned upon. Then they too began to make the patchwork quilts that the middle-class and poor women had been working on for the preceding hundred years.

The quilts that were brought by the Puritans were of sturdy fabric and simple design. Those quilts that were carried by the Cavaliers to Virginia, the Carolinas, and Maryland were more colorful.

There were quilted woolen bedcovers which today are often called linsey-woolseys, although they were not often made of that staple household fabric. Rather, they were made of a top layer of woolen or glazed worsted fabric dyed dark blue, green, or brown with a bottom layer of a coarser woolen material, either natural or a shade of yellow or buff. The filling was a soft layer of carded wool, and the three layers were held together with quilting done with a homespun linen thread. The design of the quilting was often a simple one composed of interlocking circles or crossed diagonal lines giving a diamond pattern.

The name linsey-woolsey is derived from Middle English *lynsy wolsye*. The term was usually applied to a fabric used in heavy clothing and quilted petticoats. Today we think of linsey-woolsey as a heavy, warm, quilted bedcover which is so large that it hangs to the floor. The corners are cut out at the foot of the cover so that the quilt fits snugly around the tall four-poster beds of the 1700's. The beds of that period differed from those today in being shorter and wide; they were short because people slept in a semisitting position with many bolsters or pillows, and wide because each bed often slept three or more.

The linsey-woolsey covering was found in the colder regions of the country because of the warmth it afforded. There was no central heating and most bedrooms did not have fireplaces.

The type of quilt made in the early days of America was dictated partly by the state of family finances and partly by the location of the home. Families in towns along the coast were able to obtain background fabrics more easily from the Old World than inland settlers because of the difficulty of transporting goods.

As a result, farm families were dependent upon their own production of fabrics. They planted flax in their gardens, raised sheep for fleece, and carded, spun, and wove on their own wheels and looms. The farmer's wife used native dyes, such as butternut and other vegetable colorings. She decorated the woven cloth by tying and dipping. These fabrics gave long service, as is evidenced by many that survive as patches in New England quilts and in the blocks of the pieced quilts which the colonists carried across the land.

In New Amsterdam (later New York) Dutch housewives imported materials which they decorated with fancy stitching and appliqué work. The whole cover was then interlined and quilted. The Germans who settled in what later became Pennsylvania used the same style of quilting.

Colonial quilts were the creation of women who, despite the demands and trials of everyday living, found time to do needlework that has been the delight of the generations since those hard days. Women who helped settle our country made quilts not only out of necessity, but also as a means of self-expression and as a relaxing change from more strenuous physical chores.

In the southern colonies background materials were rich, light in weight, and wide in variety. Cotton and linen, used in place of wool, gave the southern quilt a different look and feel from those of New England. Silk was often used on coverlets for guest-room beds in the great houses found on the plantations in Virginia and along the Eastern Shore of Maryland. Appliquéd designs were used in a wide variety of delicate colors.

Every inch of cloth brought from Europe in sailing vessels was valued highly and saved for later use. When the quilts and blankets which the colonists brought with them began to wear out, they were patched until the coverings could hold no more thread. New quilts were then made of these saved pieces of materials. Any size, shape, and color would do. This led to the birth of the famous Crazy Quilt.

These quilts probably were not very pretty, but there was no complaint about their durability, since they were made of strong material left over from unusable clothing. Grasses or corn husks were sometimes the only materials available as fillers.

Quilting could not be done with such fillers and so string was used to tack the top, bottom, and stuffing together. A short piece of twine was thrust down through the quilt and up again, and then tied on the front of the quilt and clipped off close to the material.

What pride must have been felt by the New England housewife of 1750 as she spread her first patchwork quilt over her bed! At this period of American history all women were expected to engage in needlework. As early as 1716 the Boston *News-Letter,* America's first newspaper, printed the following advertisement:

> This is to give Notice, that at the House of Mr. George Brownell, late School Master in Hanover Street, Boston, are all sorts of Millinary Works done; . . . and also young Gentlewomen and Children taught all sorts of fine works as Quilting, Featherwork . . . Embroidering a new way, Turkey-Work for Handkerchiefs . . . flourishing and plain Work, and Dancing Cheaper than ever taught in Boston, Brocaded Work for Handkerchiefs and short Aprons upon Muslin, artificial Flowers work'd with a Needle.

Many schools of the same type were soon opened and remained in vogue until the Revolution. Some schools advertised such courses for young gentlemen as English, writing, and arithmetic, while young ladies were taught all types of needlework. Only affluent families could afford such luxurious tutelage for their young.

In every household, rich or poor, the women sewed. The quilt in the house of plenty might be made of ribbons and silks, while the quilt in the house of little might be made of scraps of material left over from other articles.

Cloths of different weaves and textures were often used in the same quilt. The colors of thread used were as varied as the stitches, but all were soft, blending colors. The stitches were very even. The young girl was punished for making uneven stitches.

The second period of American quilting was the Revolutionary era. In tribute to our European allies French accents were introduced, such as flower sprays cut from the toile and appliquéd on the background. Martha Washington did much quilting and some of her quilts are on display at Mount Vernon. Her quilting frame consisted of four walnut bars; the larger bars were eleven feet long and one and a half inches wide, with canvas strips for attaching the quilt. The shorter two bars were nine and a half feet long and two and a half inches wide. Canvas strips were so arranged that they slid along the bars and could be tightened or loosened by use of two laces.

Among the most valuable records of colonial days are will and marriage inventories, which often provide detailed descriptions of quilts. In old account books and letters one can find lists of materials purchased for quilt-making.

Although the appliqué quilt became a great favorite, the art of patchwork quilting flourished in the period 1775-1875. Quilts came to be made in great numbers not principally as coverlets but as blankets to provide additional warmth. Tradition says that a chest filled with thirteen quilts went with each bride to her new home.

The pioneer period, roughly from 1800 through the Gold Rush days of 1849-1855, made up the third period. Gradual westward movement across the continent began soon after the first settlers arrived. From New England coastal settlements, pioneers ventured into western Massachusetts, Connecticut, and along the valley of the Mohawk River in New York. The westward movement accelerated after the American Revolution as families moved from the Eastern Seaboard to the lands of the Western Reserve and the valleys of the Ohio and Mississippi Rivers. With the housewife on her migration went the quilts and quilting patterns that were dear to her. The patchwork quilt of New England became the pieced quilt of the Middle West. Scraps of material were carefully cut and pieced together to form larger blocks, which in turn were joined together to make the cover of the quilt. Usually these smaller bits were of uniform size and shape but in contrasting colors. Beautiful geometric designs were the result.

Pioneers of the Middle West became prosperous farmers, and their women soon had more time for needlework. The result was an increase in ornamental detail which marks the quilts of that era.

With the growth of permanent farmsteads women found opportunities to exchange patterns. The quilting bee soon flourished to an even greater extent than it had in New England.

At the bees women set up and stitched beautiful quilts, some of which are now displayed in museums. In the more remote areas a loaded rifle might be balanced against the quilting frame, ready for protection against Indians or wild animals. Pioneer women still used the calicoes of their own worn-out dresses and homespun they had dyed themselves earlier in the East.

Back in the East, meanwhile, material became easier to obtain in a variety of colors and prints. Covers of the appliquéd or laid-out type rose to favor. This type of quilt pattern became the most important contribution made to the art of quilting in America.

The scrap bag became a topic of conversation among neighboring womenfolk. From it were exchanged "pieces" with neighbors—a practice which furthered not only the artistic end of quilt-making, but the spirit of community as well. As a result of the exchange most quilts made in the same locality over a period of time tend to look somewhat alike.

Quilts of that period were gay, with bold combinations of reds, greens, purples, blues, pinks, and yellows.

The fourth period of quilting in America was the Civil War era, which included the 1850's and 1860's. Mills produced inexpensive goods in plentiful supply, but women seemed reluctant to replace homemade quilts with coverings bought from a peddler or country store.

They planned the arrangement of the pieces and cut the fabrics to suit a desired design rather than allowing scrap pieces to dictate final design. Quilts of several thousand pieces could be made in a well-planned design. The quilt maker usually worked out a motif to be repeated in uniform squares. She could work on a piece whenever she had the opportunity.

The technique of making the quilt top in separate blocks then led to a special type of quilt, co-operatively produced by a number of neighbors and known as Signature, Album, Autograph, Friendship, Bride, or Presentation. Each of these was made for some special person. Everyone participating supplied a pieced or appliquéd block of her own chosen pattern, which she usually signed in India ink. Often a quilt of this type was made for a favorite minister and his wife.

In those days all property, real and personal, was controlled by the male family head. Little leeway was permitted females in thought, word, or deed. Men laid down the law and women and children obeyed.

Even in instances where comparative wealth afforded women greater ease and culture, few were permitted free expression in the decoration of their homes or in the adornment of their persons. Men ordered the material for their wives' gowns as well as the materials for their own waistcoats. But women found an outlet for creative expression in the making of quilts and in this their men did not interfere.

The oldest pattern known as Crazy Quilt underwent a great change from the original design of that name. It was no longer just a bedcover made up of all the odds and ends of materials in the house. No home of average comfort was without its crazy-patch quilt or "slumber throw," a Victorian version made of odds and ends of ribbons, silks, and velvets. Some of the loveliest quilts of all were made during this period.

No crib was complete without its snow-white quilt. Paper patterns, based on feathers, fruit, birds, bouquets, cornucopias, and baskets of flowers, could be purchased, while patterns for straight quilting such as crossbars and diamonds could be made with chalk, pencil, or even cord. Magazines and newspapers published quilt-block patterns and quilting designs over a period of years. *Godey's Lady's Book* frequently published such designs. Sometimes half a dozen designs appeared in the same quilt.

The fifth quilting period was the centennial period and began in the 1870's. At this time, except in the most remote villages and farmhouses of the Middle West and the mountain cabins of the Great Smokies and Blue Ridge Mountains, power machines and industrialized needle trade had replaced the home craft of quilting to a large extent. Women in the eastern part of the United States were concentrating on such other forms of handwork as needlepoint.

However, in 1876 the Philadelphia Centennial Exhibition exhibited handwork by the women of the eighteenth century, and this brought about a rebirth of all types of handwork. Books were published on the arts and homemade quilts again became popular.

The size of the quilts began to change, as did designs. Many of the eighteenth-century quilts were square, as the beds of that period were wider than those of the present day. Many were made of four blocks, each measuring thirty-six inches square, to which was added an eighteen-inch border; thus the finished quilt was one hundred and eight inches square. As beds became smaller, so did the size of the quilts.

In the latter years of the nineteenth century many households began to use machine-made bedcoverings. By the turn of the century quilting had become a rather rare pastime. But there were still a number of quilters' clubs where interested women could exchange patterns and ideas. Occasionally a quilting article appeared in a magazine or newspaper, and quilt contests were often held at country fairs.

The art of quilt-making continued to be practiced in the southern mountains, where life was as simple and unhurried as it had been since the day the pioneers moved there. Mountain women still practice quilt-making in that area, using their own original patterns. Many have combined to form successful co-operative quilting enterprises in Georgia, Kentucky, and Alabama, as well as in other localities.

Chapter 3

Quilting Customs and Superstitions

PIONEER WOMEN OF the early- to mid-nineteenth century centered a large part of their social lives around quilt-making activities. Quilting bees were as important socially before the Civil War as was the sewing circle during and after the Civil War. Each woman would sit at home alone, piecing together discarded patches of fabric in preparation for the day when this patchwork top would be batted (padded), backed, and quilted on the community quilting frames. These early artisans almost always completed their work together because, in most cases, only one quilting frame was available for the entire region.

Quilting bees were a purely American social custom and were unknown in foreign countries. Few events were more important than the quilting bee in villages and small towns. For many years it was the most popular form of feminine hospitality. Since there usually were four women on each side of the frame, there would be seven guests and the hostess.

When distances between families were great, the hostess sometimes waited until she had more than one quilt to piece and then invited more guests, if she could borrow an extra frame. At some time during the day, usually in the morning, female friends and neighbors gathered at the home of the woman owning the quilt and aided in laying the top (cotton or wool) and lining together, rolling it on the frame, and setting it up. Then all settled down to the stitching, sometimes with a favorite needle which had become curved through prolonged use. At noon—a rest period—dinner was served. But the needles soon began to fly again so that quilting might be finished before suppertime.

The beaux and sweethearts of the unmarried quilters and the husbands of those who were married were invited to supper, when chicken or turkey was the usual main course. The men arrived in Sunday best, and after supper there were kissing games, singing, dancing, and courting. The women had done their serious gossiping during the morning and afternoon sessions. If the quilting bee was in honor of a bride-to-be, the party following it was particularly festive.

The supper dishes were cleared away, and the quilt was brought out and held high by the young men and young women. A cat was then placed in the middle of the quilt and that young man or woman over whose head it jumped was said to be the next candidate for matrimony.

The album party is believed to have been a more formal affair, occurring more frequently in the urban than in rural localities and usually held when an Album Quilt was being prepared for the local minister.

The annual county fair encouraged quilt-making as an art. Entire families would attend. The women often entered the quilt-making competition. To win an annual fair prize was an honor for which the winner became famous throughout the county.

In New England a Freedom Quilt was often presented at a party celebrating a young man's twenty-first birthday. The quilt was a symbol of independence; he could now leave home and live his own life. No longer would he have his mother's or sister's quilts to warm his bed. So a quilt was given to him until he could find a wife who would make quilts for their bed.

The Freedom Quilt was made by the lad's female friends. His mother or sisters invited the girls he knew to spend the afternoon preceding the birthday party. They brought with them scraps of their own prettiest gowns, and from these they pieced the young man's quilt. This homely, friendly custom went out of fashion about 1825. Not many real Freedom Quilts were made after that date. These quilts went around the Horn on whaling ships, over the trails to California, and into battle with men in the Civil War. Because of the rough treatment they received, few survive today.

Another quilt that is associated with a party is the Friendship Quilt. The maker usually asked each of her friends for enough material to make one block. Often the same pattern was used throughout, but occasionally each block, while of a uniform size, was pieced or appliquéd in a different design. Thus in the same quilt could be found a Log-Cabin block, a Chimney Sweep, a Bear's Paw, as many different designs as there were blocks in the quilt. Friendship Quilts of this type were often called Friendship Medley Quilts.

Although a girl might give a Friendship Medley party for herself, it usually was her mother or some close friend who arranged such a party as a surprise for the young lady on her birthday, engagement, or wedding anniversary. Sometimes a party was planned just as a social gathering, not for any particular occasion. They were most popular prior to the Revolution.

The guests would arrive early in the day. Each brought her own material and the first order of business would be to decide who would make what blocks. Guests would vie for the honor of making the most difficult blocks as a display of skill with the needle. By suppertime the quilt was finished, gentlemen would arrive, and merriment would start.

Memory Quilts or Memorial Quilts, made of the clothing of the dead, were fairly somber in their coloring, at least around the border. All the friends of the recently departed would take part in the quilting bee.

Before 1870 no wedding dowry was complete without a Bride's Quilt. Some designs because of their names were never made for a dowry quilt. Wandering Foot was thought to be inappropriate until the name was changed to Turkey Tracks. Hearts, either in the design of the patchwork itself or in the quilting, formed the insignia of a bride. Few brides had quilts without the conspicuous use of some heart-shaped patches or quilting. Before 1840 the sign of the heart was used only for decorating things made for a bride. If the heart was used on any quilt but a Bride's Quilt, it was believed that the girl would never marry at all. Today, if one sees something old with hearts as decoration, it may be assumed that the article was originally made for presentation to a bride.

Chapter 4

Quilting in the Literature of the Times

Quilts in Colonial America

By Alice Morse Earle

Alice Morse Earle is considered one of the outstanding authorities on life in colonial America. She has written many books on the subject. This is an excerpt from one of her books, Home Life in Colonial Days, *written in 1898.*

"   The feminine love of color, the longing for decoration, as well as pride in skill of needle-craft, found riotous expansion in quilt-piecing. A thrift, economy, too, a desire to use up all the fragments and bits of stuffs which were necessarily cut out in the shaping, chiefly of women's and children's garments, helped to make the patchwork a satisfaction. The amount of labor, of carefully fitting, neat piecing, and elaborate quilting, the thousands of stitches that went into one of these patchwork quilts, are to-day almost painful to regard. Women revelled in intricate and difficult patchwork; they eagerly exchanged patterns with one another; they talked over the designs, and admired pretty bits of calico, and pondered what combinations to make, with far more zest than women ever discuss art or examine high art specimens to-day. There was one satisfactory condition in the work, and that was the quality of the cottons and linens of which the patchwork was made. They were none of the flimsey, composition-filled, aniline-dyed calicoes of to-day. A piece of 'chancey,' or 'copper-plate' a hundred years old will be as fresh to-day as when woven. Real Indian chintzes and palampours are found in these quilts, beautiful and artistic stuffs, and the firm, unyielding, high-priced, 'real' French calicoes.

A sense of idealization of quilt-piecing is given also by the quaint descriptive names applied to the various patterns. Of those the Rising-sun, Log Cabin, and Job's Trouble are perhaps the most familiar. Job's Trouble was simply honeycomb or hexagonal blocks. To set a Job's Trouble was to cut out an exact hexagon for a pattern (preferably from tin, otherwise from firm cardboard); to cut out from this many hexagons in stiff brown paper or letter paper. These are covered with the bits of calico with the edges turned under; the sides were sewed together carefully over and over, till a firm expanse permitted the removal of the papers.

The name of the pattern seldom gave an expression of its character. Dove in the Window, Rob Peter to Pay Paul, Blue Brigade, Fanmill, Crow's Foot, Chinese Puzzle, Flywheel, Love-Knot, Sugar-bowl, are simply whims of fancy. Floral names, such as Dutch Tulip, Sunflower, Rose of Sharon, Blue-Bells, World's Rose, might suggest a love of flowers. Sometimes designs are appliquéd on with some regard for coloring. I once saw a quilt that was a miracle of tedious work. The squares of white cotton each held a slender stem with two leaves of green or light brown calico, surmounted by a four-petalled flower of high-colored calico,—pink, red, blue, etc. This design was surprisingly Oriental.

When the patchwork was completed, it was laid flatly on the lining (often another expanse of patchwork), with layers of wool or cotton wadding between, and the edges were basted all around. Four bars of wood, about ten feet long, 'the quilting-frame,' were placed at the four edges, the quilt was sewed to them with stout thread, the bars crossed and tied firmly at corners, and the whole raised on chairs or tables to a convenient height. Thus around the outstretched quilt a dozen quilters could sit running the whole together with a fanciful set designs of stitching. When about a foot on either side was wholly quilted, it was rolled upon its bar, and the work went on; thus the visible quilt diminished, like Balzac's *Peau de Chagrin,* in a united and truly sociable work that required no special attention, in which all were facing together and all drawing closer together as the afternoon passed in intimate gossip. Sometimes several quilts were set up. I know of a ten days' quilting-bee in Narragansett in 1752.

In early days calicoes were not common, but every one had woolen garments and pieces, and the quilts made of these were of grateful warmth in bleak New England. All kinds of commonplace garments and remnants of decayed gentility were pressed into service in these quilts: portions of the moth-eaten and discarded uniforms of militiamen, worn-out flannel sheets dyed with some brilliant dome-dye, old coat and cloak linings, well-worn petticoats. A magnificent scarlet cloak worn by a Lord

Mayor of London and brought to America by a member of the Merritt family of Salisbury, Massachusetts, went through a series of adventures and migrations, and ended its days as small bits of vivid color casting a grateful glory and variety on a patchwork quilt in the Saco valley of Maine. To this day at vendues or sales of old country households in New England, there will be handed out great rolls of woolen pieces to be used for patchwork quilts or rag carpets, and they find purchasers.

These woolen quilts had a thin wadding, and were usually very closely quilted, so they were quite flat. They were called 'pressed quilts.' An old farm wife said to me in New Hampshire, 'Girls won't take the trouble to make pressed quilts nowadays. It's as much as they'll do to tack a puff,' that is, make a light quilt with thick wadding only tacked together from front to back, at regular intervals. A pressed quilt which I saw was quilted in inch squares. Another had a fan-pattern with sunflower leaf border; another was quilted in the elaborate pattern known as 'feather-work.'

As much ingenuity was exercised in the design of the quilting as in the pattern of the patchwork, and the marking for the quilt design was exceedingly tedious, since, of course, no drawings could be used. I remember seeing one quilt marked by chalking strings which were stretched tightly across at the desired intervals, and held up and snapped smartly down on the quilt, leaving a faint chalky line to guide the eye and needle. Another simple design was to quilt in rounds, using a saucer or plate to form a perfect circle.

The most elaborate quilt I know of is of silk containing portions of the wedding-dress of Esther Powel, granddaughter of Gabriel Bernon; she was married to James Helme in 1738. When her granddaughter was married in 1795, the quilt was still unfinished, and a woman was hired who worked on it for six months, putting a miracle of fine stitches in the quilting. I think she must have been very old and very slow, for the wages paid her were but twenty cents a week and 'her keep,' which was very small pay even in that day of small wages. When Washington came to Newport, this splendid quilt was sent to grace the bed upon which the hero slept.

I said a few summers ago to a farmer's wife who lived on the outskirts of a small New England hill-village: 'Your home is very beautiful. From every window the view is perfect.' She answered quickly: 'Yes, but it's awfully lonely for me, for I was born in Worcester; still I don't mind as long as we have plenty of quiltings.' In answer to my questions, she told me that the previous winter she had 'kept count,' and she had helped at twenty-eight 'regular' quiltings, besides her own patchwork and quilt-making, and much informal help of neighbors on plain quilts. Any one who has attended a country fair (one not too modernized and spoiled) and seen the display that intricate patchwork and quilting will make in country homes can see that it is not an obsolete accomplishment.   ,,

The Minister's Wooing

By Harriet Beecher Stowe

Harriet Beecher Stowe's book is of interest to quilters for its chapter which describes a New England quilting-bee.

The rattling of wheels was heard at the gate, and Candace, Mrs. Marvin's cook, was discerned, seated aloft in the one-horse wagon, with her usual complement of baskets and bags.

'Well, now, dear me! if there isn't Candace!' said Miss Prissy; 'I do believe Miss Marvin has sent her with something for the quilting!' and out she flew as nimble as a humming bird, while those in the house heard various exclamations of admiration, as Candace, with stately dignity, disinterred from the wagon one basket after another, and exhibited to Miss Prissy's enraptured eyes sly peeps under the white napkins with which they were covered. And then, hanging a large basket on either arm, she rolled majestically towards the house, like a heavy-laden Indian-man coming in after a fast voyage.

'Good-mornin', Miss Scudder! Good-mornin', Doctor!' she said, dropping her curtesy on the doorstep; 'Good-mornin', Miss Mary! Ye see our folks was stirrin' pooty early dis mornin' and Miss Marvin sent me down wid two or three little tings.'

Setting her baskets on the floor, and seating herself between them, she proceeded to develop their contents with ill-concealed triumph. One basket was devoted to cakes of every species, from the great Mont-Blanc loaf-cake, with its snowy glaciers of frosting, to the twisted cruller and puffy doughnut. In the other basket lay pats of golden butter curiously stamped, reposing on a bed of fresh green leaves, while currants, red and white, and delicious cherries and raspberries, gave a final finish to the picture. From a basket which Miss Prissy brought in from the rear appeared cold fowl and tongue delicately prepared, and shaded with feathers of parsley. Candace, whose rollicking delight in the good things of this life was conspicuous in every emotion, might have furnished to a painter, as she sat in her brilliant turban, an idea for an African Genius of Plenty.

'Why, really, Candace,' said Mrs. Scudder, 'you are overwhelming us!'

'Ho! Ho! Ho!' said Candace, 'I's tellin' Miss Marvin folks don't git married but once in der lives, (gin'ally speakin', dat is) an' den dey oughter had plenty to do it wid.'

'Well, I must say,' said Miss Prissy, taking out the loaf-cake with busy assiduity, 'I must say, Candace, this does beat all!'

'I should rader tink it oughter,' said Candace, bridling herself with proud consciousness; 'ef it don't, 'taint 'cause old Candace hain't put enough into it. I tell ye, I didn't do nothin' all day yisterday but jes' make dat ar cake. Cato, when he got up, he begun to talk some-h'n 'bout his shirt buttons, an' I jes' shet him right up. I says, 'Cato, when I's r'ally got a cake to make for a great 'casion, I wants my mind *jest* as quiet an' *jest* as serene as ef I was agoin' to de sacrament. I don't want my no 'arthly cares on it. Now,' says I, 'Cato, de ole Doctor's gwine to be married, and dis yer's his quiltin' cake; an' Miss Mary, she's gwine to be married, an' dis yer's *her* quiltin' cake. An' dar'll be eberybody to dat ar quiltin', an' ef de cake ain't right, why, th' would be puttin' a candle under a bushel, An' so,' says I, 'Cato, your buttons must wait.' An' Cato, he sees de 'preity ob it, 'cause, dough he can't make cake like me, he's a 'mazin' good judge on't, an' is dreful tickled when I slips out a little loaf for his supper.'

'How is Mrs. Marvin?' asked Mrs. Scudder.

'Kinder thin and shimmery; but she's about,—habin' her eyes eberywar 'n' lookin' into eberyting. She jes' touches tings wid de tips ob her fingers an' dey seem to go like. She'll be down to de quiltin' dis aternoon. But she tole me to take de tings an' come down an' spend de day here; for Miss Marvin an' I both knows how many steps mus' be taken sech times, an' we agreed you oughter favor yourselves all you could.'

'Well, now,' said Miss Prissy, lifting up her hands, 'if that ain't what 't is to have friends! Why, that was one of the things I was thinking of, as I lay awake last night; because, you know, at times like these, people run their feet off before the time begins, and then they are all limpsey and lop-sided when the time comes. Now, I say, Candace, all Miss Scudder and Mary have to do is to give everything up to us, and we'll put it through straight.'

'Dat's what we will!' said Candace. 'Jes' show me what's to be done, an' I'll do it.'

Candace and Miss Prissy soon disappeared together into the pantry with the baskets, whose contents they began busily to arrange. Candace shut the door, that no sound might escape, and began a confidential outpouring to Miss Prissy.

'Ye see,' she said, 'I'se *feelin's* all de while for Miss Marvin; 'cause, ye see, she was expecting', ef eber Mary was married—well—dat 'twould be to somebody else, ye know—our Mass'r Jim.'

By two o'clock a goodly company began to assemble. Mrs. Deacon Twitchell arrives, soft, pillowy, and plaintive as ever, accompanied by Cerinthy Ann, a comely damsel, tall and trim, with a bright black eye and a most vigorous and determined style of movement. Good Mrs. Jones, broad, expansive, and solid, having vegetated tranquilly on in the cabbage garden of the virtues since three years ago when she graced our tea party, was now as well preserved as ever, and brought some fresh butter, a tin pail of cream, and a loaf of cake made after a new Philadelphia receipt.

The quilt-pattern was gloriously drawn in oak leaves, done in indigo; and soon all the company, young and old, were passing busy fingers over it, and conversation went on briskly.

Madam de Frontignac, we must not forget to say, had entered with hearty *abandon* into the spirit of the day; she would have her seat and soon won the respect of the party by the dexterity with which she used her needle; though, when it was whispered that she learned to quilt among the nuns, some of the elderly ladies exhibited a slight uneasiness, as being rather doubtful whether they might not be encouraging papistical opinions by allowing her an equal share in the work of getting up their minister's bed-quilt; but the younger part of the company were quite captivated by her foreign air, and the pretty manner in which she lisped her English; and Cerinthy Ann even went so far as to horrify her mother by saying that she wished she'd been educated in a convent herself,—a declaration which arose less from native depravity than from a certain vigorous disposition, which often shows itself in young people, to shock the current opinions of their elders and betters. Of course, the conversation took a general turn, somewhat in unison with the spirit of the occasion; and whenever it flagged, some allusion to a forthcoming wedding, or some sly hint as the future young Madame of the parish, was sufficient to awaken the dormant animation of the company.

Cerinthy Ann contrived to produce an agreeable electric shock by declaring that for her part she never could see into it, how any girl could marry a minister; that she should as soon think of setting up housekeeping in a meeting house.

'Oh, Cerinthy Ann!' exclaimed her mother, 'how can you go on so?'

'It's a fact,' said the adventurous damsel; 'now other men let you have some peace, but a minister's always around under your feet.'

'So you think the less you see of a husband, the better?' said one of the ladies.

'Just my views,' said Cerinthy Ann, giving a decided snip to her thread with her scissors. 'I like the Nantucketers, that go off on four-years' voyages and leave their wives a clear field. If I ever get married, I'm going up to have one of those fellows.'

'You'd better take care, Cerinthy Ann,' said her mother. 'They say that 'those who sing before breakfast will cry before supper.' 'Girls talk about getting married,' she said, relapsing into a gentle didactic melancholy, 'without realizing its awful responsibilities.'

'Oh, as to that,' said Cerinthy Ann, 'I've been practising on my pudding now these six years, and I shouldn't be afraid to throw one up a chimney with any girl.'

This speech was founded on a tradition, current in those times, that no young lady was fit to be married till she could construct a boiled Indian pudding of such consistency that it could be thrown up a chimney and come down on the ground outside without breaking; and the consequences of Cerinthy Ann's sally was a general laugh.

'Girls ain't what they used to be in my day,' sententiously remarked an elderly lady. 'I remember my mother told me when she was thirteen she could knit a long cotton stocking in a day.'

'I haven't much faith in these stories of old time—have you, girls?' said Cerinthy, appealing to the younger members at the frame.

'At any rate,' said Mrs. Twitchell, 'our minister's wife will be a pattern; I don't know anybody that goes beyond her either in spinning or fine stitching.'

Thus the day was spent in friendly gossip as they quilted and rolled and talked and laughed, and as the afternoon sun cast lengthening shadows on the grass Mary and Miss Marvin went into the great kitchen, where a long table stood exhibiting all that plenitude of provision which the immortal description of Washington Irving has saved us the trouble of recapitulating in detail.

The husbands, brothers, and lovers had come in, and the scene was redolent of gayety. When Mary made her appearance, there was a moment's pause, till she was conducted to the side of the Doctor; when, raising his hand, he invoked a grace upon the loaded board.

Unrestrained gayeties followed. Groups of young men and maidens chatted together, and all the gallantries of the times were enacted. Serious matrons commented on the cake, and told each other high and particular secrets in the culinary art, which they drew from remote family archives. One might have learned in that instructive assembly how best to keep moths out of blankets; how to make fritters of Indian corn undistinguishable from oysters; how to bring up babies by hand; how to mend a cracked teapot; how to take out grease from a brocade; how to reconcile absolute decrees with free will; how to make five yards of cloth answer the purpose of six; and how to put down the Democratic party. All were busy, earnest, and certain, just as a swarm of men and women, old and young, are in 1859.   "

The Quilting at Miss Jones's

By Josiah Allen's Wife

Marietta Holley, better known as Josiah Allen's Wife, was one of the outstanding comic writers of the late 1800's. At the age of 24, she wrote this piece for the July 1868 issue of Godey's Lady's Book.

"   Our minister was married a year ago, and we have been piecing him a bed-quilt; and last week we quilted it. I always make a pint of going to quilting, for you can't be backbited to your face, that's a moral sertenty. I know wimmen jest like a book, for I hev been one a good while. I always stand up for my own sect, still I know sertin effects follow sertin causes, to wit, and namely, if two bricks are sot up side by side, if one tumbles over on to the other one, the other one can't stand, it ain't natur'. If a toper hold a glass of likker to his mouth, he can't help swallerin', it ain't natur'. If a young man goes slay-riding with a pretty girl, and the Buffelo robe slips off, he can't help holin' it round her, it ain't natur'. I might go on illustratin', but enuff; quiltin' jest sets wimmen to slanderin' as easy and beautiful as enything you ever see'. So I went. There wasn't anybody there when I got there. For reason, I always go early.

I hadn't been there long before Miss Deacon Graves came, and then the Widder Tubbs, and then Squire Edwards's wife, and Maggie Snow, and then the Dobb girls (we call 'em *girls,* though it would be jest as proper to call mutton lamb, for forty summer hev gilded their heads if one has gilt 'em). They was the last that come, for Miss Brown's baby had the mumps, and otherwise couldn't leave; and the Ripleys had unexpected company. But with Miss Jones, where the quiltin' was held, and her girls, Mary Ann and Alzina, we made as many as could set round the quilt comfortable.

The quilt was made of different kinds of calico; all the wimmen round had pieced a block or two, and we took up a collection to get the batten and linin', and the cloth to set it together with, which was turkey red, and come to quilt it, it looked well; we quilted it herrin'-bone, and a runnin' vine round the border. After the path-master was detorelized, the school-mistress tore to pieces, the party to Ripley scandelized, Miss Brown's baby voted an unquestionable idiot, and the rest of the unrepresented neighborhood dealt with, Lucinder Dobb spoke up, and sez she:—

'I hope tha minister will like the bed-quilt' (Lucinder is the one that studies mathematics to discipline her mind, and has the Roman nose).

'It ain't noways likely he will,' sez her sister Ophelia (she is the one that has her hair frizzled on top, and wears spectacles). 'It ain't noways likely he will—he is a cold man, a stone statute.'

Now, you see, I set my eyes by the minister, he is always doin' good to somebody, besides preachin' more like a angel than a human bein'. I can't never forget— nor I don't want to—how he took hold of my hand, and how his voice trembled and the tears stood in his eyes, when my little Joe died; pretty little lamb, he was in his infant class, and he loved him; you see such things cut deep, and there is some lines you can't run down; you see it riled up the old Smith blood, and when that is riled, Josiah says he always takes his hat and leaves till it settles. And I spoke up, and sez I:—

'Lucky for him he was made of stone before he was married, for common flesh and blood, sez I, would have gin out a hundred times chaste round by the girls as he was' (you see it was the town's talk how Ophelia Dobb acted before he was merried, and she almost went into a decline, and took heaps of mother wort and fetty).

'I don't know what you mean, Miss Allen,' sez she, turning red as a brick. 'I never heard of his bein' chaste; I know I never could bear the sight of him.'

'The distant sight,' sez Mary Ann Jones.

Ophelia looked so mad at that, that I don't know but she would have pricked her with her quiltin' needle, if old Miss Graves hadn't spoke up. She is a fat old lady with a double chin, 'mild and lovely' as Mount Vernen's sister. She always agrees with everybody; Thomas Jefferson, Josiah's boy by his first wife, called her 'Woolen Apron,' for one day he sez he heard her say to a neighbor, 'I don't like woolen aprons, do you?' 'Why, yes, Miss Graves, I do' 'Wal, so do I' But good old soul, if we was all such peacemakers as she is, we should be pretty sure of Heaven, though Thomas H. said that if Saten should ask her to go the other way, she would go rather than hurt his feelings; I jest told him to shet his weekedness, and he shet up.

As I said, she looked smiling up over her spectacles and nodded her purple cap ribbons two or three times, and said, 'Yes,' 'Jest so, Ophelia.' And then to change the subject, sez she, 'Has the minister's wife got home yet?'

'I think not,' said Maggie Snow, 'I was to the village day before yesterday, and she had not come then.'

'I suppose her mother is well off,' sez the Widder Tubbs, 'And as long as she stays there she saves the minister five dollars a week. I should think she would stay all summer.'

The widder is about as savin' a woman as belongs to the meetin'-house.

'It don't look well for her to be gone so long,' sez Lucinder Dobb, 'I am very much afraid it will make talk.'

'Mebby it will save the minister five dollars a week,' sez Ophelia, 'and extravagant as she is in dress—as many as four silk dresses she has got, and folks as good as she is in the congregation hain't got but one, and a certain person *full* as good as she is, that hain't got any' (Ophelia's best dress is poplin), 'it won't take her long to run out the minister's salary.'

'She had her silk dresses before she was married, and her folks was wealthy,' said Miss Squire Edwards.

'As much as we have done and are still doing for them, it seems ungrateful in her,' sez Lucinder, 'To wear such a bonnet as she wore all last summer—a plain white straw with a little bit of white ribbon in it; it looked so scrimped and stingy. I have thought she wore it on purpose to mortify us before the Baptists, jest as if we couldn't afford to dress our minister's wife as good as they did their.'

Maggie Snow's cheeks were gettin' red as fire, and her eyes begun to shine jest as they did that day we found some boys stonin' her cat. You see she and the minister's wife are the greatest friends that ever was. And I see she couldn't hold in much longer; she was jest openin' her mouth to speak, when the door opened, and in walked Betsy Babbet.

'Why, it seems to me you are late, Betsy,' said Miss Jones, 'but walk rite into the spare bed-room and take off your things.'

'Things!' said Betsy, 'who cares for things?' And she dropped into the nearest rockin'-chair and commenced rockin' violently.

Betsy Babbet was a humble critter. But we hadn't no time to meditate on her, for as Miss Jones asked her agin to take off her things, she broke out:—

'Would that I had died when I was an infant babe!'

'Amen!' whispered Mary Ann Jones to Maggie Snow.

'Do tell us what is the matter, Betsy,' said Miss Jones.

'Yes, do,' said Miss Deacon Graves.

'Matter enuff!' sez she; 'no wonder there is earthquakes and jars! I heard the news jest before I started, and it made me weak as a cat; I had to stop to every house on the way down to rest and not a soul had heard of it till I told 'em. Such a turn as it give me, I sh'nt get over it for a week; but it is jest as I always told you; I always said the minister's wife wasn't any *too good*. It didn't surprise me—not a bit.'

'You can't tell me one word against Mary Linden that I will believe,' said Maggie Snow.

'You will admit that the minister went North last Tuesday, won't you?'

Seven wimmen spoke up to once, and said, 'Yes, his mother was took sick, and they telegraphed for him.'

'So he said,' sneered Betsy Babbet, 'so he said; I believe it's for the good.'

'Oh dear!' shrieked Ophelia Dobb, 'I shall faint away; ketch hold of me, somebody.'

'Ketch hold of yourself,' said I, severely, and then sez I to Betsy, 'I don't believe he's run away any more than I believe I am the next President of the United States.'

'Well, if he hain't, he'll wish he had,' sez she. 'His wife came night before last on the cars.'

Four wimmen said 'Did she?' two said, 'Do tell?' and three opened their mouths and looked at her speechless; amongst the last was Miss Deacon Graves. I spoke in a kolected manner, and sez I, 'What of it?'

'Yes, what of it?' said she. 'I believe the poor man mistrusted it all out, and run away from trouble and disgrace.'

'How dare you!' sez Maggie Snow, 'speak the word disgrace in connected with Mary Linden?'

'How dare I?' sez Betsy Babbet. 'Ask Jake Coleman, as it happened I got it from his own mouth, it didn't come through two or three.'

'Get what?' sez I; 'If you can speak the English language, Betsy Babbet, and have got sense enuff to tell a straight story, tell it and be done with it,' sez I.

'Well, jest as I come out the gate to our house,' sez she, 'Jake Coleman came along, and sez he, "Betsy, I have got something to tell you. Miss Linden has got home, and she didn't come alone, neither." Sez I, "What do you mean?" He looked as mysterious as a ghost, and sez he, "I mean what I say," sez he, "I mean I drove the carriage home from the depot," sez he, "as sure as my name is Jake Coleman, I heard her talking to somebody she called Hugh (you know her husband's name is Charles); I heard her tell this Hugh that she loved him, loved him better than the whole world." And then he made me promise not to tell; but he said he heard not only one kiss, but fourteen or fifteen. 'Now,' sez Betsy, 'What do you think of the minister's wife?'

'Good heavens!' cried Ophelia Dobb, 'Am I deceived? is this a phantagory of the brain, or have I got ears? Have I got ears?' she kontinude, wildly glaring at me.

'You can feel and see,' said I, shortly.

'Will he live with the wretched creature?' kontinude Ophelia, 'No, he will get a divorcement from her; such a tender-hearted man as he is too. If ever a man wanted a comforter in a tryin' time he is the man, and to-morrow I will go and comfort him.'

'I guess you will find him first,' said Betsy Babbet. 'And I guess if he was found, there is a certain person he would be as glad to see as he would another certain person.'

'There is some mistake,' said Maggie Snow. 'Jake Coleman is always joking.'

'It was a male,' said Lucinder Dobb, 'Else why did she call him Hugh? You have all heard the minister say his wife hadn't a relative on earth, except her mother and a maiden aunt; it couldn't have been her mother, and it couldn't have been the maiden aunt, for her name was Martha instead of Hugh. Besides,' she kontinude, for she had so hardened her mind with mathematics, that she could grapple the hardest fact and floor it, so to speak. 'Besides,' sez she, 'the maiden aunt died a year and a half ago, that settled the matter conclusively it was not the maiden aunt.'

'I have thought something was on the minister's mind all the spring,' said Widder Tubbs, 'I have spoken to sister Ann about it a number of times.' Then she kinder rolled up her eyes, jest as she does in class-meetin', and sez she, 'It is an awful dispensation, but I hope he'll turn it into a means of grace; I hope his speritooil strength will be renewed. But,' Sez she, 'I have worryed a good deal of trouble about his bein' so handsome; I have noticed that handsome ministers don't turn out well, they most always have somethin' happen to 'em sooner or later; but I hope he'll be led.'

'Well, I never thought that Miss Linden was any *too* good,' said Betsy Babbet.

'Neither did I,' said Lucinder Dobb.

'She has turned out jest as I always thought she would,' said Ophelia, 'and I have jest as good an opinion of her as I have for them that stand up for her.'

Maggie Snow spoke up then; jest as clear as a bell her voice sounded; she ain't afraid of anybody, for she is Lawyer Snow's only child, and has been to Boston to school. Sez she, 'Aunt Allen' (She is a little related to me on her mother's side), 'Aunt Allen, why is it that, as a general rule, the very worst folks are the first ones to suspect other folks of being bad?'

Sez I, 'Maggie, they draw their pictures from memory. They want to pull down other folkses' reputations, for they feel as if their own goodness is in a totterin' condition, and if they fall, they want something to fall on, so as to come down easier like.'

Maggie Snow laughed, and so did Miss Edwards, and the Joneses, but Betsy Babbet and the Dobb girls looked black as Erobious. And, sez Betsy Babbet me, sez she: 'I shouldn't think, Josiah Allen's wife, that you would countenance such conduct.'

'I will first know there is wrong conduct,' sez I. 'Miss Linden's face is jest as innocent as a baby's, and I ain't a-goin' to mistrust any evil out of them pretty brown eyes till I am obleeged to.'

Jest at this minute the hired girl came in and said supper was ready, and we all went out to eat it. Miss Jones said there wasn't anything on the table fit to eat, and she was afraid we couldn't make out, but we did have a splendid supper, good enough for the Zero of Rushy.

We hadn't got up from the supper table and back into the parlor, when we heard a knock onto the front door. Miss Jones went and opened it, and who, of all the live world, should walk in but the minister! The faces of the wimmen as he entered would have been a study for Michael Angelico, or any of the old painters. Miss Jones was so flustrated that she asked him the first thing to take his bonnet off, then she bethought herself, and sez she, 'How's your mother?' before she had got him a chair or anything. But he looked jest as pleasant and composed as ever, though his eyes kinder laughed. And he thanked her and told her he left his mother, the day before, a good deal better; and then he turned to Maggie Snow, and sez he:—

'I have come after you, Miss Maggie,' sez he. 'My wife came home night before last, and wanted to see you so bad, that I told her as I had business past your house and I would call for you as I went home, and your mother told me you was here. I think I know,' sez he, 'why she wants to see you so very much now, she is so proud of our boy she can't wait till'—

'Your boy?' gasped nine wimmen to once.

'Yes,' sez he, smiling more pleasant than I ever see him. 'I know you will all wish me joy. We have a nice little boy, little Hugh, for my wife has named him already for her father. He is a fine, healthy little fellow—almost two months old.'

'It wouldn't have done any good for Michael Angelico to have been there then, nor Mr. Ruben, nor none of the rest of them we read of, for if they had their paletes and easeles all ready they never could have done any justice to the faces of Betsy Babbet and the Dobb girls, and, as for Miss Deacon Graves, her spectacles fell off unnoticed, and she opened her mouth so wide that it was very doubtful to me if she could ever shet it agin. And, as fer me, I was truly happy enuff to sing the Te Deus.

Maggie Snow flew out of the room to put on her bonnet, with her face shin' like a cherubin, and, as I lived half a mile on the road they was goin', and the quilt was most off, and he had two horses, and insisted, I rode with 'em and I hain't seen none of the quilters sense.

"

✳ ✳ ✳
Grandma's Patchwork Quilt

In 1868 George E. Crowell first published the magazine Household. *Its masthead bore the words "Be it ever so humble, there's no place like home." In a short period of time the magazine became a household necessity, especially in the New England area. In the October 1881 issue, under the section devoted to "The Dressing Room," this piece was published:*

Here it is, old, faded, and torn. It shows the marks of wear and time, but it is dear to me because of the many pleasant thoughts connected with it. It was made many years ago when grandma was a girl, as part of her wedding outfit. How diligently she gathered scrap after scrap of calico and bright cambric, to add light and beauty to the mystic line of stars and squares.

Grandma was young and handsome then. Those silver white locks were luxuriant, curling tresses, those dim eyes flashed then with health and youth, the form not bent and slender, was then full and delicately rounded, the step quick and elastic that is now so slow and faltering. Her soft, white fingers held the shining needle, weaving a romance as she sewed the bits of cloth. Were we but gifted with the power of divination, we should find therein a story sweeter than any ever written.

And were those dreams of life, peace, and happiness ever to be realized? It is not for us to know. We see her now, a peaceful loving old lady. If she had passed through sorrow and disappointment, they have left no trace on her except to render her more gentle and lovable. She had nobly lived down all petty cares and trials, always having a word of cheer for the distressed, charity for the needy, and consolation for the afflicted, and putting by her own crosses, she has come to be like gold seven times refined.

Here is a scrap of her mother's blue calico. How lovingly her fingers shaped this diamond, and how she was thinking, as she stitched it in, of her she was soon to leave, to cast her lot with one who was more to her than father, mother, sister, or brother! In this square is a bit of bright pink cambric. 'Tis a piece of her baby brother's dress. He only lived till he had learned to lisp the names of sister and mother, and then God took him to dwell with Him. So she went on, day after day, adding square and diamond. We will not describe them all, though there are tender recollections connected with each one. Finally it was pronounced large enough. Then it was lined, marked out in that wonderful shell pattern, and made ready for the friends to quilt.

It is a rare, meet day in June. In one of the large front rooms of her mother's house, a score of fair maidens have gathered. There is much chatter and more laughter, but that does not hinder the busy working of the needles. No sewing machines then to do row after row of fine stitching. So they talk and work, and many are the sly jokes, which call up the blushes to the face of the bride expectant.

The sunbeams fall aslant the room, the work is nearly finished, and the center is reached. How anxious each one is to put in the last stitch! It is decided at last that her friend, Lizzie Smith, who is to become her sister soon, by marriage, shall have the coveted privilege.

Now it is taken from the frame, brushed, and admired, the room swept out, and everything is put in order for the reception of the young gentlemen, who have been invited to tea. They come by twos and threes, bashfully seat themselves in corners, and look as though they knew not what to do with their hands and feet, and the girls are, to tell the truth, quite as much embarrassed as the boys.

The supper table is spread in the long kitchen, and fairly groans with its load of good things. As they gather round the board, tongues are loosened, and joke and repartee pass from lip to lip. Supper finished, they engage in the old-fashioned games of 'twirl the platter,' and 'button.' They seem to enjoy themselves much, though some of the faces turn painfully red as the 'journey to Rome' slowly progresses.

All things must have an end. They are going home, and those boys who have mustered sufficient courage take each a dear little girl on his arm. Only grandpa lingers to talk a while with the chosen one of his heart and life. Thus we leave them. Let us hope the day fulfilled the promise of the dawn. **"**

Aunt Jane of Kentucky

By Eliza Calvert Hall

In 1898 Eliza Calvert Hall wrote Aunt Jane of Kentucky. *Its Chapter III, "Aunt Jane's Album," is treasured by those who collect quilts.*

" They were a bizarre mass of color on the sweet spring landscape, those patchwork quilts, swaying in a long line under the elms and maples. The old orchard made a blossoming background for them, and farther off on the horizon rose the beauty of fresh verdure and purple mist on those low hills, or 'knobs,' that are to the heart of the Kentuckian as the Alps to the Swiss or the sea to the sailor.

I opened the gate softly and paused for a moment between the blossoming lilacs that grew on each side of the path. The fragrance of the white and purple blooms was like a resurrection-call over the graves of many a dead spring; and as I stood, shaken with thoughts as the flowers are with the winds, Aunt Jane came around from the back of the house, her black silk cape fluttering from her shoulders, and a calico sunbonnet hiding her features in its cavernous depth. She walked briskly to the clothes-line and began patting and smoothing the quilts where the breeze had disarranged them.

'Aunt Jane,' I called out, 'are you having a fair all by yourself?'

She turned quickly, pushing back the sunbonnet from her eyes.

'Why, child,' she said, with a happy laugh, 'you come pretty nigh skeerin' me. No, I ain't havin' any fair; I'm jest givin' my quilts their spring airin'. Twice a year I put 'em out in the sun and wind; and this mornin' the air smelt so sweet, I thought it was a good chance to freshen 'em up for the summer. It's about time to take 'em in now.'

She began to fold the quilts and lay them over her arm, and I did the same. Back and forth we went from the clothes-line to the house, and from the house to the clothes-line, until the quilts were safely housed from the coming dewfall and piled on every available chair in the front room. I looked at them in sheer amazement. There seemed to be every pattern that the ingenuity of woman could devise and the industry of woman put together,—four-patches, nine-patches, log-cabins, wild-goose chases, rising suns, hexagons, diamonds, and only Aunt Jane knew what else. As for the color, a Sandwich Islander would have danced with joy at the sight of those reds, purples, yellows, and greens.

'Did you really make all these quilts, Aunt Jane?' I asked wonderingly.

Aunt Jane's eyes sparkled with pride.

'Every stitch of 'em, child,' she said, 'except the quiltin'. The neighbors used to come in and help some with that. I've heard folks say that piecin' quilts was nothin' but a waste o' time, but that ain't always so. They used to say that Sarah Jane Mitchell would set down right after breakfast and piece till it was time to git dinner, and then set and piece till it was time to git supper, and then piece by candle-light till she fell asleep in her cheer.

'I ricollect goin' over there one day, and Sarah Jane was gittin' dinner in a big hurry, for Sam had to go to town with some cattle, and there was a big basket o' quilt pieces in the middle o' the kitchen floor, and the house lookin' like a pigpen, and the children runnin' around half naked. And Sam he laughed, and says he, "Aunt Jane, if we could wear quilts and eat quilts we'd be the richest people in the country." Sam was the best-natured man that ever was, or he couldn't of put up with Sarah Jane's shiftless ways. Hannah Crawford said she sent Sarah Jane a bundle o' caliker once by Sam, and Sam always declared he lost it. But Uncle Jim Matthews said he was ridin' along the road jest behind Sam, and he saw Sam throw it into the creek jest as he got on the bridge. I never blamed Sam a bit if he did.

'But there never was any time wasted on my quilts, child. I can look at every one of 'em with a clear conscience. I did my work faithful; and then when I might of set and held my hands, I'd make a block or two o' patchwork, and before long I'd have enough to put together in a quilt. I went to piecin' as soon as I was old enough to hold a needle and a piece o' cloth, and one o' the first things I can remember was settin' on the back door-step sewin' my quilt pieces, and mother praisin' my stitches. Nowadays folks don't have to sew unless they want to, but when I was a child there warn't any sewin' machines, and it was about as needful for folks to know how to sew as it was for 'em to know how to eat; and every child that was well raised could hem and run and backstitch and gather and overhand by the time she was nine years old. Why, I'd pieced four quilts by the time I was nineteen years old, and when me and Abram set up housekeepin' I had bedclothes enough for three beds.

'I've had a heap o' comfort all my life makin' quilts, and now in my old age I wouldn't take a fortune for 'em. Set down here, child, where you can see out o' the winder and smell the lilacs, and we'll look at 'em all. You see, some folks has albums to put folks' pictures in to remember 'em by, and some folks has a book and writes down the things that happen every day so they won't forgit 'em; but, honey, these quilts is my albums and my di'ries, and whenever the weather's bad and I can't git out to see folks, I jest spread out my quilts and look at 'em and study over 'em, and it's jest like goin' back fifty or sixty years and livin' my life over agin.

'There ain't nothin' like a piece o' caliker for bringin' back old times, child, unless it's a flower or a bunch o' thyme or a piece o' pennyroy'l—anything that smells sweet. Why, I can go out yonder in the yard and gather a bunch o' that purple lilac and jest shut my eyes and see faces I ain't seen for fifty years, and somethin' goes through me like a flash o' lightnin', and it seems like I'm young agin jest for that minute.'

Aunt Jane's hands were stroking lovingly a nine-patch that resembled the coat of many colors.

'Now this quilt, honey,' she said, 'I made out o' the pieces o' my children's clothes, their little dresses and waists and aprons. Some of 'em's dead, and some of 'em's grown and married and a long way off from me, further off than the one's that's dead, I sometimes think. But when I set down and look at this quilt and think over the pieces, it seems like they all come back, and I can see 'em playin' around the floor and goin' in and out, and hear 'em cryin' and laughin' and callin' me jest like they used to do before they grew up to men and women, and before there was any little graves o' mine out in the old buryin'-ground over yonder.'

Wonderful imagination of motherhood that can bring childhood back from the dust of the grave and banish the wrinkles and gray hairs of age with no other talisman than a scrap of faded calico.

The old woman's hands were moving tremulously over the surface of the quilt as if they touched the golden curls of the little dream children who had vanished from her hearth so many years ago. But there were no tears either in her eyes or in her voice. I had long noticed that Aunt Jane always smiled when she spoke of people whom the world called 'dead,' or the things it called 'lost' or 'past.' These words seemed to have for her higher and tenderer meanings than are placed on them by the sorrowful heart of humanity.

But the moments were passing, and one could not dwell too long on any quilt, however well beloved. Aunt Jane rose briskly, folded up the one that lay across her knees, and whisked out another from the huge pile in an old splint-bottomed chair.

'Here's a piece o' one o' Sally Ann's purple calicker dresses. Sally Ann always thought a heap o' purple caliker. Here's one o' Milly Amos' ginghams—that pink and white one. And that piece o' white with the rosebuds in it, that's Miss Penelope's. She give it to me the summer before she died. Bless her soul! That dress jest matched her face exactly. Somehow her and her clothes always looked alike, and her voice matched her face, too. One o' the things I'm lookin' forward to, child, is seein' Miss Penelope agin and hearin' her sing. Voices and faces is alike; there's some that you can't remember, and there's some you can't forgit. I've seen a heap o' people and hear a heap o' voices, but Miss Penelope's face was different from all the rest, and so was her voice. Why, if she said Good mornin' to you, you'd hear that Good mornin' all day, and her singin'—I know there never was anything like it in this world. My grandchildren all laugh at me for thinkin' so much o' Miss Penelope's singin', but then they never heard her, and I have: that's the difference. My grandchild Henrietta was down here three or four years ago, and says she, "Grandma, don't you want to go up to Louisville with me and hear Patti sing?" And says I, "Patty who, child?" Says I, "If it was to hear Miss Penelope sing, I'd carry these old bones o' mine clear from here to New York. But there ain't anybody else I want to hear sing bad enough to go up to Louisville or anywhere else. And some o' these days," says I, "I'm goin' to hear Miss Penelope sing." '

Aunt Jane laughed blithely, and it was impossible not to laugh with her.

'Honey,' she said, in the next breath, lowering her voice and laying her finger on the rosebud piece, 'Honey, there's one thin' I can't git over. Here's a piece o' Miss Penelope's dress, but where's Miss Penelope? Ain't it strange that a piece o' caliker'll outlast you and me? Don't it look like folks ought o' hold on to their bodies as long as other folks holds on to a piece o' the dresses they used to wear?'

Questions as old as the human heart and its human grief! Here is the glove, but where is the hand it held but yesterday? Here is the jewel she wore, but where is she?

Strange that such things as gloves, jewels, fans, and dresses can outlast a woman's form.

'Behold! I show you a mystery—the mystery of mortality.' And an eery feeling came over me as I entered into the old woman's mood and thought of the strong vital bodies that had clothed themselves in these fabrics of purple and pink and white, and that now were dust and ashes lying in sad, neglected graves on farms and lonely roadside. There lay the quilt on our knees, and the gay scraps of calico seemed to mock us with their vivid colors. Aunt Jane's cheerful voice called me back from the tombs.

'Here's a piece o' one o' my dresses,' she said; 'brown ground with a red ring in it. Abram picked it out. And here's another one, that light yeller ground with the vine runnin' through it. I never had so many caliker dresses that I didn't want one more, for in my day folks used to think a caliker dress was good enough to wear anywhere. Abram knew my failin' and two or three times a year he'd bring me a dress when he come from town. And the dresses he'd pick out always suited me better'n the ones I picked.

'I ricollect I finished this quilt the summer before Mary Frances was born, and Sally Ann and Milly Amos and Maria Petty come over and give me a lift on the quiltin'. Here's Milly's work, here's Sally Ann's, and here's Maria's.'

I looked, but my inexperienced eye could see no difference in the handiwork of the three women. Aund Jane saw my look of incredulity.

'Now, child,' she said, earnestly, 'you think I'm foolin' you, but, la! there's jest as much difference in folks' sewin' as there is in their handwritin'. Milly made a fine stitch, but she couldn't keep on the line to save her life: Maria never could make a reg'lar stitch, some'd be long and some short, and Sally Ann's was reg'lar, but all of 'em coarse. I can see 'em now stoopin' over the quiltin' frames—Milly talkin' as hard as she sewed, Sally Ann throwin' in a word now and then, and Maria never openin' her mouth except to ask for the thread or the chalk. I ricollect they come over after dinner, and we got the quilt out o' the frames long before sundown, and the next day I begun bindin' it, and I got the premium on it that year at the Fair.

'I hardly ever showed a quilt at the Fair that I didn't take the premium, but here's one quilt that Sarah Jane Mitchell beat me on.'

And Aunt Jane dragged out a ponderous, red-lined affair, the very antithesis of the silken, down-filled comforter that rests so lightly on the couch of the modern dame.

'It makes me laugh jest to think o' that time, and how happy Sarah Jane was. It was way back yonder in the fifties. The crops was all fine that season, and such apples and pears and grapes you never did see. The Floral Hall was full o' things, and the whole county turned out to go to the Fair. Abram and me got there the first day bright and early, and we was walkin' around the amp'itheater and lookin' at the town-folks and the sights, and we met Sally Ann. She stopped us, and says she, "Sarah Jane Mitchell's got a quilt in the Floral Hall in competition with yours and Milly Amos'." Says I, "Is that all the competition there is?" And Sally Ann says, "All that amounts to anything. There's one more, but it's about as bad a piece o' sewin' as Sarah Jane's, and that looks like it'd hardly hold together till the Fair's over. And," says she, "I don't believe there'll be any more. It looks like this was an off year on that particular kind o' quilt. I didn't get mine done," says she, "and neither did Maria Petty, and maybe it's a good thing after all."

'Well, I saw in a minute what Sally Ann was aimin' at. And I says to Abram, "Abram, haven't you got somethin' to do with app'intin' the judges for the women's things?" And he says, "Yes." And I says, "Well, you see to it that Sally Ann gits appointed to help judge the caliker quilts." And bless your soul, Abram got me and Sally Ann both app'inted. The other judge was Mis' Doctor Brigham, one o' the town ladies. We told her all about what we wanted to do, and she jest laughed and says, "Well, if that ain't the kindest, nicest thing! Of course we'll do it."

'Seein' that I had a quilt there, I hadn't a bit o' business bein' a judge; but the first thing I did was to fold my quilt up and hide it under Maria Petty's big worsted quilt, and then we pinned the blue Ribbon on Sarah Jane's and the red on Milly's. I'd fixed it all up with Milly, and she was jest as willin' as I was for Sarah Jane to have the premium. There was jest one thing I was afraid of: Milly was a good-hearted woman, but she never had much control over her tongue. And I says to her, says I: "Milly, it's mighty good of you to give up your chance for the premium, but if Sarah Jane ever finds it out, that'll spoil everything. For," says I, "there ain't any kindness in doin' a person a favor and then tellin' everybody about it." And Milly laughed, and says she: "I know what you mean, Aunt Jane. It's mightly hard for me to keep from tellin' everything I know and some things I don't know, but I'm never goin' to tell this, even to Sam." And she kept her word, too. Every once in a while she'd come up to me and whisper, "I ain't told it yet, Aunt Jane," jest to see me laugh.

'As soon as the doors was open, after we'd all got through judgin' and puttin' on the ribbons, Milly went and hunted Sarah Jane up and told her that her quilt had the blue ribbon. They said the poor thing like to fainted for joy. She turned right white, and had to lean up against a post for a while before she could git to the Floral Hall. I never shall forget her face. It was worth a dozen premiums to me, and Milly, too. She jest stood lookin' at that quilt and the blue ribbon on it, and her eyes was full o' tears and her lips quiverin', and then she started off and brought the children in to look at "Mammy's quilt." She met Sam on the way out, and says she: "Sam, what do you reckon? My quilt took the premium." And I believe in my soul Sam was as much pleased as Sarah Jane. He came saunterin' up, tryin' to look unconcerned, but anybody could see he was might well satisfied. It does a husband and wife a heap o' good to be proud of each other, and I reckon that was the first time Sam ever had cause to be proud o' pore Sarah Jane. It's my belief that he thought more o' Sarah Jane all the rest o' her life jest on account o' that premium.

'Me and Sally Ann helped her pick it out. She had her choice betwixt a butter-dish and a cup, and she took the cup. Folks used to laugh and say that the cup was the only thin' in Sarah Jane's house that was kept clean and bright, and if it hadn't been solid silver, she'd 'a' wore it all out rubbin' it up. Sarah Jane died o' pneumonia about three or four years after that, and the folks that nursed her said she wouldn't take a drink o' water or a dose o' medicine out o' any cup but that. There's some folks, child, that don't have to do anything but walk along and hold out their hands, and the premiums jest naturally fall into 'em; and I reckon nobody but the Lord and Sarah Jane knows how much happiness she got out o' that cup. I'm thankful she had that much pleasure before she died.'

There was a quilt hanging over the foot of the bed that had about it a certain air of distinction. It was a solid mass of patchwork, composed of squares, parallelograms, and hexagons. The squares were of dark gray and red-brown, the hexagons were white, the parallelograms black and light gray. I felt sure that it had a history that set it apart from its ordinary fellows.

'Where did you get the pattern, Aunt Jane?' I asked. 'I never saw anything like it.'

The old lady's eyes sparkled, and she laughed with pure pleasure.

'That's what everybody says,' she exclaimed, jumping up and spreading the favored quilt over two laden chairs, where its merits became more apparent and striking. 'There ain't another quilt like this in the State o' Kentucky, or the world, for that matter. My granddaughter Henrietta, Mary Frances' youngest child, brought me this pattern *from Europe.*'

She spoke the words as one might say, 'from Paradise,' or 'from Olympus,' or 'from the Lost Atlantic.' 'Europe' was evidently a name to conjure with, a country of mystery and romance unspeakable. I had seen many things from many lands beyond the sea, but a quilt pattern from Europe! Here at last was something new under the sun. In what shop of London or Paris were quilt patterns kept on sale for the American tourist?

'You see,' said Aunt Jane, 'Henrietta married a mighty rich man, and jest as good as he's rich, too, and they went to Europe on their bridal trip. When she come home she brought me the prettiest shawl you ever saw. She made me stand up and shut my eyes, and she put it on my shoulders and made me look in the lookin'-glass, and then she says, "I brought you a new quilt pattern, too, grandma, and I want you to piece one quilt by it and leave it to me when you die." And then she told me about goin' to a town over yonder they call Florence, and how she went into a big church that was built hundreds o' years before I was born. And she said the floor was made o' little pieces o' colored stone, all laid together in a pattern, and they called it mosaic. And says I, "Honey, has it got anything to do with Moses and his law?" You know the Commandments was called the Mosaic Law, and was all on tables o' stone. And Henrietta jest laughed, and says she, "The minute I stepped on that pavement I thought about you, and I drew this pattern off on a piece o' paper and brought it all the way to Kentucky for you to make a quilt by." Henrietta bought the worsted for me, for she said it had to be jest the colors o' that pavement over yonder, and I made it that very winter.' Aunt Jane was regarding the quilt with worshipful eyes, and it really was an effective combination of color and form.

'Many a time while I was piecin' that,' she said, 'I thought about the man that laid the pavement in that old church, and wondered what his name was, and how he looked, and what he'd think if he knew there was a old woman down here in Kentucky usin' his patterns to make a bed quilt.'

It was indeed a far cry from the Florentine artisan of centuries ago to this humble worker in calico and worsted, but between the two stretched a cord of sympathy that made them one—the eternal aspiration after beauty.

'Honey,' Aunt Jane said suddenly, 'did I ever show you my premiums?'

And then, with pleasant excitement in her manner, she arose, fumbled in her deep pocket for an ancient bunch of keys, and unlocked a cupboard on one side of the fireplace. One by one, she drew them out, unrolled the soft yellow tissue-paper that enfolded them, and ranged them in a stately line on the old cherry center-table—nineteen sterling silver cups and goblets. 'Abram took some of 'em on his fine stock, and I took some of 'em on my quilts and salt-risin' bread and cakes,' she said, impressively.

To the artist his medals, to the soldier his cross of the Legion of Honor, and to Aunt Jane her silver cups. All the triumph of a humble life was symbolized in these shining things. They were simple and genuine as the days in which they were made. A few of them boasted a beaded edge or a golden lining, but no engraving or embossing marred their silver purity. On the bottom of each was the stamp: 'John B. Akin, Danville, Ky.' There they stood, filled to the brim with precious memories—memories of the time when she and Abram had worked together in field or garden or home, and the County Fair brought to all a yearly opportunity to stand on the height of achievement and know somewhat the taste of Fame's enchanted cup.

'There's one for every child and every grandchild,' she said, quietly, as she began wrapping them in the silky paper, and storing them carefully away in the cupboard, there to rest until the day when children and grandchildren would claim their own, and the treasures of the dead would come forth from the darkness to stand as heirlooms on fashionable sideboards and damask-covered tables.

'Did you ever think, child,' she said, presently, 'how much piecin' a quilt's like livin' a life? And as for sermons, why, they ain't no better sermon to me than a patchwork quilt, and the doctrines is right there a heap plainer'n they are in the catechism. Many a time I've set and listened to Parson Page preachin' about predestination and free-will, and I've said to myself, "Well, I ain't never been through Centre College up at Danville, but if I could jest git up in the pulpit with one of my quilts, I could make it a heap plainer to folks than parson's makin' it with all his big words." You see, you start out with jest so much caliker; you don't go to the store and pick it out and buy it, but the neighbors will give you a piece here and piece there, and you'll have a piece left every time you cut out a dress, and you take jest what happens to come. And that's like predestination. But when it comes to the cuttin' out, why, you're free to choose your own pattern. You can give the same kind of pieces to two persons, and one'll make a nine-patch and one'll make a wild-goose chase, and there'll be two quilts made out o' the same kind o' pieces, and jest as different as they can be. And that is jest the way with livin'. The Lord sends us the pieces but we can cut 'em out and put 'em together pretty much to suit ourselves, and there's a heap more in the cuttin' out and the sewin' than there is in the caliker. The same sort o' things comes into all lives, jest as the Apostle says, "There hath no trouble taken you but is common to all men."

'The same trouble'll come into two people's lives, and one'll take it and make one thing out of it, and the other'll make somethin' entirely different. There was Mary Harris and Mary Crawford. They both lost their husbands the same year; and Mary Crawford set down and cried, and worried and wondered what on earth she was goin' to do, and the farm went to wreck and the children turned out bad, and she had to live with a son-in-law in her old age. But Mary Harris, she got up and went to work and she managed the farm better'n it ever had been managed before, and the boys all come up steady, hard-workin' men, and there wasn't a woman in the county better fixed than Mary Harris. Things is predestined to come to us, honey, but we're jest as free as air to make what we please out of 'em. And when it comes to puttin' the pieces together, there's another time when we're free. You don't trust to luck for the caliker to put your quilt together with; you go to the store and pick it out yourself, any color you like. There's folks that always looks on the bright side and makes the best of everything, and that's like puttin' your quilt together with blue or pink or white or some other pretty color; and there's folks that never see anything but the dark side, and always lookin' for trouble, and treasurin' it up after they git it, and they're puttin' their lives together with black, jest like you would put a quilt together with some ugly color. You can spoil the prettiest quilt pieces that ever was made jest by puttin' them together with the wrong color, and the best sort o' life is miserable if you don't look at things right and think about 'em right.

'Then there's another thing. I've seen folks piece and piece, but when it comes to puttin' the block together and quiltin' it and linin' it, they'd give out; and that's like folks that do a little here and little there, but their lives ain't of much use after all, any more'n a lot o' loose pieces o' patchwork. And then while you're living your life, it looks pretty much like a jumble o' quilt pieces before they're put together; but when you git through with it, or pretty nigh through, as I am now, you'll see the use and the purpose of everything in it. Everything'll be in its right place jest like the squares in this four-patch, and one piece may be pretty and another one ugly, but it looks right when you see it finished and joined together.'

Did I say that every pattern was represented? No, there was one notable omission. Not a single crazy quilt was there in the collection. I called Aunt Jane's attention to this lack.

'Child,' she said, 'I used to say there wasn't anything I couldn't do if I made up my mind to it. But I hadn't seen a crazy quilt then. The first one I ever seen was up in Danville, at Mary Frances', and Henrietta says, "Now, grandma, you've got to make a crazy quilt; you've made every other sort that ever was heard of." And she brought me the pieces and showed me how to baste 'em on the square, and said she'd work the fancy stitches around 'em for me. Well, I set there all the mornin' trying to fix up that square, and more I tried, the uglier and crookeder the thing looked. And finally I says: "Here, child, take your pieces. If I was to make this the way you want me to, they'd be a crazy quilt and a crazy woman, too" '

Aunt Jane was laying the folded quilts in neat piles here and there about the room. There was a look of unspeakable satisfaction on her face—the look of the creator who sees his completed work and pronounces it good.

'I've been a hard worker all my life,' she said, seating herself and folding her hands restfully, 'But 'most all my work has been the kind that "perishes with the usin'," as the Bible says. That's the discouragin' thing about a woman's work. Milly Amos used to say that if a woman was to see all the dishes that she had to wash before she died, piled up before her in one pile, she'd lie down and die right then and there. I've always had the name o' bein' a good housekeeper, but when I'm dead and gone there ain't anybody goin' to think o' the floors I've swept, and the tables I've scrubbed, and the old clothes I've patched, and the stockin's I've darned. Abram might 'a' remembered it, but he ain't here. But when one o' my grandchildren or great-grandchildren sees one o' these quilts, they'll think about Aunt Jane, and, wherever I am then, I'll know I ain't forgotten.

'I reckon everybody wants to leave somethin' behind that'll last after they're dead and gone. It don't look like it's worth while to live unless you can do that. The Bible says folks "rest from their labors, and their works do follow them," but that ain't so. They go, and maybe they do rest, but their works stay right here, unless they're the sort that don't outlast the usin'. Now, some folks has money to build monuments with—great, tall, marble pillars, with angels on top of 'em, like you see in Cave Hill and them big city buryin'-grounds. And some folks can build churches and schools and hospitals to keep folks in mind of 'em, but all the work I've got to leave behind me is jest these quilts, and sometimes, when I'm setting here, workin' with my caliker and gingham pieces, I'll finish off a block, and I laugh and say to myself, "Well, here's another stone for the monument."

'I reckon you think, child, that a caliker or a worsted quilt is a curious sort of a monument—'bout as perishable as the sweepin' and scrubbin' and mendin'. But if folks values things rightly, and knows how to take care of 'em, there ain't many things that'll last longer'n a quilt. Why, I've got a blue and white counterpane that my mother's mother spun and wove, and there ain't a sign o' givin' out in it yet. I'm going to will that to my granddaughter that lives in Danville, Mary Frances' oldest child. She was down here last summer, and I was lookin' over my things and packin' 'em away, and she happened to see that counterpane, and says she, "Grandma, I want you to will me that," And says I: "What do you want with that old thing, honey? You know you wouldn't sleep under such a counterpane as that." And says she, "No, but I'd hang it up over my parlor door for a—" '

'Portière?' I suggested, as Aunt Jane hesitated for the unaccustomed word.

'That's it, child. Somehow I can't ricollect these new-fangled words, any more'n I can understand these new-fangled ways. Who'd ever 'a' thought that folks'd go to stringin' up bed-coverin's in their door? And says I to Jane, "You can hang your great-grandmother's counterpane up in your parlor door if you want to, but," says I, "don't ever make a door-curtain out o' one o' my quilts." But la! the way things turn around, if I was to come back fifty years from now, like as not I'd find 'em usin' my quilts for window-curtains or door-mats.'

We both laughed, and there rose in mind a picture of a twentieth-century house decorated with Aunt Jane's nine-patches and rising suns. How could the dear old woman know that the same esthetic sense that had drawn from their obscurity the white and blue counterpanes of colonial days would forever protect her loved quilts from such a desecration as she feared? As she lifted a pair of quilts from a chair near by, I caught sight of a pure white spread in striking contrast with the many-hued patchwork.

'Where did you get that Marseilles spread, Aunt Jane?' I asked, pointing to it. Aunt Jane lifted it and laid it on my lap without a word. Evidently she thought that here was something that could speak for itself. It was two layers of snowy white cotton cloth thinly lined with cotton, and elaborately quilted into a perfect imitation of a Marseilles counterpane. The pattern was a tracery of roses, buds, and leaves, very much conventionalized, but still recognizable for the things they were. The stitches were fairylike, and altogether it might have covered the bed of a queen.

'I made every stitch o' that spread the year before me and Abram was married,' she said. 'I put it on my bed when we went to housekeepin'; it was on the bed when Abram died, and when I die I want 'em to cover me with it.' There was a life-history in the simple words. I thought of Desdemona and her bridal sheets, and I did not offer to help Aunt Jane as she folded this quilt.

'I reckon you think,' she resumed presently, 'that I'm a mean, stingy old creetur not to give Janie the counterpane now, instead o' hoardin' it up, and all these quilts too, and keepin' folks waitin' for 'em till I die. But, honey, it ain't all selfishness. I'd give away my best dress or my best bonnet or an acre o' ground to anybody that needed 'em more 'n I did; but these quilts—why, it looks like my whole life was sewed up in 'em, and I ain't goin' to part with 'em while life lasts.'

There was a ring of passionate eagerness in the old voice, and she fell to putting away her treasures as if the suggestion of losing them had made her fearful of their safety.

I looked again at the heap of quilts. An hour ago they had been patchwork, and nothing more. But now! The old woman's words had wrought a transformation in the homely mass of calico and silk and worsted. Patchwork? Ah, no! It was memory, imagination, history, biography, joy, sorrow, philosophy, religion, romance, realism, life, love, and death; and over all, like a halo, the love of the artist for his work and the soul's longing for earthly immortality.

No wonder the wrinkled fingers smoothed them as reverently as we handle the garments of the dead.　　　　　　　　　　　　　　　　　　　　　　　　　　　　　　　　　　　　　　　**"**

* * *

The Comfort Club

By Elizabeth Rhodes

In 1911 the magazine Pictorial Review *ran a quilting contest with a first prize of $10.00, a second prize of $5.00, and prizes for runners-up of $1.00 each. The contest was conducted in the column called "The Comfort Club," by Elizabeth Rhodes. Here are some excerpts:*

"　　The Quilting-Bees, which were held at the home of the members, who competed for the cash prizes offered by *Pictorial Review*, are now of 'dreams of long ago,' but remember that the Quilting-Bee we held in New York, to award the prizes, is still very fresh in our memories. And so I am going to tell you all about it.

To begin at the end, as it were, the prize winners are pictured on the next page; but decisions were not reached in a minute. How I wish that you could have attended to our very novel Quilting-Bee!

Picture to yourselves a great, big office building in New York, where five hundred busy people are working. On one floor of that building you will find the editor's room, and there, amid pictures and manuscripts and ink-wells and paste-jars, we held the Bee. There were not enough chairs for all the judges to sit on, so some of us sat on the tables, one or two leaned up against the desk; while others sat on a big packing-box which held some pictures. Patchwork may be an old story in your part of the country, but it is really a novelty in an editorial office; so every one was interested and wanted to come.

We Invited the Men to Help

Oh, Yes, I must confess that we invited the men to help us. After all, it is a poor party with no men around, and anyway they would have come snooping in without an invitation. They really were not much practical help and we did not pay much attention to their opinions, but they did not know it, so the party broke up without any unkind words. Some of the reasons they gave were really very funny, and I must tell you about them.

Mr. Blank, who can add up the longest list of the figures in the shortest possible time, declared that the log-cabin quilt should get first prize, because he had made one when he was a child and could still remember how very difficult it was! We told him he might be all right in the accounting-room but as a judge of quilts he was a failure.

Then the editor spoke up, and of course we all expected something just right from him, because he was a country boy and really ought to have known something about quilts. I suppose he slept under them until he was a grown man, but you never can tell! He declared that the Cherokee Rose should be given first prize, because he remembered a pair of portières in his grandmother's sitting-room made after that pattern. As the Queen Bee in this little part, I felt that I could afford to speak my mind right then and there, even to the editor; so I very sarcastically reminded him that this was not a portière exhibit but a quilting-bee.

Quilting and Workmanship Counted

Finally we decided that the men could stay, but that their opinions on quilts were not all we had hoped for, and from that moment on the women took charge. We spent over an hour going over each quilt, examining it from several standpoints—color, quilting, piecing, and binding, and we sincerely hope that everyone will be satisfied with the results. We were as honest as could be and if you are content write me.

Some of the life stories which were woven into the quilts were heart-rending, and some of them held only the happiest memories. One woman sent me a quilt from Iowa and with it went this story:

Her father died when she was about twelve years old and her mother was an invalid. This child went to work for a dressmaker, and did all the housework except the cooking for which the dressmaker paid her in scraps of silk. At that time they seemed perfect treasures, as the brilliant-colored silks were about the only bright things that came into her life. And when she had finished her work, she used to sit and piece quilts. But I fear her little fingers were very weary when the beds were made, the stairs swept down, for the stitches were not very even and the piecing was—well not exactly straight. But think what that quilt represents to this woman. Years of a young life that should have been spent making mud pies and dressing curly-wigged doll babies!

Another quilt had been made in a prison in Newfoundland, by a model prisoner. She was a young girl, who, in a moment of weakness and temper, had committed some wrong. The pieces were given to her by visitors to the institution, and when the quilt was actually finished, the authorities allowed her to sell it to the woman who had submitted it to us. Think of the sorrow and heartache that is sewn into that calico covering!

But among the happy stories stitched into a quilt was one made of white satin. The girl who pieced it said it was made from pieces of her grandmother's wedding-gown, her mother's wedding-gown, and her own bridal dress! It was odd to see the various shades which the satin had taken on in the flight of years. Some of it was so yellow that it was corn-color. And we imagined that we could pick out the quality which made the oldest and the newest frock, just from the texture of the satin which changes with the fashions.

One Quilt Pieced by a Man

Still another was pieced by a man! He had been very ill, and when he was convalescing his wife was piecing a quilt, but was doing it by hand. He suggested that he run up the pieces on the machine, and so his wife let him do it. He became so interested in it that when it was all together he wanted to do the quilting by machine. The effect was really very good, but of course could not compete with hand quilting. I had a long letter from him the other day and I really think he was a most disappointed contributor. Just as if we would give a man the prize, even if his quilt was a good one!

One quilt was submitted which was a winner of a one-dollar prize, but I am sorry to say that it is not pictured among the winners. It was sent in by Mrs. Peter Efferts of Minnesota, but because of the coloring, it could not be photographed well enough to reproduce. It was a beautiful little quilt to fit a baby's crib, and made of the softest white muslin and tiny squares of pale-blue satin. And the quilting was wonderful. . . . We hope that you had as good a time at your quilting-bee as we did at ours. 〞

Chapter 5

Origin and Variety of Quilt and Pattern Names

EVERY QUILT PATTERN has a name. Many were designed to commemorate great events, political parties and their candidates, ethnic origins, and regional loyalties.

The oldest pattern, the Crazy Quilt, popular in the 1800's, is now enjoying a resurgence of interest. Then came the average geometric quilting patterns universally repeated.

Until the westward march of the pioneer, New England, Pennsylvania, and the Southern regions had their own characteristic quilts. The New England woman made pictorial patterns, while in the South the quilts were examples of exquisite needlework.

The Star and Crescent is characteristic of Pennsylvania Dutch quilts, always highly individualistic. It requires tedious and most exacting work and was never popular with New England women, for all their industrious ways. The women of New England made quilts by the dozen, and exceedingly beautiful ones, but they also read, attended community singing schools, and shared to a considerable degree the general life of the day.

This was not so with the Pennsylvania Dutch housewife, whose time was spent largely on work which would show material results. Pennsylvania Dutch quilts are the easiest to identify, as they are of bold colors, elaborate designs, pieced more often than appliqués, and quilted beautifully. Two of their favorite quilts are Full Blown Tulip and Princess Feathers.

Many quilt names were taken from the Bible. World Without End is a name taken from a phrase in the Book of Common Prayer. Examination of this attractive all-over pattern reveals the endless "worlds," which are interlocking circles constructed of triangles and squares.

The Star of Bethlehem, Jacob's Ladder, and Job's Tears are some other quilts with Biblical names. Others were named The Star and the Cross, King David's Crown, Golgotha, The Three Crosses, Cross Upon Cross, and Cross and Crown.

Some of these designs are common only to the communities of their origin, while many others acquired new names with only slight changes and so ran the number of designs into the hundreds. To be sure, some of the most interesting of the older patterns have been lost because of changing conditions and migrations. There are several similar designs all known as Joseph's Coat, alike in their wonderful colors and degree of difficulty. The Rose of Sharon quilt patterns are innumerable. Almost every pattern that has any resemblance to a rose has at one time or another been called Rose of Sharon. The same is the case with star patterns and their association with the name Star of Bethlehem.

Early American quilters reproduced scenes of military action and adventure when they designed The Burgoyne Surrender, Underground Railway, Whig's Defeat, Lincoln's Platform, and Rocky Road to California.

War or unexpected political events brought on a rash of new quilt patterns. Often they were old patriotic patterns renamed. Eagles, stars, and soldiers were introduced into the basic patterns to produce a new design. Quilters tried to keep up with the times and hurried their quilting in order to complete it by the time another outstanding event would occur.

The Lobster, which was named for a fancied resemblance to that creature, was developed along the seacoast early in the colonial period. However, it became a popular design in all of the states during the War of 1812 when the British attacked Washington. It seems that the British military man was called Lobsterback by the Americans; so the design came into being as a rebuff to the British.

The quarrel between the United States and British Canada over the division of the Pacific Northwest in 1846 resulted in the pattern known as 54-40 or Fight. This pattern is still popular.

The Lincoln-Douglas debates of 1854 inspired The Little Giant and Lincoln's Platform. These two designs are still being used. Other politically named designs are Washington's Quilt, Jackson's Star, Tippecanoe and Tyler Too, and Free Trade Block.

Trades and occupations of the times also became a good source of quilt names. The Carpenter's Wheel, The Double Monkey Wrench, The Anvil, The Saw Tooth, and The Churn Dash are examples. The Reel was named after the reel used by women to wind thread into skeins.

The Dusty Miller immortalized the old roadside mill and miller. Water furnished the power for the mill. Natural mill sites, therefore, were of great value. Very often the location of a village or town was determined by the location of the mill.

Swing-in-the-Center and Eight Hands Round were taken from recreation and leisuretime pursuits. These two names are names of figures and calls for the square dance that finished off many an evening after a quilting bee, a husking bee, or a barn-raising.

The more romantic quilters worked on Cupid's Arrow, Bridal Stairway, The Eternal Triangle, and finally Double Wedding Ring.

Some quilts were named after foreign countries, expressing, perhaps, women's desire to travel. Some of the patterns were Dutch Mill, Chinese Puzzle, Arabian Star, and World's Without End.

Almost every flower has a quilt named after it, such as Tulip, American Beauty Rose, Morning Glory, Mountain Laurel, and Primrose Path. Vegetable names inspired Corn and Beans, Strawberry Quilt, Melon Patch, and Tobacco Leaf.

Birds and insects as well as animals were used as a source of names. Honey Bee, Flying Swallows, Bear Tracks, and Wild Goose Chase are representative. Dove-in-the-Window dates back to the time when a barn had round holes cut in the gable with a tiny platform beneath to house the pigeons.

A name might be chosen to honor the quilter's favorite heroine. Barbara Fritchie Star, Dolly Madison Star, Martha Washington's Star, Mrs. Cleveland's Choice are named for such famous ladies. Lady of the Lake is named after the novel of the same name by Sir Walter Scott.

Quilts were even named after the sun. Why the Rising Sun pattern is so complicated one cannot say, but it is one of the most difficult designs to work out. Only a true expert attempts to make that quilt. There are two ways to construct the Rising Sun quilt. Some favor the single Rising Sun, which consists of one large sun with rays radiating from the center of the quilt to the edges. The longest ray often measures four feet in length with a six-inch base. The second method is to construct many smaller suns, often one to a block.

The Setting Sun, however, is a simple pattern. The blocks of this quilt are always set together and sewed into strips; then they are joined so that each seam comes in the exact middle of the block of the strips adjoining above and below.

Each of the states has quilts named for it. Many cities are likewise honored by quilt names, such as Georgetown Circles, Chicago Star, and Philadelphia Pavements.

The easiest part of designing a new pattern was naming it. There are always historical events, pioneer struggles, and social events to fall back on. A single popular name was often applied to many patterns. Conversely, a popular pattern might have many names, each one correct for a particular locality or time. This is the case of two patterns, the Shoo-fly and Star-Spangled Banner. The Shoo-fly is called by its regular name when done in any color combination except green and yellow on white; when pieced in these colors, it becomes Chinese Coin. The Star pattern when done in red, white, and blue is called Star-Spangled Banner and Golden Splendor when done in three shades of yellow.

A design might have a different name in each region in which it was quilted.

The Bear's Paw in Pennsylvania was called Duck's Feet in the Mud on Long Island, where there were no bears but plenty of ducks. Another example is a pattern that appeared first in New England as Wood's Lily. In Pennsylvania it became Pennsylvania Tulip; in North Carolina it was North Carolina Lily; in Ohio, Tiger Lily; and in parts of the Midwest it became Meadow Lily. Through all these name changes, the pattern varied not one bit.

The Garden design was to appliqué what a Star of Bethlehem or Rising Sun was to pieced patchwork. Other popular appliqué designs were Birds of Paradise and Horn of Plenty. These are all-over designs and are not made in separate blocks. Garden Wreath is an appliquéd quilt constructed from individual blocks. One of the popular methods for producing striking effects in appliqué was to use four great yard-square blocks, such as Spice Pink and Rose of Sharon. Rose of Sharon was usually a bride's quilt, being the most often used of all appliqué for that final touch to a dowry.

A woman's inspiration for choosing a quilt pattern might come from a design used by her neighbor; she might revise a pattern of her European ancestors, or copy a design from *Godey's Lady's Book*. More often than not, her design would depend to a great extent upon what scraps of material she had collected.

Although the basic pattern might be the same, every quilt is different in detail from every other quilt. The colors and sizes vary. The sewing work is individualized. A woman's stitch is like her signature. Some quilts took months to make, others a few weeks—depending on the skill of the worker, the sophistication of her tools, and whether or not she had help.

In the late Victorian era entirely new quilt names were added to the old familiar ones. The Spanish-American War brought closer ties among Cuba, the Philippine Islands, and the United States. The Battle of Manila, in 1898, made George Dewey a household word and the quilt pattern The Dewey resulted. Other quilt patterns directly related to the Spanish-American War were the Cuban Quilt, the Manila Quilt, and The Philippines.

During this period baseball grew to be a national pastime. So, of course, the quilt pattern Baseball was created.

All was not serene during the Gilded Age. The unemployment rate was high. A large band of unemployed dissidents, led by Jacob S. Coxey of Ohio, began a march on Washington to petition the government for reforms. They arrived at their destination on May 1, 1894. The quilt Coxey's Camp commemorates the event.

From about 1879 the temperance movement was a powerful force on the American scene. Its influence was felt, even in the highest circles. President Rutherford B. Hayes lived in a "dry" White House during the years 1877 to 1881. Public officials, who were forced to attend White House social functions, slyly referred to the President's wife as "Lemonade Lucy," much to the consternation and horror of their very proper and genteel Victorian wives. So it is not surprising to find that there was a quilt named W.C.T. Union.

Several outstanding exhibitions were held during the late Victorian era. The

Philadelphia Centennial Exhibition in 1876 inspired the creation of such quilt patterns as Centennial and Centennial Wreath. The Columbian Exposition at Chicago in 1893 had a Women's Building in which was displayed outstanding needlework from all over the world. Several new quilt patterns resulted from the event, including The World's Fair Block, World's Fair, Columbian Star, and The World's Fair Puzzle.

During this same period many prominent English authors came to America for lecture tours. Charles Dickens, who made the trip in 1842, was one of the first. By the late 1800's Rudyard Kipling and Oscar Wilde spent some time here. Wilde's reputation preceded him; so American women designed a quilt called Oscar's Crazy Quilt. Oscar Wilde had worked hard to popularize the sunflower; so this mosaic quilt was made with an appliquéd and embroidered sunflower decorating each block.

The tragedy of President Garfield's assassination was immortalized in a quilt called Garfield's Monument.

New patterns are being designed today by many women, but they have not yet been popularized. Perhaps with the growing interest in quilts these new patterns will be exhibited and copied.

There are so many quilt and pattern names that a complete list is impossible. A few of the more popular ones are described here:

The Album: A real old-timer. Its original purpose was as a gift to a bride-to-be. Each friend of a bride would piece a block and embroider her own name upon it. Since each of the many squares was created by a different individual, the quilt often had an unusual look about it.

Baby Blocks: This design used the diamond motif, with its patches carefully pieced to bring their corners exactly together. It produces a puzzling geometric effect.

The other names of the pattern were Box Quilt, Cube Works, Tea Chest. When care was used in the shading of the blocks, the pattern was known as The Heavenly Steps.

Bear's Paw: This is unquestionably of frontier origin. Perhaps the pioneer father told of such a track and the mother thought to herself, "How interesting!" Then she drew the pattern on linsey-woolsey, or hickory-dyed jean, using the unworn parts of much-patched garments to make a sturdy quilt block. This design is also known as Duck's Food in the Mud.

In Pennsylvania the Friends called the pattern Hand of Friendship. By curving its angles, others created a lovely block called Hands All Around.

Beggar Block: This design of many small pieces probably arose from the neighborly custom of begging one's friends for scraps of frocks or for old neckties to sew into a quilt.

Blazing Star: Along the New England coast this pattern is called The Ship's Wheel and is said to have originated on Cape Cod. Inland it is known as The Harvest Sun. Among seafarers the blocks represented the ship's wheel. The projections were the steering handles grasped by the helmsman. To the pioneers who settled in Ohio, Illinois, and Kansas the pattern looked like the sun that ripened their grain.

Bride's Quilt: Fashionable in the mid-nineteenth century, it included hearts in its design—almost the only design that did, since it was considered unlucky to use the heart in any other quilt lest the young girl would have a broken engagement.

In the dower chest of every bride-to-be was a "baker's dozen" of quilts. All but one would be made for everyday use. But there would be a special one elaborate in design and execution. Throughout her girlhood the maker would lay top after top in her chest as fast as they were completed. Until a girl became engaged, people felt that there was no point in supplying the material for the wadding and back, or in doing the quilting. When the neighbors were invited to quilt a girl's tops, they knew that she planned to be married.

California Rose: This quilt is also called Whig Rose, Democratic Rose, or Tea Rose, depending upon its area of origin.

Crazy Quilt: From worn and discarded woolen clothing women cut small patches of sound material and sewed them together "crazy fashion." The back and padding or interlining was fastened to the top at intervals with stitches of varicolored yarn in the manner known as "knotting."

The nineteenth-century development of the Crazy Quilt occurred when silks and velvets were basted upon a cambric foundation and the edges fastened together with embroidery stitches. The more elaborate the handwork, the more beautiful the finished quilt. These quilts were usually made in large squares, which were then sewn together to produce quilts used as "slumber robes" or "couch throws."

Crewelwork Quilt: Crewelwork of multicolored wools is appliquéd to the top of this quilt, which is then quilted.

Cubework: A diamond pattern, which was a special favorite in New England, reserved for the best quilts of that region.

The Delectable Mountains: This quilt originated in New England. The name had its inspiration in the following lines from *Pilgrim's Progress* by John Bunyan: "They went till they came to the Delectable Mountains . . . behold the gardens and orchards, the vineyards and fountains of water."

Falling Star: Also called Flying Star, Flying Swallow, and Circling Swallows. It is a great favorite in New England and Pennsylvania.

French Star: Canadian pattern combining an eight-pointed star of diamond-shaped blocks and a small melon-shaped piece of the background color or of contrasting hue. The melon-shaped pieces in turn form a wreath and may divide the star into two colors.

Friendship Quilt: Each block might contain a different design. The final result might be a quilt that would be more interesting than beautiful. Following a girl's engagement, a friend, or perhaps her mother, would arrange a friendship medley surprise party. Each guest brought materials for a block, but the hostess provided material for the set. The guests would work quickly, for although no two blocks would be alike they had to be finished and set together before supper was served. Often the same guests were invited to return to a quilting bee when the bedcover was ready to be stitched.

Full-blown Tulip: The peacock and the tulip were Pennsylvania Dutch motifs, the bird representing to some the "eye of God." A block similar to Full-Blown Tulip with petals square instead of rounded is called Caesar's Crown. Only a woman thoroughly experienced in piecing could make such a quilt.

Hit and Miss: This quilt used the rectangular patch in an all-over pattern. This and Roman Stripe and Brick Wall are called one-patchers. When the square is cut diagonally in half and arranged to form a pattern, the design is called Two-Patch.

Honeycomb: Hexagon patches sewed together without any attempt at color arrangements are the basis of this pattern. This is one of the earliest of the pieced quilt patterns and was an excellent means of using small but precious scraps of material.

Ice-Cream Bowl: This pattern is made up of triangular-shaped pieces of various sizes to give the effect of cut glass.

Lafayette Orange Peel: This quilt is also known as Orange Peel. The story is that once when the Marquis de Lafayette was feted in Philadelphia, a fair guest at the banquet took home as her souvenir an orange imported from Barcelona. To preserve her treasure and the memory of the day, she carefully made a pattern from the pared rind and this pattern comes down to us as the Orange Peel quilt block. This design is also known as Rob Peter to Pay Paul, a general name for a block in which the cut part of one section appears to pay the part robbed from another.

Le Moyne Star: Some variation of the diamond or square forms the base of all star patterns, which far outnumber all other designs. The simplest form is an eight-pointed star known as the Star of Le Moyne. The name alludes to the LeMoyne brothers who in 1718 founded the city of New Orleans. In New England the name was shortened to Lemon Star.

Log Cabin: This is an excellent pattern for using small silk scraps. The block, carefully shaded in light and dark, is made with a square center, while four "logs" graduated in length are built up on each of its four sides. A different placing of light and dark corners produced the Straight Furrow and the Barn Raising.

Many colonial homes had at least one of these geometrically arranged quilts made from scraps of silk. It was highly prized and used only for "company best."

Ohio Star Quilt: Miniature triangles are pieced together to form four squares. These, plus one solid, center square, comprise an eight-pointed star. Four white corner blocks are added to make the basic Nine-Patch design within a three-inch square. Alternate blocks are set on point to give an over-all checkerboard diamond effect.

Old Maid's Puzzle: This is a genuinely antique pattern. Triangles of two sizes are arranged so that the large triangles form an Hourglass.

Pieced Star: The versions of star quilt piecing vary from four points to eight.

Some of the star blocks are named Northumberland Star, California Star, St. Louis Star, Chicago Star, Dolly Madison's Star, and the Cowboy's Star.

Presentation Quilt: A form of quilt in the album class to convey regard and respect, usually given to the local minister and his wife.

Peony or Piney: Peony pattern is a combination of patchwork and appliqué, usually red and green blossoms being pieced and the green leaves and stems whipped onto the white foundation of the four-part block. The flowers make up three-fourths of the entire block and are made of eight diamond-shaped patches, the arrangement of colors suggesting the red petals and green calyx. This pattern is a very old design common to many parts of the country. It was the inspiration for countless patterns that appear in different places under various names.

Roman Stripe: Rectangular scraps of silk of varying widths sewn together into strips and set lengthwise with strips of a contrasting color.

Scripture Quilt: Each block contains a verse, a Bible quotation, or admonition written in indelible ink.

Star of Bethlehem: A pattern formed from eight perfectly matched diamonds cut from a single square.

Swastika: Frontier women ingeniously converted this ancient symbol of good luck into a quilt pattern which is made simply from two triangles. Sometimes it is called Fly Foot. The swastika, an ancient symbol believed to represent the sun, was a popular device brought over from Germany. The Whirling Swastika appeared on Pennsylvania-German barns and is locally referred to as *Hexfiess*, or witches' feet, painted on barns to ward off evil spirits. While these figures no doubt originally possessed symbolic meaning, today they are merely ornamental.

Tree of Life: One of the oldest designs in Massachusetts for a pieced quilt. In pre-Revolutionary days The Pine Tree and The Tree of Life were popular designs for quilts. The Weeping Willow, symbolic of mourning, embroidered in silk was sometimes used. The Tree of Life used on quilts is thought to have originated in the motif so frequently found in Oriental rugs which graced the eighteenth-century homes in the colonies or in the enormous tree pattern of the palampores brought by sea captains returning from the East Indies. Such designs were cut from India chintz and appliquéd on a quilt top as fancy dictated but never used in their entirety.

Tulip: About the middle of the sixteenth century the tulip traveled to Europe from Asia Minor and immediately became popular in the gardens of England, the Low Countries, and Germany. When the Mennonites brought the tulip to Pennsylvania, it was one of the most frequently used designs in Pennsylvania Dutch art, for even untrained hands could follow the simple outlines of the flower. Some believed the tulip had a religious meaning, the three tulips symbolizing the Trinity. It is said that in Germany the tulip is regarded as a variation of the Holy Lily.

In patchwork all the pieced Lily and Tulip designs were based on the famous Star of Le Moyne. These geometrical flowers were formed from diamond-shaped pieces. In its journey across the continent one lily pattern used in quilts changed its name at least eight times, varying with the wild lily common to each region.

Variable Star: When the question of the annexation of Texas wrecked the political hopes of Calhoun and Clay and placed the dark-horse James K. Polk in the Presidential chair, this pattern was rechristened The Lone Star or Texas.

Weathervane: This pattern of patchwork dates back to the time when the weathervane was used to forecast weather.

Wild Goose Chase: The three-cornered patch was a recognized bird symbol. Variations included Hovering Hawks, Ducks and Ducklings, and Birds-in-the-Air.

Windmill: The windmill is made by cutting four squares of a light four-patch and those of a dark four-patch diagonally across and then combining the resulting triangles in an alternating color arrangement. If one stares at the design for a while, all the little "windmills" seem to revolve and give a pin-wheel effect.

Wreath of Rose: The wreath design was a delight to the colonial quilt-maker, who varied the motif to suit her fancy. Sometimes the flowers represented hollyhocks, dahlias, or carnations instead of roses.

The Zigzag: It is also known as Streak of Lightning or Rail Fence. The diamond is cut to form triangles, the arrangement of light and dark giving the zigzag effect.

Part II
QUILT BASICS

Chapter 6

Patchwork

PATCHWORK IS THE result of sewing together small pieces of fabric to form a useful article, such as a quilt, counterpane, cushion, or tea cozy. When materials were scarce and expensive, practically unobtainable to the peasants of Europe, women saved every scrap of cotton, linen, wool, or silk, and built precious inventories later to be made into bedcoverings and other household necessities. When an old garment wore out, sound pieces were cut from it and added to the stockpile.

At first the pieces probably were sewn together haphazardly. But as collections of scraps grew, women began to join their patchwork pieces into pleasing and colorful patterns. The most artistic creations were copied by others and preferences for certain patterns resulted in their being widely copied, named, and passed on for generations.

As it developed, patchwork took on a slightly different style in each country. In Britain it was always closely linked with quilting. When the Pilgrims left Holland to found their New World Colony, the women took their skills and scraps of fabric with them to produce bedcoverings that kept them warm in the bleak winters.

One of the most striking things about patchwork quilts is their combination of gay and harmonious colors. Amazing too is the patience of the early quilt makers, who combined as many as sixteen hundred small patches into a single quilt, sewn together so accurately that the whole makes a perfect square.

A young wife would save a piece from every garment she possessed, beginning with her wedding dress, adding to these pieces from her children's clothes until the day when she would combine them into a patchwork quilt that recorded her married life history. Some women made patchwork for their daughters, using pieces from every dress a daughter had worn, beginning with the christening robe. A plain cotton patch might temporarily occupy the central position, to be replaced later by a piece of white satin from the daughter's wedding gown.

The earliest type of patchwork in this country is believed by some to have been *crazy patchwork*. In this sort every scrap of material can be used, and sometimes wool, cotton, and silk are found together. All the pieces are sewn onto a foundation, and often the seams are covered with an embroidery stitch such as the feather stitch or herringbone.

Many references to patchwork are to be found in the household lists of the seventeenth century, but the greatest period of this craft was between about 1795 and 1870.

Mosaic patchwork is actually the original type and the method of joining the pieces has changed very little over the centuries.

In all forms of patchwork good design depends on careful thought and planning, so that the arrangement of the pieces displays color and tone to their best advantage. Sometimes inspiration can be gained from ceramic mosaics. It is usually helpful to arrange the patchwork pieces in different positions, pinned to a piece of cork, and experiment until a successful arrangement is discovered.

Shades of the same color are attractive, or plain and patterned materials can be used together. Stripes, checks, and spots in different combinations make interesting patterns. The careful distribution of colors with regard to both tone and contrast is most important. Use more plain than printed fabrics, or the design will become "restless."

In working patchwork you should never mix materials that will not launder with those that will launder easily. For this reason, never mix cotton and rayon, or cotton and silk, though silk and velvet are occasionally used together. It is also best to avoid having too many textures in the same piece of work. It is best to use the same type of fabric throughout, simply varying the size and shape of the patches. To join them you need a # 80 or # 100 thread, to match the main color of the patches, and a very fine needle.

Hexagons, squares, diamonds, triangles, octagons, lozenges, stars, crescents, and rectangles are some of the shapes used for patches. Long diamonds, long hexagons, and long octagons are also common. Templates or patterns for these can be drawn on cardboard and cut very accurately, though today precut or plastic ones are available. It is useful to have a mask to go with each template, which can be used as a guide when you cut out your pieces of patterned fabrics. The mask, ¼" larger all around than the template, allows for the turning on the patch, and the hole in the middle of it enables you to position flowers or parts of a printed pattern.

When you have decided which templates you want to use, paper shapes need to be cut for each patch. It is most important that these should be absolutely accurate, pieces of similar shapes being identical. Thick notepaper can be used. In the past women are said to have used their love letters, and in some of the old quilts the papers were left in after the quilt was finished. This no doubt gave extra warmth, but quilts of this kind could not be washed.

Very thin card stock can be used if you prefer. The metal or plastic templates can be placed on top of two layers of paper (never cut more than two shapes at once) and cut round with sharp scissors or a razor blade. It is essential that the papers be accurately cut. If you are going to make a large piece of work, such as a quilt, each paper can be used several times to save the labor of cutting one for each piece.

The patches are then cut, leaving ¼″ to ½″ turnings. Use an iron to press the turnings over the paper; then remove the pattern. It is helpful to mark on the template the way of the grain of the fabric so that the warp of all the pieces runs the same way. This is vital with large pieces, but for those with a diameter of one inch or less it is not so important, and sometimes with a striped or patterned material it may be necessary to use some of the patches on the cross to obtain an interesting effect.

Arrange the patches to form the pattern and then begin joining them. Place the right sides of the patches together and stitch the edges along the crease (by hand or by machine), using very small stitches on the wrong side. Take up only one or two threads of the fabric in each stitch. When all seams have been sewn, press the seams flat on the wrong side.

If decorative stitchery, such as herringbone or feather stitch, is added on the right side to cover the joins (seams), the threads should be of a color which will enhance the design of the work.

Patchwork always needs a lining. If warmth is needed, an interlining of wool or wadding can be used and a little quilting added to hold the layers firmly together.

Shell or scale patchwork is unlike mosaic patchwork in that the pieces are lapped and joined on the right side. A single template is used to produce an all-over pattern. The pieces are cut as for mosaic patchwork, but the top edge is carefully turned down on the wrong side. It is best to place the template on the right side of the fabric, then carefully turn the edges to the wrong side, making very small pleats as you go around the curved edge. This turning is then tacked down. When all the shells are prepared in this way, pin them on a piece of cork, one row at a time. Accurate placing is essential. Then hem down the top edges, one row at a time. Each scale overlaps the row above. An interesting diagonal effect is achieved by using alternate light and dark patches. This type of patchwork is not often used, and more skill in joining the patches is necessary than for mosaic patchwork.

Applied or appliquéd patchwork can, if carefully planned, be very effective. Sometimes templates are used, as for mosaic patchwork; the shapes are cut freely, joined, and applied. In this work the whole is not made up of pieces; the patchwork is used instead to decorate a piece of fabric.

In 1879 a book called *Treasure in Needlework* was published. Its authors, Mrs. Warren and Mrs. Pullen, wrote this about patchwork:

" The materials necessary for patchwork are such portions of wearing apparel, whether of cloth, calico, linen, Holland, silk, velvet, cotton prints, &c., as would other wise be thrown away, or saved for the rag-man. No matter how small the portion, it has its use. . . .

The materials should be arranged into shades and qualities. After having been cut to the requisite sizes, and the irregularities of the edges remedied, they are ready for use.

The patterns may be varied *ad infinitum,* if the person possess the least talent for drawing and designing, but for the sake of those who may not be thus gifted, we submit . . . simple and effective designs, to be executed in any of the materials. [*EDITOR'S NOTE: There is a complete section of Patchwork Designs.*]

To make the Patchwork.—The pattern should be placed before the person, and the shades being selected, the several pieces arranged so as to form the design, and the edges then neatly sewn together; after which they are either pressed, or ironed, the papers removed, and the lining proceeded with.

When silks and velvets are employed, it improves the effect to combine the two, taking the silk for the lighter, and the velvet for the darker shades, and two velvets for the others, shaded to pattern.

A very pretty effect is produced by combining Holland and calico, silk and satin, satin and velvet, and rough and fine cloth. "

In her book, *The Ladies' Guide to Needlework, Embroidery, etc.,* published in 1877, S. Annie Frost said about patchwork:

" Although this work seems to come more under the head of plain than fancy needlework, this little book would scarcely be complete were all reference to it be omitted. It is generally our first work and our last—the schoolgirl's little fingers setting their first crowded or straggling stitches of appalling length in patchwork squares, while the old woman, who can no longer conquer the intricacies of fine work, will still make patchwork quilts for coming generations.

But the calico squares whose combinations and varieties would fill a volume are not the only patchwork that is made. Silk is also used in variously shaped blocks and patterns, for the covers of chairs and bed-quilts, although we know many pieces, started in tiny pieces to make an enormous bed-quilt, end ignominiously in a very small pincushion.

The taste is one that nearly died out, although some beautiful specimens are still seen at fancy fairs, the work of tasteful brains and industrious fingers. . . .

It is a great improvement upon the huge and unwieldly quilting-frames of the days of our grandmothers, to make the patchwork for a quilt in bound squares. Each one is lined, first with wadding, then with calico quilted neatly, and bound with strips of calico. These squares being then sewed together, the quilt is complete. Album quilts made in this way, with the name of the giver neatly written upon a small square of white in the centre of each piece, are much more acceptable than when they must all be quilted together in a huge frame.

"

In 1882 *The Dictionary of Needlework* had a fairly large section devoted to patchwork. Excerpts of the article are reproduced here. The section that deals with the various patterns has been left intact.

Patchwork.—This needlework, which consists in sewing pieces of material together so as to form a flat, unbroken surface, possesses many advantages, as it is not only useful and ornamental, but it forms out of odds and ends of silk, satin, or chintz, that would otherwise be thrown away, a handsome piece of needlework. Its manipulation requires both patience and neatness and also calls into place both the reasoning and artistic faculties, as the designs chiefly depend for their beauty upon the taste displayed in the arrangement and selection of the shades of colour used to produce them. Patchwork originally only aimed at joining together any kinds of materials in the shapes they happened to have retained, so that when arranged a flat surface was produced; but, at the present time much more is required from the worker.... The designs so worked out are necessarily geometrical, as it is essential that they should reply to fixed and accurate measurements, and the figures elected are the angles formed by squares, diamonds, and hexagons, in preference to the curved lines formed by circles and ovals, as the joining together of ovals and rounds in perfectly correct patterns is much more difficult to accomplish than when points are fitted into angles, as is done with the first-named figures....

... The working out of the design and the manner of making up the patches is the same, whatever the material or size of the patches used, they being increased or decreased for the occasion. In the work, the great essential is that every piece should be cut with perfect uniformity....

Patchwork patterns can be made from geometrical figures, and are chiefly copied from old Mosaic or Parquetrie designs; however the designs can be made as elaborate as the worker likes, and have been carried to the extent of working coats of arms in their natural colours, and pictures containing large sized figures.... The following patchwork patterns are amongst the best, and can be enlarged, or decreased in size as required.

American or Canadian.—This particular pattern in patchwork is one that in Canada is known as Loghouse Quilting. It is a variety made of several coloured ribbons instead of pieces of silk or cretonne, and these ribbons are arranged so as to give the appearance of different kinds of wood formed into a succession of squares. To work, as shown in Figure 1, cut out in lining a square of 12 inches, and tack to it in its centre a small square of plain colour 1½ inches in size. Procure ribbon three-quarters of an inch wide, and two shades of every colour used, take the two shades of one colour and tack the darkest shade right down one side of the small square and over-lapping three-quarters of an inch beyond at both ends; sew to this and to the square a dark piece at the bottom and a light piece at the top, and allow both to overlap beyond the square on the left side for three-quarters of an inch; completely surround the square by filling it with the light colour for the side not already filled up. Change the ribbons, and again surround the square with two shades of the same colour, putting the darkest underneath the dark part and lightest against the light part, and arrange their manner of overlapping (always allowing three-quarters of an inch extra for the same) according to the design. Seven rows of ribbon are needed to

Fig. 1. American or Canadian Patchwork

fill the 12-inch square; diversify these as to colour and design, but always make two shades of one colour form a square, and place the darkest of such shades underneath each other. Prepare a large number of these 12-inch squares, and then sew them together as ordinary patches, but so that the light side of one square is next to the light side of another, and the dark against the dark, thus giving the look of alternate squares of light and dark colours. Make large pieces of work such as counterpanes with the 12-inch square and the three-quarter inch ribbon, but small pieces, such as cushions, make with narrow ribbon and a 5-inch square.

Box.—This design is sometimes known as Block pattern. It is made by arranging diamonds so that three of them form a solid raised block, of which two sides and the top are shown; and this look is given to the flat surface entirely by the arrangement of the diamonds as to colour. To form: Procure a number of pieces of silk of three shades of one colour, such as yellow, deep gold, and chestnut, or pale blue, peacock blue, and indigo blue, and cut out from each shade an equal number of diamonds. These must be made 3 inches in length, 2 inches in width, and 2 inches from corner to corner. Join a chestnut colour silk to a deep gold silk, so as to make a straight line between them, the slant of the diamond in each going upward; put the dark colour on the right hand, the lighter upon the left hand. These two diamonds form the sides of the Block. Take the light yellow diamond, and make with it the top of the Block, fit it into the angle formed by the upward slant of the sides, so that it lies across them, the points of its width being upwards, and those of its length horizontal. Make a number of these blocks, shading them all the same way, and then join them together, thus: On the left side, left unattached of the light yellow top, join the under side of a chestnut piece, and to the right side of the yellow top the under side of a deep golden piece. This will produce the effect of a number of successive blocks of wood arranged diagonally across the work. The dark side of these blocks is often made with velvet, and by this arrangement the sections stand out with great boldness.

Check.—This design is worked to imitate a chess or draught board, and is one of the easiest of the patterns, being formed of squares sewn together. To work: cut out a number of 2-inch squares in pale yellow, and a number of the same size in brown. Sew the brown square to the yellow square, and underneath and above the brown sew a yellow one, and underneath and above the yellow square sew a brown one. Continue to join the pieces together in this manner so that no squares of the same hue are next to each other. Any two colours can be used, or varieties of two colours, but it is advisable not to employ more.

Cloth.—Cloth Patchwork is used for carriage rugs and tablecloths, and can be made extremely effective, either as a bordering to these articles or as entirely forming them. As cloth is of too thick a substance to allow of turning under the raw edges, each patch has to be bound with either a narrow ribbon or braid before it is sewn into its right position in the work, and as the material is only made plain or with patterns that would not look well if inserted, bright self-coloured foundations are selected, which are embroidered with designs worked out with silks or narrow braids. To work: Select a large sized pattern either of a Hexagon or Mosaic shape, and cut the pieces out in the ordinary way and embroider them in Satin Stitch; bind each round with a braid matching it in colour, and then stitch it into its proper position. No lining is required.

Diamonds.—The diamond (next to the Hexagon) is the most used design in Patchwork, and looks well when made of two materials, such as silk and velvet or silk and chintz. It is the easiest of all the figures. To work: Cut out a number of Diamonds 3 inches in length and 2½ inches in width. Make half of them in dark materials and half in light, join them together so that they form alternate rows of light and dark colours across the width of the article, or join four pieces of one shade together so as to make a large Diamond, and sew this to another large Diamond made of four pieces of a contrasting colour to the one placed next it.

Embroidered.—This kind of work is only suitable for small articles, such as cushions, handkerchief cases, and glove cases. It is formed by sewing together squares of different colours after they have been ornamented with fancy stitches. To work: Cut a number of 3-inch squares in dark velvet and silk or satin, and upon each satin or silk square work a spray of flowers or a small wreath in satin stitch and in filoselles matching the colours of the flowers; make each spray or wreath of a different kind of flower and upon a different coloured satin, but care must be taken that the colours of the satins used will blend together. Take the dark velvet squares (these should be all of one shade) and work a pattern upon each of their sides in lines of coral, herringbone, or chain stitch, and then join the velvet and satin squares together—a satin and a velvet patch alternately. A simpler pattern in Embroidery is made as follows: Cut out either in silk or satin small 2-inch squares of various colours, sew these together, and, when all are secured, work a railway stitch in coloured filoselles from each corner of the square to the centre, and a satin stitch on each side of it; this, when repeated in every square, will make a pretty design. Another manner of embroidering squares is to make them of holland and plush alternately, and to work a line of herringbone or coral on two sides of the holland square, but leave the velvet plain.

Honeycomb or Hexagon.—(1) The pattern known by this name is the one commonly used in Patchwork, as it is easily executed, produces many varieties of devices, according to the arrangement of the colours, and is a shape into which most remnants of silk or cretonne may be cut. To make as shown in Figure 2: Cut out a number of hexagons, and make each of their six sides three-quarters of an inch in length. Take a dark-coloured patch and sew round it six light patches. These should agree in their shade of colour, but need not as to pattern. Into the angles formed on the outside of these light Hexagons sew dark-coloured patches, and continue to work so as to give the appearance of a dark patch surrounded with a set of light patches.

Fig. 2. Honeycomb or Hexagon Patchwork

(2) Another variety of the same pattern is made with hexagons, and arranged so as to form light-coloured stars upon a dark velvet ground. It is useful when only a few, but good, pieces of brocade or satin are available, and makes handsome sofa cushions or banner screens. The hexagons are all of the same size, and should be

three-quarters of an inch upon each side. To make: Cut out a number of hexagons in deep maroon velvet or dark peacock-blue velvet to form the ground; then take the satin scraps, and from them cut out the same sized hexagons. Pick up one of these and surround it with six other pieces, arranged as follows: Should the centre piece be pale blue, surround it with old gold; should it be crimson, with yellow-pink; should it be lavender, with purple; should it be yellow, with chestnut. Make a set of these stars, and then reverse the colours, putting the centre colour as the outside colour. Arrange as follows: Sew on two rows of the ground, and for the third row sew on the stars already made and put one of the ground coloured hexagons between each star; for the next two rows only use the ground coloured patches, and then recommence the stars. Arrange these so as to contrast with the ones first placed, and to come between them, and not directly underneath.

(3) In this variety of the same pattern it is intended to produce the appearance of Raised Work without the stuffing. To work: All the pieces are made of equal-sided hexagons, three-quarters of an inch to every side. Cut out a number of hexagons all in one light colour, and of the same material—these should be either of French grey, maize, or sky blue—then cut out a number of hexagons in the dark maroon velvet, and a few in brocaded silks, either pale blue, green, chocolate, flame colour, or peach. If brocade cannot be procured for these last pieces, work each with a small flower in silks and in satin stitch. Arrange as follows: Surround each brocaded hexagon with six dark velvet ones, and make them all up in this way. Then stitch all round these a row of the light silk patches, so that every dark section is separated from its corresponding section with a border of light silk. Finish this pattern with a straight border worked with flowers and a ball fringe.

Jewel.—The pattern shown in Figure 3 is intended to give the appearance of large precious stones, set round with smaller ones, and a plain setting. Each of the large squares represent a cut stone with the light falling upon it, and to produce this effect is made either of two shades of blue satin brocade, two of ruby brocade, emerald, or yellow brocade. The small squares are made of any colours, and should

Fig. 3. Jewel Patchwork

be much varied; the long lines of plain brown gold satin. To work: Cut out in paper a perfect square, measuring 2 inches each way, run a line across this from the left hand top point to the right hand bottom point and horizontally across its centre. Cut down the diagonal line from the left hand top corner to the centre of the square; cut across to the right on the horizontal line. The two pieces the square is thus divided into will be the two sizes required for the centres of the pattern; have them copied in tin, and cut from the smallest piece half the light shades of satin and half the dark shades, and from the larger half the dark shades of satin and half the light shades required. For the straight pieces, cut out lengths of two inches an inch wide; and for the small squares an inch every way. Join the light satin to the dark, so as to make a perfect square, and put the light colour on the right side of the dark colour for three patches on one line, two patches on the next line, and one patch on the third line of the work, and reverse it for the next three rows; surround a square thus made with the long brown pieces and fill in the four corners with four little squares, then join on another large square and surround that on the three sides left open with the straight pieces of brown satin and the small squares.

Kid.—This Patchwork is generally confined to the making of such small articles as pincushions, slippers, or mats, as the kid generally used for the purpose is cut from old gloves, and therefore is not of a large size; but if the pieces can be obtained of sufficient size cushions, footstools, and other larger articles may be attempted. To work: Select an easy geometric pattern, and cut out from a tin plate a number of kid patches without allowing for any turnings, sew these together upon the wrong side without turning any of the kid under, and iron the work over when finished; then take a narrow cord of gold thread or silk braid and couch this down to the kid with a silk thread matching it in colour, so that it follows and conceals all the lines of stitches. Where it is not possible to turn the cord or braid, make a hole with a stiletto, and push it through this hole to the back and fasten it off there. If the kid is stitched together with great neatness, and a very fine needle used, the outline cord will not be required; it is only used to hide the stitches where their size or irregularity would spoil the look of the work.

Leather.—Patchwork made with leather scraps differs in one essential from true patchwork, as the pieces have to be glued to a foundation instead of stitched together, as in the other kinds, but the patterns used and the manner of cutting out the sections are the same. The leather used is morocco, and is procured at bookbinders and leather dressers, and the articles formed are chessboards, folding screens, flower mats, note cases, &c. To work: Having obtained scraps of leather, fix upon some easy geometrical pattern that the scraps will most easily lend themselves to make; draw this pattern quite correctly out upon a sheet of millboard, and mark out what coloured scrap is to cover each space. Arrange the scraps on a table in their proper order, make hot some common glue (that is free from impurities and of equal consistency), spread it upon the backs of the leather, and lay the leather in its proper place upon the millboard. Work with despatch, but be careful that every point is glued down, and that they are all accurately arranged; then lay the millboard into a linen press, and keep it there until the glue has quite dried. The millboard can be covered upon its wrong side either with silk or water paper pasted down upon it; the edges at the sides should either have narrow ribbon pasted upon them before the leather is put on, or they should be gilded with shell-gold when the work is finished. A fringe made of cutting strips of thin narrow leather into close one-eighth of an inch lines should be used for edging mats, and any flat articles that would be improved by such a finish.

Lozenge or Pointed Oblong.—A useful shape for using up small scraps of material, and one that is easily made. The lozenge is a figure of six sides, and is an oblong with pointed instead of straight ends, the points being in the centre of the width and formed with two angles. To work: Cut out a number of these figures, make them 3 inches from point to point, 1½ inches across, and 1½ inches for the side lines, and 1 inch for the lines from the point to the side. Sew these together in rows, placing a light lozenge next to a dark one. In the next row arrange the lozenges in the same way, so that when all the patches are arranged diagonal lines of alternate shades will cross the material.

Mosaic.—(1) The pattern shown in Figure 4 is formed with squares and acute-angled triangles. It is a good pattern to use for cretonne-patches and for small pieces of silk and satin, the large square being made with pieces of cretonne or flower

Fig. 4. Mosaic Patchwork No. 1

designs, and the small triangles of various coloured silks. Cut out the squares and make them 6 inches each way. Cut the triangles out, and make their base 6 inches, their height 3 inches. Take a cretonne square and sew to each of its sides the base of a dark triangle, and fill in the triangle with three other triangles; turn all their points inwards, and make a perfect square with their bases. Make this kind of square to the four sides of the centre, and fill in the sides of the cross thus made with four large cretonne squares. Join a number of pieces together in this manner, and then sew them to each other and make a variegated pattern by using various patterned and coloured cretonne and silk in different sections.

(2) Another variety of Mosaic is composed of three differently cut pieces, viz., squares, parallelograms, and unequal sided hexagons. To work: Cut out the squares

in pale yellow silk, and make them 1½ inches in length. Make the parallelograms 2 inches long, and 1 inch wide. The two sides lines are upright and of equal lengths, but the left hand line commences before the right hand one, and ends before it. The top and bottom lines join these slants together; cut half the number required in dark brown silk brocade, and half in old gold silk brocade, and make the angles slope different ways in the two colours. Cut the unequal hexagons all from the same silk or brocade, which should either be dark blue, crimson, or black—their two sides are 2 inches long, their width 2 inches, and the four lines that form the angles 1½ inches each; join four parallelograms together at their long sides, the light colour to the left of the dark, and arrange their shades alternately; let their short lines slope upwards and form angles, join a number of these together in this way before placing them. Take two squares and fit them into the upper angles made by the parallelograms; and, into the angle made between the two squares, fix the pointed end of the hexagons. To the left of the hexagons sew the dark side of a set of four parallelograms, to the right, the left side of another set, and to the top fit in the angle made by the second and third pieces of a set of parallelograms. Repeat the pattern until the size required is made. Then join a piece of silk to the top and bottom as a border, and make it straight at one side, and vandyked at the other so as to fit into the angles of the pattern for the sides; cut some half hexagons and fit them in, and finish with a plain straight border.

(3) The pattern shown in Figure 5 is intended to be used in making counterpanes and other large articles, and should be worked with cretonnes or gaily-coloured chintzes. It is made with squares of two different sizes and of pointed oblongs. To work: Cut out in a tin a square of 6 inches, and form a face 1¾ inches in length at each corner by cutting away the point of the square. Choose a flower-patterned chintz with bunches of flowers, and from this cut the large squares, so that each has a bunch of flowers in the center. Cut from various coloured chintzes a number of small

Fig. 5. Mosaic Patchwork No. 3

squares 1¾ inches in size, and from a coloured chintz of one shade, the pointed oblongs make 6 inches from point to point, 2⅓ inches wide, and 3⅓ inches upon each side; join five of the small squares together, place the lightest coloured square in the centre, and surround it with four of a darker shade, and fit into the four angles that are thus made the point of four of the oblongs, and into the four corners of the outer squares the angles of four of the large squares which have been so cut as to join on the straight sides of the oblong; join the pieces together so that every large square is surrounded with the ornamental border made by the oblong and small squares.

This pattern can be varied almost indefinitely by altering the colouring, and the material composing the patches; thus all the large squares can be made of a ground colour, and differently coloured and shaped flowers Appliquéd on to them, and the oblongs may be formed of different shades of the one colour instead of one shade only, while the small squares can be made of velvet or satin, instead of chintz, with the centre square of plain material, and the four outer squares of variegated, or *vice versa*.

(4) A pretty set pattern made with three different sized patches, and forming a combination of squares, crosses, and hexagons. To work as shown in Figure 6: Cut out in black satin a number of perfect squares 1½ inches in width and length, and some of the same size in yellow satin. Cut out in red silk lozenge-shaped or pointed

Fig. 6. Mosaic Patchwork No. 4

oblong patches, each measuring 3 inches from point to point, 1½ inches across, 1½ inches for the long line, and three-quarters of an inch for the short lines that form the right angle. Take some violet silk and cut a number of larger lozenges 4 inches from point to point, 2 inches across, 3 inches for the long lines, and 1½ inches for the short lines that form the right angle. Join together five squares as a square cross, and one dark square being in the centre, and four light ones round it; take a black square and join to it four red lozenges, and sew the points of the lozenges to each other. Sew the cube thus made to the outside of one of the arms of the cross, so that the centre square is on the same line as the centre of the cross, and fill in the spaces on the sides of the cubes and cross with the violet lozenges. Continue the pattern by connecting a cross to a cube, and a cube to a cross, always filling up with the violet lozenges. The pattern measures across one cube and a cross 9 inches, and as each design takes four light squares, two dark squares, four red lozenges, and four violet lozenges, a brief calculation will give the number of patches required for a given space, to which must be added a few extra of all the sizes to fill in corners, etc.

Puzzle.—The pattern shown in Figure 7 is an extremely useful one for using up odds and ends of material, but it is a difficult one to adjust. To work: Prepare a number of pieces of cretonne or silk 4 inches long and 3 inches wide, and slope off one corner of some of these so as to form a curve, and leave the rest perfectly square. Cut a few larger pieces 5 inches long by 3 inches wide, and out of scraps cut some odd-shaped pieces either of the right length or width. Arrange these various pieces upon a lining so as to form the design shown in the illustration; but instead of

Fig. 7. Puzzle Patchwork

stitching two pieces together, as in ordinary patchwork, lay one over the other and turn under the edges of the top pieces, and run it to the bottom. When all are in position and run to each other and the lining, work round the edge of every patch with herringbone stitches made with bright coloured filoselle. The whole beauty of this design depends upon the judicious selection of the colours and patterns of the patches used.

Raised.—This is also known as Swiss patchwork, and is made by stuffing the patches with wadding so that they are well puffed up. The shapes selected for the patches should be either good sized hexagons or diamonds, and only one shape should be used as intricate patterns made by combining various sized pieces render the work troublesome. To work: Cut out the hexagons or diamonds, from a tin plate pattern, from pieces of silk or brocade, size of diamonds 2½ inches upon each side, of hexagons 1½ inches along each of the six sides; cut the same shapes out in old lining and make a small slit in the centre of each, sew the lining patches to the silk patches, and join each lined patch together in the pattern selected. When finished, sew a piece of silk 5 inches wide all around the work, and ornament with coral, herringbone, and other fancy embroidery stitches; this border need not be lined. Take soft wadding and push it into every slit made in the lined patches until they are well puffed out and quite hard. Fill them in thoroughly, and be careful that the corners are not neglected. Tack over the hole made in the lining to prevent the wadding coming out, and then line the whole of the work, including the straight border, with a piece of old silk, or red, or blue twill, or cretonne. A more difficult plan, but one that does not need the extra or second lining, is as follows: Cut out the shapes from the tin plate in silk or brocade, and cut out cretonne or good twill linings to fit them, join these linings to the patches, but leave one side in all of them unsecured. Join the patches together as a row, leaving the open side of them exposed. Into this stuff the wadding, taking care to make each section quite hard and full. Sew the lining up, tack on another row of patches and stuff them out as before, and continue to sew on row after row and stuff them until the size required is made.

Right Angles.—The principle of the pattern shown in Figure 8 is much the same as that of the box pattern, but in this case the diamonds forming the design are cut away so as to form a number of right angles. To work: Procure a number of pieces of silk three shades of one colour, such as pink, crimson, and maroon, of which the darker shade is brocaded. Cut out a diamond on paper, length 3 inches, width 2 inches, from point to point; out of one side of this cut out a right angle, leaving 1 inch thus making the shape required for the design. Have this cut in tin, and from that cut out an equal number of sections from each coloured silk, and then join them together, according to the pattern; sew together the straight side of a ruby and crimson section with the cut out edge to the right and left, and fit a pink section into the angle at the

Fig. 8. Right Angles Patchwork

top of these two, with its cut out edge upright; make up all the pieces in this manner, and then join the figures together. The cut out edge of the light pink of one figure will fit into the bottom angle of the crimson and maroon colours, and the angles at the sides of these sections will fit into the sides of a fresh row of figures. In making this pattern care must be taken that the position of the colours is never altered.

Twist.—This pattern is formed of eight-sided cubes and squares, which are separated from each other by long narrow patches cut so as to appear to twist or interlace each other and twine round the squares and cubes. To work, as shown in Figure 9: Cut a number of squares measuring 1¼ inches each way, and eight-sided

Fig. 9. Twist Patchwork

cubes measuring 1¼ inches at top, bottom, and side lines, but only three-quarters of an inch across the lines that form the four corners. Make these cubes and squares of dark coloured pieces of satin and brocade. Cut out in light silk or satin the large narrow stripes, make these half an inch in width and 2 inches in length on one side, and 2¾ inches in length on the other. Cut them so that one side of the width is quite straight and the other pointed. Take one of the squares, stitch to it on the left a long narrow piece. Turn its short or 2-inch length to the square, make it even on its straight width with the bottom line of square, and let the overlap and the point come at the top; to this end, but not to the point, join another long piece in the same way, fit it into the overlap where it is straight, and join its short 2-inch length to the top of the square, allowing the overlap and the point to be on the right hand. Come down the right side of the square and put a piece on at the bottom of the square; in the same manner join the long pieces to all the squares. Now arrange the cubes as to colour, and join them to the long pieces. The short corners of the cubes will fit into the points of the long pieces, four different cubes will join the four different points, and the straight parts will fit into the straight lines of the long pieces.

In the second half of the nineteenth century many magazines were introduced expressly for women readers and a number of books were published on the subject of needlework.

Godey's Lady's Book featured patchwork designs made expressly for that very popular periodical.

Fig. 10. Godey Design for Patchwork

Our page compels us to reduce the size of the pattern; but, by a little attention, sections may easily be cut out of any dimensions desired. Take a piece of clean stout white paper, and fold it in all parallel sloping lines seen in our engraving. These may be at any distance from each other; only regular and equal. It will be seen that a line drawn exactly between every pair of parallels will take in the point.

Draw these lines with a pencil, to distinguish them from those caused by the folding, and the proper form can be readily obtained. Cut them out, and from them others in card-board, if for a large piece of work, and you have all your sections ready, without the possibility of a misfit. The two eight-pointed figures are differently arranged. 'A' may be filled up in eight pieces, while 'B' should be composed of nine—a star of eight points to the centre, and eight diamonds round it. Or, if on a sufficiently large scale, the inner star may be of eight pieces. Two very distinct shades of the same color will look better for 'A' than many different tones. 'B' may have a dark centre and bright points, or *vice versa*. The intermediate figure 'C' should be of such neutral tints or dark shades as may throw up the brilliant hues of which the star should be composed.

,,

Fig. 11. Godey Designs for Patchwork

Fig. 12. Godey Designs for Patchwork

Fig. 13. Godey Designs for Patchwork

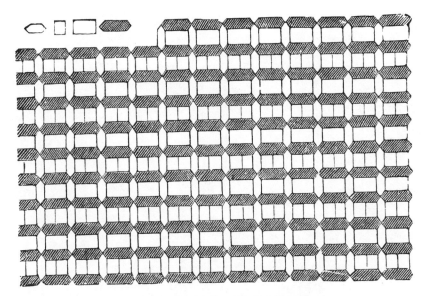

Fig. 14. Godey Design for Patchwork

Fig. 15. Godey Design for Patchwork

Fig. 16. Godey Designs for Patchwork

Peterson's Magazine was as popular as *Godey's Lady's Book,* partly because of the excellent designs found in this magazine.

Fig. 17. Macaroon Patchwork in Silk and Velvet

"   This is a new and beautiful pattern, for a species of work that is economical as well as fashionable; for it enables the fair worker to use up odd bits of velvet and silk that otherwise would be lost.

It is called the Macaroon Patchwork. It is made up of two shapes, independently of the round of velvet from which it received its title. The arrangement of color must depend upon individual taste, but the depth of shade must be carefully remembered. The interior square must be of a neutral tint, half of the side-pieces light, the other half dark, or black, which last has a very good effect.

The round, or macaroon of velvet, must be laid upon the central square of silk before it is tacked on to its paper shape, which is done by passing the needle through the centre, and making a long overcast-stitch, which reaches to the outer rim, repeating this so as to form as many divisions as appear in our illustration. This is to be done in deep-maize-color, or scarlet silk.

When completed, this silk patchwork will be found to produce an excellent effect for cushions, tablecovers, and various other articles.

This patchwork, of course, may be made of any size; but that which we give is the best for most purposes. By sewing together as many squares as are necessary, a cushion, tablecover or other article may be made large or small.

For beginners in fancy work, patchwork is especially suitable, for there are few who cannot do it.

Fig. 18. Peterson Design for Patchwork

Fig. 19. Peterson Design for Patchwork

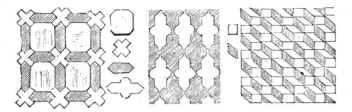

Fig. 20. Peterson Design for Patchwork

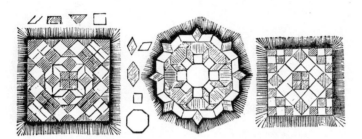

Fig. 21. Peterson Design for Patchwork

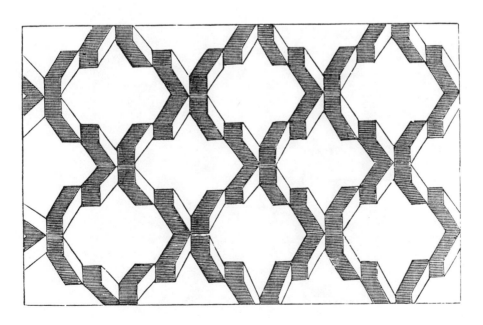

Fig. 22. Peterson Design for Patchwork

Fig. 23. Peterson Design for Patchwork

Fig. 24. Peterson Design for Patchwork

Fig. 25. Peterson Design for Patchwork

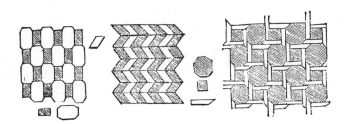

Fig. 26. Peterson Design for Patchwork

Treasures in Needlework was published in 1870. A number of its pages were devoted to combination designs for patchwork. They are very simple to follow, as each design first gives the basic components of the design and then demonstrates how to put them together.

Fig. 27. Combination Designs

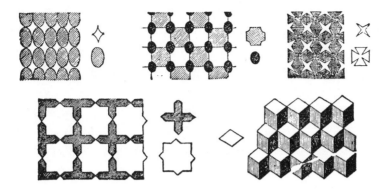

Fig. 28. Combination Designs

The materials for this design may . . . be pieces of silk; . . . to give the proper effect two shades of each of two colours plus one other colour and black will be required.

A reference to the engraving will show that in the stars one-half of each section is lighter and the other darker. This part should be worked in two shades of some rich colour. The black part may be done by laying black velvet or narrow satin ribbon on,

Fig. 29. Patchwork in *Treasures in Needlework*

after the work is otherwise completed; and in this case, as a matter of course, the pieces which they edge must be proportionally larger. Each quarter of the square is also done in two shades, those with the horizontal lines being the darkest. A third colour is to be used for the small diamonds. As every shade of colour can be obtained in silks, the following combinations will be found pretty:—two violets for the star, 2 ambers for the square, and a rich emerald green for the diamonds; or these latter colours may be reversed. Rich blue and brown, or blue and cerise, with amber diamonds would also look well. The various sections may be enlarged to any required dimensions; doubled or even trebled; and the squares may be worked in different colours, if a very gay effect is desired.

During this same period there were many pamphlets published on patchwork and its designs. The following are taken from some of these pamphlets and are easily followed.

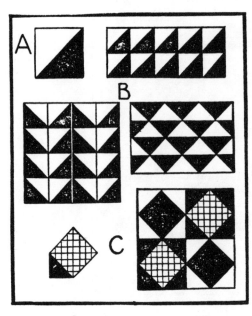

Fig. 30. Various Combinations of Patchwork

Fig. 31. Various Combinations of Patchwork

DIAMOND PATTERN

BOX PATTERN

PAVEMENT PATTERN

CHINESE BLOCK PATTERN

STAR PATTERN

DRYAD

Fig. 32. Various Combinations of Patchwork

Chapter 7

Appliqué

DURING THE HUNDRED-YEAR span of 1775-1875 appliqué as a method of quilt-making was equally popular with patchwork in America. Patchwork involves assembling hundreds of individual patches side by side into a large overall design. In the appliqué technique the parts of the design, such as hearts, flowers, leaves, birds, and vases, are cut from fabrics and sewn onto the background fabric of the spread with simple overcasting, buttonhole, or seed stitch. Before stitching, the edges of the design pieces are turned under to form a hemmed edge.

Women who could afford to cut designs from material tended toward appliqué, while those who saved leftover scraps made patchwork quilts.

It has been said that appliqué was used because quilt makers became bored with sewing in straight lines. Workmanship in appliqué quilts is usually superior to that found in patchwork quilts.

The earliest appliqué coverlets were made by sewing design elements cut from printed chintzes and imported Oriental calicoes to white cotton or linen spreads, which were then quilted to make the appliqué more outstanding. An example of such a quilt is to be found in the Valentine Museum in Richmond, Virginia. It is the West-over-Berkeley coverlet. It is made of fine unbleached cotton and contains squares, triangles, and strips which are joined by narrow bands in a red calico print. The chintz appliqué and silk embroidery are very elaborate and were made by the women of the two neighboring plantations, Berkeley and Westover.

According to documents, this spread was made sometime before the American Revolution. The ladies of both estates met every fortnight to work on the spread. The corners were embroidered with pineapples, the emblem of hospitality, and cornucopias, and horns of plenty. There are sprays of hops, tiny birds on trailing branches of flowers, and a chipmunk.

In addition to Wedding Quilts done in appliqué, there were Friendship Quilts, Freedom Quilts, and Family-Record Quilts. Some quilts illustrate, in appliqué, the history of a family or a town. In the Shelburne Museum, Shelburne, Vermont, there is a quilt which illustrates the Lincoln-Douglas debates.

In the early nineteenth century appliqué quilts were made in Hawaii. The single appliqué on one of those quilts fills the entire spread.

Appliqué work is the ideal way to obtain a quick, bold effect. It produces the maximum effect with the minimum labor. It is excellent for covering large areas, and can be very gay for wall panels, pictures, curtains, fire screens, and similar furnishings. Appliqué work is not suitable for articles that will have to be laundered frequently.

Appliqué is now enjoying another wave of popularity, since it offers a wide scope for individual expression, admitting no limit to subject or material. Any kind of material—plain and printed cotton, silks, braid, buttons, felt, leather—is used. If the article is not to be washed, several kinds of material can be used on the same piece of work.

The beauty of this work depends upon a well-planned, well-executed design with its colors pleasingly distributed before the embroidery stitches are considered. If you start with a good design, no matter how simple, the work will be a success. Finishing touches of stitchery to embellish the smaller details are quite sufficient and should be worked on the applied motifs and the foundation material after the preliminary work is completed. Bold conventional shapes with simple outlines lend themselves readily to the technique and any attempt to reproduce naturalistic flowers should be avoided.

Use a simple geometric pattern tastefully put together to make a design. You can also fold a piece of material several times and cut out pieces, as is done in kindergarten.

The appliquéd motifs need not be of the same material as the background—use contrasting colors or different shades of one color. If the appliqué is the same color but a different material from the background, it will stand out, but make certain that the materials are compatible.

A very good material to use for appliqué motifs is felt, since it does not fray and looks attractive even on coarse linen or canvas. Use simple designs. A flower effect can be obtained, for example, by placing three circles of felt in graded sizes over one another and securing them in the center with a French knot.

Almost any material can be used for the ground. Firm materials with clean-cut edges that do not fray are easiest to apply. In all appliqué work it is essential that every piece of applied fabric should be cut with the warp and weft corresponding to the warp and weft of the background. If this is not done, the applied pieces may later stretch or pull out of shape.

Material that is inclined to fray easily, or stretch out of shape, can be thin-pasted on the back and allowed to dry thoroughly. A mixture of a little gum arabic or resin and cold water should be made, then brought slowly to the boil, while it is stirred all the time. It should be allowed to cool before use. For fragile or transparent fabrics take a piece of tissue paper or muslin and paste it sparingly with a very thin solution of cold paste made from wheat flour. Be certain that there are no lumps and use only a very thin smear—just enough to stick the tissue paper or muslin to the wrong side of the fabric that is to be applied. Be careful that the paste does not penetrate to the right side of the fabric so that spots are visible. Lay the fabric quite flat on the tissue paper or muslin, and press flat with a clean cloth. Cover with several layers of clean paper, and put between two drawing boards to press for a day or two until quite dry. When thin fabrics are being appliquéd, it is best to tack them in place and sew around them before cutting away the extra fabric.

Any thread can be used for outlining the work; the thickness should vary with the texture of the material being used. Cottons and silks of all kinds are suitable, and wools can be very effective for bold work. Most appliqué work can be done in the hand, but for very large pieces a frame may help.

Blind appliqué is the name given to appliqué which has very little added embroidery. The pieces applied are secured by small back stitches, or blind stitches. Plain materials are usually used. It is a very simple, quick way of decorating articles, and is especially suitable for big pieces of work, such as bedspreads and curtains. Each piece of material is cut out with narrow turnings, and is pinned and tacked in place. The raw edges of the fabric can be tucked under with the point of the needle, and slipstitched in position with ordinary matching thread.

Figure appliqué is very similar to blind appliqué, but the satin stitch is used around the edges instead of slipstitch. Minute satin stitches are worked so close together that the stitches touch each other. Either the raw edges can be tucked in with the needle, or satin stitch can be worked around the outline before the fabric is cut away very close to the stitching. Any extra embroidery is worked after the appliquéd pieces have been fixed.

Hemmed appliqué. It is possible to fix firm materials down with ordinary hemming stitches, if one uses a fine thread in self-color. The edges should first be turned under to prevent fraying.

Chapter 8

Quilting

THE WORD "QUILTING" came into the English language from the old French *cuilte,* which in turn was derived from Latin *culcuitra*—a stuffed mattress or cushion. From *culcuitra* came *cotra* or *coutre,* whence *countre pointe,* which then was changed into "counterpane."

Quilting is a very ancient craft. The Persians used it at an early date for such articles as práyer rugs, carpets, and draperies of linen, silk, and satin. The practice of stitching three layers of fabric together was originally in the interest of warmth.

Oriental quilting designs reached Europe through the early Portuguese traders and missionaries who traveled to the East Indies. Before the eleventh century little is known of quilting and appliqué or patchwork, but after that date they became more and more used in Western Europe.

It was usual in the Middle Ages to wear thickly padded and quilted coats and hoods under armor in order to ease the pressure of the heavy, unyielding metal plates. The Crusaders discovered these quilted articles of clothing and brought the idea back to Europe and the British Isles.

In the fourteenth century the Great Freeze descended on all of Europe. Rivers that never froze before did so and remained frozen all winter. The Great Freeze produced extremely cold winters for many years, which caused Europeans to seek methods of producing greater warmth in both clothing and bed. Quilted garments and spreads were one answer.

The quilting frame was devised and became a common piece of household equipment. At first the stitching was in simple and diagonal lines, but soon it became more elaborate and decorative. Central ornamental motifs surrounded with sprays and scrolls were developed. In Italy a special quilting stitch was developed, known as Trapunto quilting.

Silks and damasks were quilted in France and Italy, brocades and velvets in Spain.

Although there are few quilts left today to show the work done at the time, account books and inventories of many English homes mention quilts as valued items. Often we find descriptions of quilted valances, side-bed curtains, and bedspreads and quilts.

In England the early quilts used in both cottage and castle were of hand-woven linen. Through the quality of the weave one is able to distinguish between the quilts used in the castle and those of the cottage. Aristocrats preferred the finer-textured linen, although it was not so sturdy.

English women used many designs in their quilts. Geometric forms were preferred in Wales, while nature patterns such as wheat, birds, and leaves were favored in the south. One pattern is based on the sea. When geometric forms were used, they covered the entire quilt; while in nongeometric designs the main motif was found in the center of the quilt, with a different pattern for a border.

In England the wife was the keeper of the quilting frame and custodian of the quilting designs. Daughters of the household were taught quilting by their mothers after other chores were done. Even the youngest girls took their places along the quilting frame. The mother acted as the teacher, while the children did the actual work.

Every girl knew that she must quilt the coverlets to use on the beds in her home when she became married. Each girl started quilting early so as to produce a supply of bedcoverings to last until she had daughters old enough to begin quilting. For each the goal was a baker's dozen—thirteen—quilts before marriage. The first twelve were planned when the young girl was tiny. Each quilt was unique, though all followed designs handed down in her own family. The first design was simple; complexity increased with each additional spread as the young girl grew older and more competent. When the girl was pledged to marry, the thirteenth spread was designed and quilted. This was called the Bride's Quilt and was the most elaborate one in her dowry.

If one were to look at these thirteen quilts, one would see that as the young girl grew older, the border patterns would have not broken ends or twisted lines of stitching, since it was believed at that time that these were omens of trouble to come.

In parts of England there was a popular quatrain which reads as follows:

"At your quilting, maids, don't tarry,
Quilt quick if you would marry,
A maid who is quiltless at twenty-one,
Never shall greet her bridal sun!"

Early settlers of New Amsterdam (New York), New England, Virginia, and the Carolinas introduced the art of quilting into America as they remembered it from their European homes. The colonies created patterns that reflected the feelings of the people of the new country. Quilting, particularly in all-white designing, became a high form of applied art in the late eighteenth century, with bas-relief "puffing." The pineapple, pomegranate, and fern-leaf motifs symbolized hospitality. Plenty was represented by the cornucopia motifs and charm through the use of floral forms. These patterns appear most frequently in a variety of arrangements.

There are very few examples of these quilts now available since it was difficult to buy the cotton material for this use. Only occasionally could one find pieces of cotton which were either large enough to make a 6 x 7-foot bedcover, or equally matched in pure whiteness to be suitable for use as a bedcover.

To make an all-white quilt was a work that required skill with the needle and exquisite taste on the part of the maker. The women would take weeks just to draw out in advance a design that they liked and wanted to copy.

Occasionally patriotic notes would creep into the design. One such quilt is the famous Secession Quilt, made in 1860 by Mrs. P. D. Cook of South Carolina, who both designed and worked it. She used charcoal to sketch the intricate pattern of cornucopias, pomegranates, grapes, and roses. These motifs were worked into garlands bordering the squares. There is a spread eagle above the figure of Liberty. The arms of South Carolina appear on shields in the four corners, and above them are stitched the names of the governors who served the state from 1830 to 1838. George Washington's name appears above the head of Liberty, while the name of General P. D. Cook appears at the base of the centerpiece. The inscription "Secession-Yancey, 1860" is found below the name of George Washington. From the beak of the spread eagle flutters a scroll on which is written "E Pluribus Unum." This quilt is a monumental work of art and love.

During the eighteenth and early nineteenth centuries baskets filled with flowers were in vogue in quilt designs. The baskets were generally puffed with padding through the homespun linen on the reverse side. Another popular theme was a basket filled with the flowing branches of flowers spaced over the entire area of the bedcover. Well-known motifs of mid-eighteenth-century designs were Princess Plume, Pineapple, Rope, and Bell Flower.

Quilting patterns were used for window hangings and bed curtains, to keep out cold drafts. Chair seats and table covers were quilted to add a decorative note to the home. Clothing was quilted to lessen the sting of a cold winter's day in New England.

Quilted "petti-skirts" or underskirts were worn beneath brocaded or chintz top skirts in the eighteenth century. These skirts were often ornately quilted. The top part often had allover diamond or block stitching. A flower or leaf motif was spotted over the area, after the manner of the flowers scattered on brocade designs. The background of the border around the bottom was frequently worked in tiny allover quilting, with grape vines or flower scrolls in a larger puffing effect circling around the skirt in silhouette against the smaller stitches.

Although at first the stitches in quilting were purely utilitarian, their importance as an element of design rapidly increased. Some women found that quilting was more effective if worked on plain white or pale-colored fabric rather than on patterned cotton. Quilting became important in work other than patchwork.

In the early 1800's quilting patterns printed on thin paper became available. A tracing wheel was used to transfer them to the right side of the work. Toward the end of the nineteenth century women's magazines and newspapers began to print quilting designs which readers could transfer.

Many of these old quilting designs were so intricate as to make the wrong side of the quilt almost as interesting as the right. Thus it happened that when colored counterpanes began to go out of style in the 1870's, many women turned their red-and-green masterpieces wrong side up, thereby achieving the fashionable look of plain white.

Long before 1870, however, quilting of itself was so highly prized as an art that not infrequently the all-white quilt, best of backgrounds for fine stitchery, was made. White quilts without exception were elaborately done and used as counterpanes, though they never equaled in popularity the all-white "candlewick" or "tufted" spreads, save in the instance of layettes. At one time no crib was complete without its own snow-white quilt.

Since the workmanship was so exacting, the designs were very carefully worked out. White quilts seldom made use of transfer patterns. More and more, certain motifs were found and began to take on special significance. The pineapple became known as the symbol of hospitality. The acanthus leaf was borrowed from a favorite architectural detail and waves lines were adopted from the Atlantic tides. The dove of peace came to represent a social tea; the feather ring derived from the plume worn by women as a formal headdress; the oak leaf symbolized strength and virility; and the pine tree represented the spirit of America.

Simple patterns were made for quilting by using diagonal lines. These ran across the weave and showed to good advantage. They also prevented the effects of wear in the material better than those parallel to the weave. The crossing of diagonal lines with others in opposite directions in a pattern of diamonds were found in such patterns as double and triple diamonds and the hanging diamond. Circles, segments of circles, hexagons, octagons, imbrication, and wavy lines were all used for quilting patterns.

In the absence of stencil or paper patterns, various household implements were used. Teacup quilting takes its name from a set of circles made by using a teacup as a pattern. The marking of a quilt top for elaborate quilting required special skill. Women who developed this knack were well paid for their time and efforts.

Plates, saucers, and coins were used to make circles and segments of circles by drawing or chalking around the items. Straight lines made a good finish to the edges of articles and for borders.

The usual way of making a quilt ready for quilting was first to trace the design on the top either by means of a roweled dressmaking wheel—it was said that a riding spur served in early days—or with a pencil or chalk. When the lining or back was pinned into the frames, the wadding laid on it evenly in the desired thickness, and the top stretched over all and pinned to the frames, the piece was finally ready for quilting.

The design could be worked on a frame to make the finished work reversible, the stitches being taken through both layers of fabric and the thin layer of wadding between them.

Quilting was done in a running stitch with a fairly long needle. With the left hand under the quilt and the right hand manipulating the needle, the quilter ran several stitches before pulling the thread through—not an easy task.

Today the design can be needle marked on the top layer of fabric. Back stitch, running stitch, or chain stitch can be used throughout. If chain stitch is used, it should be worked from the back, leaving an unbroken line of back stitches on the front. Every stitch must be made in two movements, upward and downward, going through all three layers of fabric. Each stitch should be as regular and as even as possible. Begin with a knot that is pulled through the lower layer.

Repeatedly pushing so slender a bit of steel as an ordinary sewing needle through so many thicknesses of cloth bent it, but this was considered desirable by quilters in the past. A curved needle was the more easily forced down and up through a taut flat surface. Therefore women always "broke in" quilting needles by using them first on the coarser everyday patchwork. Those that became nicely bent were jealously saved for the curves and flourishes of intricate needlework lavished on best quilts.

Patterns in the form of a stencil were used not long ago. They were cut from a thick, open-mesh material, known as mill-net, heavily filled with glue or starch. Quite as stiff as Bristol board but more easily handled in that it was pliable and would not crack, mill-net accurately guided the marking chalk or pencil. It could be pinned to the quilt top, thus preventing the pattern from slipping while the marking was being done. The lead-blackened edges and their many pinholes of old patterns are evidence of their long and frequent use. Many women may have this form of stencil handed down to them, which still can be used.

It was mentioned previously that the object of quilting is to hold three different layers of material firmly in position. Thus the design must be planned to cover the entire surface. On the following pages are a number of designs that can be used for this purpose.

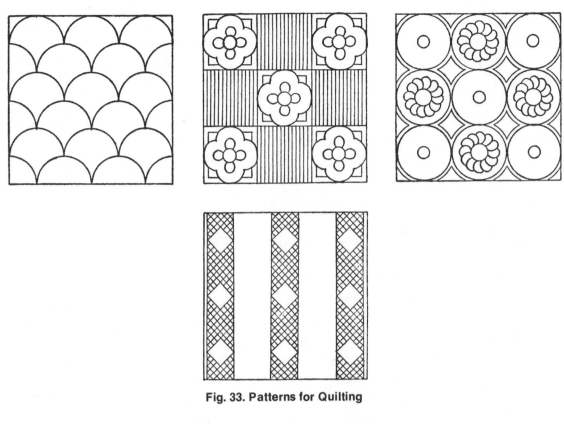

Fig. 33. Patterns for Quilting

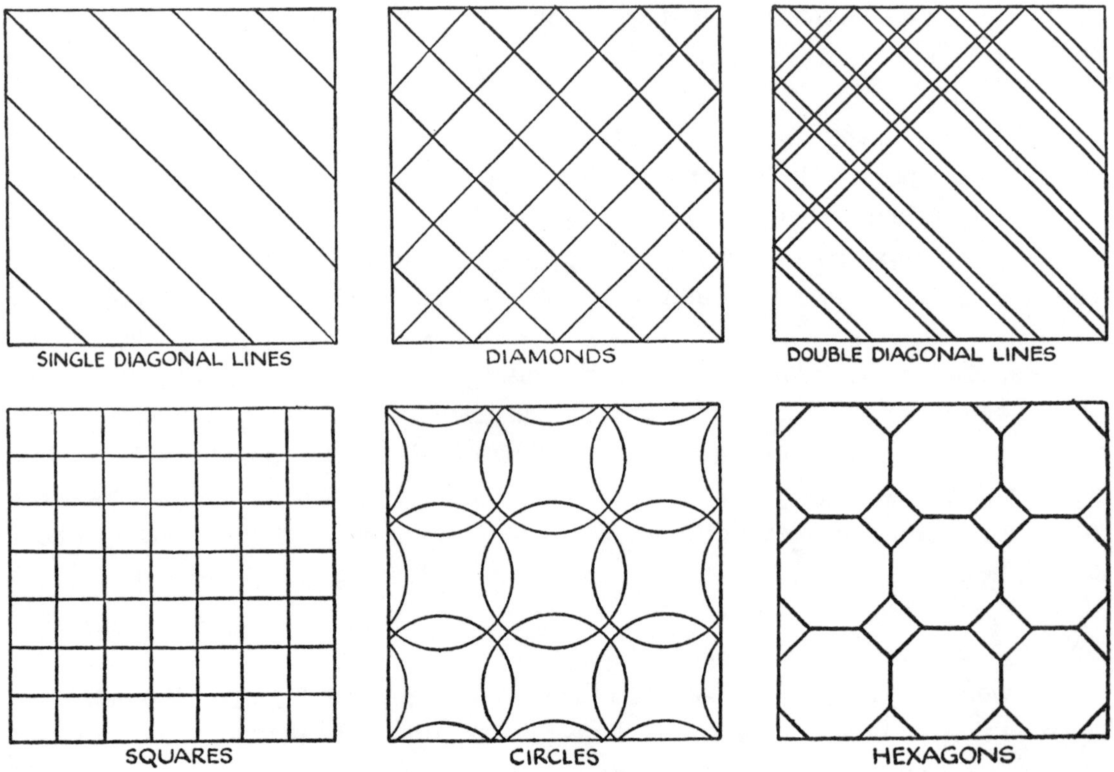

SINGLE DIAGONAL LINES	DIAMONDS	DOUBLE DIAGONAL LINES
SQUARES	CIRCLES	HEXAGONS

Fig. 34. Patterns for Quilting

Fig. 35. Patterns for Quilting

Fig. 36. Patterns for Quilting

Fig. 37. Patterns for Quilting

Fig. 38. Patterns for Quilting

Fig. 39. Patterns for Quilting

107

Fig. 40. Patterns for Quilting

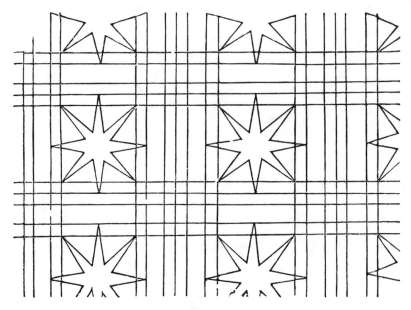

Fig. 41. Pattern for Quilting

Although styles change, quilt designs seem to retain their appeal forever. Perhaps this is because traditional quilt patterns follow important rules of good design: rhythm, balance, unity, harmony, and function. It is important to keep these basic design principles in mind when you are planning a quilt, because if you depart from them you risk failure.

Rhythm: Rhythm is basic to good design. Its elements are repetition and emphasis. Simple rhythm is exemplified by the drumbeat. It can be found in a quilt in which every block is exactly alike. A pieced quilt which is set with alternate colored and plain blocks shows a more complicated rhythm. Parts A and B of Figure 42 show how pieced blocks of alternate colors provide the accent of emphasis.

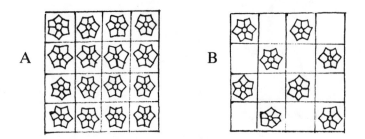

Fig. 42. Quilt Design Rhythm

In addition to the measured rhythm in these examples, another type of rhythm has a flowing quality, such as that found in appliquéd quilts with graceful, curved lines. Figure 43 illustrates flowing rhythm. It contains repetition and emphasis.

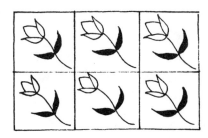

Fig. 43. Quilt Design Rhythm

Both the measured and the flowing rhythm in design lead the eye to move from one part of the design to another. This is very important to remember when you are selecting colors and fabrics for a quilt. The eye should move along the whole quilt, and not be stopped by a distracting color or a fabric inappropriately placed. Figure 44 shows how colors may be used to provide rhythm. You can also see how poor

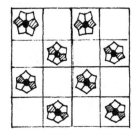 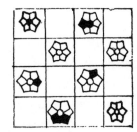

Fig. 44. Quilt Design Rhythm

placement of dark and light colors can spoil the rhythm, and make the design look "choppy." Dark colors, used without plan, call attention to themselves and distract the eye from the entire quilt.

Balance: It is essential to balance the various colors, shapes, sizes, and textures in a quilt top. Most quilt tops, especially pieced ones, contain symmetrical balance due to the nature of their design. Improper use of color, however, can destroy it. Figure 45A shows how the use of dark colors makes the quilt look weighted on the bottom. In Figure 45B the dark colors on the left are balanced with dark colors on the right.

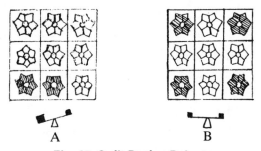

Fig. 45. Quilt Design Balance

In making appliqued blocks, shapes and colors may be balanced against one another. You can balance a large piece of a dark color with a small piece of a bright color, or two small pieces with one large piece of the same color.

Poor balance is sometimes found in quilts containing pieced or appliqued blocks set together alternately with plain blocks. Parts A and B of Figure 46 show the wrong and right ways to design a quilt of this type.

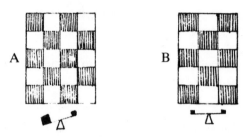

Fig. 46. Quilt Design Balance

Dark and light colors used without plan call attention to themselves and distract the eye from the whole quilt. It is the whole quilt one should be thinking of as each block is planned, and how the blocks can be set together in balance.

Unity and Harmony: Unity is the quality in a design that makes it self-consistent and complete. For example, in a ceramic mosaic unity is achieved by the grout that binds all the tiles together. In a quilt top unity can be created by using pieces of the same color, print, or texture in every block.

To achieve unity one must create a design with a definite objective in mind before beginning the work. In the case of Friendship or Sampler Quilts, in which every block comes from a different maker, or is made from a different pattern, the blocks can be unified by setting them together with strips of a neutral color. These strips serve the same purpose as the grout between mosaic tiles. Although the quilt may contain many colors and shapes, they are made harmonious by the unifying effect of the neutral element.

Another means of achieving unity is to limit the number of colors, sizes, and shapes used in the quilt top. This is not an infallible rule, because many beautiful quilts are made from a variety of colors and pattern shapes. However, if you are having design trouble, particularly in appliqué you may solve the problem by eliminating one or two of the colors or pieces you had planned to use.

The quilt designer must learn to manipulate colors, lines, sizes, and shapes—varying, emphasizing, and removing them where necessary, choosing a motif and developing it to its fullest effect, leaving other ideas for other quilts.

If you want to make a scrapbag quilt, you should choose a pattern which looks best in a wide variety of colors and prints, such as an overall design. In general, scraps should be made into pieced quilts of simple geometric shapes, not into appliquéd quilts. Remember, even scrapbag quilts usually look better if they contain a single plain color to unify the many prints used.

You may wish to follow a traditional pattern but become discouraged by the number of small pieces it requires. You wonder if you would have the time or patience to sew all those pieces together. As a result, perhaps you don't even bother to try the pattern.

However, there is a way to streamline an old pattern so that the desired effect may be achieved with much less time and effort.

Decrease the number of pieces per block. Some patterns use several small pieces where one large piece could do. These patterns were probably designed originally to use up small scraps because scarcity of new materials made it essential to use up every tiny piece on hand. Since this is no longer necessary, there is no need to be bound by this restriction.

The Road to Oklahoma is an example of a pattern which can be changed in this way. The block pattern originally called for twenty pieces, as in illustration 47A. By consolidating the *light* pieces which adjoin into one piece, and the *medium* adjoining pieces into one piece, the total number of pieces in the block can be cut down to twelve, as in illustration 47B.

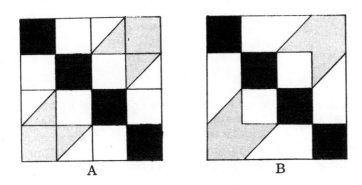

Fig. 47. How to Decrease the Number of Pieces

Here's how to consolidate adjoining pieces: Pin or Scotchtape to a piece of paper or cardboard the pattern pieces to be merged so that their seam lines touch. Draw around the outlines of the entire shape, to make the new pattern piece.

It might become necessary to clip the seam into corners, as in the two gray pieces in 47B, to make the pieces fit smoothly.

Chapter 9

The Making of a Quilt 1890 and Today

In the late 1800's instructions for quilt-making were usually handed down from mother to daughter and not much was written about the art. However, there was one book, Household Discoveries, *by Sidney Morse, published in 1890, that contained instructions.*

" QUILTS AND COMFORTERS IN 1890

The modern factory system has taken out of the home one by one practically all of the domestic arts that occupied so large a portion of the time and attention of our grandmothers. Their place is being taken partly by fancy work and partly by the various activities of the different kinds of woman's clubs and similar forms of associated effort.

The use of blankets and factory-made puffs, that are cheap, light, and warm, bids fair to displace in time to come the old-fashioned pieced quilt, crazy quilt, or comfortable of our grandmothers. But the custom of piecing and typing quilts still holds its own in many localities, partly on the score of economy—as a means of utilizing old pieces of various fabrics—and partly as a pleasant and useful occupation for time that would otherwise pass heavily. For the guidance of those who still find it worth while to make homemade quilts and comforters, and as a memorial of one of the last of the domestic arts to pass away, a few suggestions may be order.

Sorting Pieces

Sort the accumulated pieces that are no longer required for patching, putting goods of the same general character, as ginghams, woolens, calicoes, silks, and the like, in separate lots. Quilts made of similar goods are more satisfactory than if various kinds of good are mingled together, and may be used for different purposes. Silk quilts may be used for couches and sofas, woolen quilts for the guest chambers, gingham and calico quilts for everyday wear, and quilts from old stockings for summer quilts, porches, and hammocks.

To Line Quilts

Quilts may be made from blocks cut in various designs by means of patterns or made crazy fashion, filled with cotton or cotton batting or with an old blanket, lined with new goods of calico or similar material, and quilted or tied. A helpful suggestion as to filling and lining quilts is to make rather large blocks. Fill and line each block separately. Have the blocks (which may be made of smaller blocks sewed together) two or three feet square. Cut lining the same size, put the pieces together, and sew around three sides to make a bag open at one end. Now turn the bag right side out, leaving the seams inside. Introduce one or more thicknesses of cotton batting, tie at intervals to keep the cotton in place, and when the blocks are completed sew them together and cross stitch the seam with silk or worsted. The advantage of this method is that the blocks, being relatively small, may be tied without quilting frames.

Or make a foundation for a quilt or comforter by sandwiching cotton batting between two thicknesses of cheese-cloth and basting all together. This makes a cheese-cloth comforter or pad. Cover this with the patchwork quilt and line in the usual manner. This method is preferable, as the cheese-cloth keeps the cotton in place with very little quilting or tying. The cover will need some fastening, but a very few knots will be sufficient; hence the cover may be easily removed and washed or replaced.

Cheap Quilts

Where the greatest warmth is desired with the least number of quilts and absolute economy is necessary, a number of thicknesses of newspapers between two pieces of cheese-cloth, with or without one or more thicknesses of cotton batting, will give as much warmth as an additional pair of blankets. Paste all together and cover with a pieced quilt and line in the usual manner.

Or use large sheets of tissue paper. But as the quilt is worn the newspapers will crumple and cease to rattle.

Or else old blankets for summer comforters, cover with silkoline or other soft, washable material, and tie.

To Make Crazy Quilts

Use as a foundation old flour sacks sewed together, old sheets, or any strong, waste, washable material. Trim odd-sized pieces in any shape, mixing small and large together. But use materials of the same general quality, as silk, woolen, and the like, and either stitch them to the foundation by hand or stitch around the edge of each piece on the sewing machine. Afterwards feather stitch the blocks and squares together. Line with any suitable material and tack with cotton wadding to the lining. The advantage of this method is that it saves time and the necessity of using quilting frames.

Crazy quilts may be made of old calico pieces, pieces of summer dress goods, or woolen dress goods, silk neckties, ribbons, or the like, or the tops of woolen, silk, or cotton stockings, and used for a variety of purposes. Baste or pin the pieces on to the cloth ground before placing them in the sewing machine or stitching them by hand, and mingle the colors so as to get a pleasing effect. Turn the edges under to form a hem before stitching them to the background, and work fancy stitches about the edges of each.

To Protect Quilts

Bed quilts and comforters become worn and soiled mainly at the ends, by contact with the face and hands when in use, and also when the beds are opened, aired, and made up. Hence protect the ends by saving an extra piece of the lining material sufficient to cover the quilt for six inches deep on each side of the end. Or tack on a piece of calico, cheese-cloth, or other suitable material over each end to a depth of five or six inches. Tack this on by hand, or attach with feather stitches.

When soiled this protective strip may be ripped off, washed, and replaced, and the quilt itself will not require washing for a long time. These strips do not injure the appearance of the quilt when in use, as the lower end is tacked under the mattress and the upper end covered by the pillows or turned back under the top sheet if the bed is partly opened.

In regions where the temperature is variable it is usually better to make quilts and comforters and plenty of them, than to have a smaller number of relatively heavy quilts. From two to four pounds of cotton for each quilt may be used, according to climate.

Homemade Quilting Frames

To make a quilting frame, order from a lumber yard or sawmill four strips of hard pine 1 inch thick, 3 inches wide, and 6½ feet long. These could not cost more than twenty-five cents. [*EDITOR'S NOTE: This was in 1890!*] Tack a piece of muslin along the edge of each strip. Buy four clamps for a dime at a hardware store, or have them made by a blacksmith, and you have a cheap set of frames that will last a lifetime.

To Tie Quilts

In summer arrange a shady place out of doors to stretch the frames. Teach the children how to tie the knots and have them assist. One of the most regrettable things about the passing of the domestic arts is the loss of their great educational influence in forming habits of industry in children and preparing them by a sort of domestic apprenticeship to take their places in the industrial arts and crafts in later life. If the quilt has no blocks or other regular pattern as a guide in tying the knots, a piece of cheese-cloth of the same size as the quilts may be marked off into squares with crayon or by drawing threads, and holes may be clipped with buttonhole scissors where the lines intersect. Stretch this over the quilt and tie through the holes.

Or use an old sheet for this purpose. The cheese-cloth or sheet may be removed, rolled up, and used again. In this way several persons can work at the same time, and each will know where to tie.

To Tie a Quilting Knot

Thread the needle with yarn or silkateen. Double pull through the quilt as usual, leaving the end about one inch long. Form a loop of the long end over the left forefinger and thumb, and through this loop pass the short end, drawing the thread up tight at the same time with the other hand. Repeat this, beginning with fingers on the other side of the thread as before, thus forming a reverse loop. This makes the knot square, which it would not be if the second loop was begun on the same side of the yarn as the first. This will never loosen and saves drawing the long thread its full length as in the old way. "

HOW TO MAKE A QUILT TODAY

Some of the following instructions are adapted from Barbara Taylor's book on Quilting, *published by Taylor Bedding Manufacturing Company of Taylor, Texas. It gives helpful information about how to make a quilt today.*

How to Begin

THE first step is to decide on a pattern. A pieced pattern is made by sewing together small pieces to form a pattern, usually geometric in design. An appliquéd quilt is made by sewing various pieces of colored or printed cloth onto a solid background. The appliqués can be made on a solid background of one piece, or on blocks joined together to form the background. You may even wish to combine pieced and appliquéd work, or choose to do a quilted counterpane with only the quilting forming the design.

Once the pattern is decided, the next choice is which colors to use. Many appliquéd patterns are of floral design. It is preferred that you stay as closely as possible to the garden colors of these flowers. However, it is not necessary to do so.

Modern quilts usually measure 81″ x 96″. If you wish to make a smaller quilt, you can omit a row of blocks and if you wish to make a larger quilt, you can enlarge the border or add an extra row of blocks. It is best to enlarge a pattern by adding an outside border or an extra row of blocks.

Use the best materials available. You will put a lot of work into the quilt so why not make it a long-lasting heirloom? Use only color-fast materials.

Choose only closely woven fabrics with a firm weave and a soft texture such as calico, percale, chintz, muslin, or gingham. Avoid heavy sheeting, satins, and sateens. The quilting of these materials would be very difficult and the result would not be as effective.

If there is any danger of shrinkage, wash and iron your material before starting. Remember when your quilt is completed you cannot redo any of the work.

How to Make A Pattern

The number of units you need for each pattern will be specified in your instructions for the specific design. Trace the design onto a piece of tracing or tissue paper. Then place the pattern onto sandpaper to form your master pattern. Lay these parts together to become familiar with the manner in which they fit together. Hold the pattern on the sandpaper firmly with your left hand and cut around the paper pattern. Make a number of patterns at one time so that when one pattern is worn a second is available.

How to Cut Units

In order to make certain the material is absolutely even, tear off about 1″ from the cut end. Tearing the material across the width will make the edge even. Then iron the material through a damp cloth. Familiarize yourself with the lengthwise and crosswise grains in the material. Place the pattern on the lengthwise grain of the material and with a pencil or tailor's chalk, make a tracing line around the pattern.

Trace the number of units needed for each block, making certain that you leave a half inch on all sides between each tracing line for seam allowance. Cut out the units one-half inch from the tracing line on all sides.

Continue cutting pieces until enough are cut to finish the quilt top.

As each piece is cut, place the pattern directly over the tracing of the cut unit and with a moderately hot iron press back the seam allowance over the pattern, thus making a distinct guide line for sewing.

Piecing Blocks

When joining the pieces of a quilt, first pin the corners exactly, then pin the lines of the side together. Ease in any slight fullness. Check both sides of the seams to make certain that the lines are accurately pinned. Pieced blocks may be sewed, either by hand or machine. To hasten the piecing, all similar parts may be assembled at one time and joined later. For example, the print patches in the double wedding ring design may be sewed together first, then sewed to the oval section, and last to the center section. Or you may choose to complete one block at a time. Use whichever method is easiest for you. After the pieces have been joined, press the seams open.

Most pieced quilts are done in recurring pattern, making them popular with many quilt makers because they are done block by block and assembled as the rows of blocks are completed. The Crazy Quilt is one in which the pieces are usually made from scraps of materials joined together in a "crazy" pattern. This type of quilt gives one an opportunity to display all types of embroidery since feather stitching, buttonholing, or any fancy stitches may be used with embroidery floss over the seams.

Appliquéing

If you are doing appliqué, cut designs as you would for the blocks. Many quilters prefer to appliqué rather than piece, even if the appliquéd quilt is designed geometrically.

As you mark the pieces for appliquéing, mark the right side of the material. The marking lines will be your guide for turning under the seams. When basting the seams clip the material to the pencil lines on curves to avoid puckering. When one part covers another, do not turn under the seam. Appliqué one part of the seam over the seam of another part. Turn under the seams, baste, and press with a warm iron.

To apply the design in its correct position, fold the block in half and crease with thumb nail, then unfold and fold in the opposite direction and crease. Fold from corner to corner and then fold from corner to corner in the opposite direction.

All designs are applied in relation to the center and to the lines which have been creased. Leaf ends are first tucked under the stem, stem ends are then covered with buds or flowers, and all raw ends are turned under. When applying a curved unit, baste ⅛ " away from outside edge and pull slightly to form a curved edge; or clip well into fold on the curves to make the pieces lie flat.

When the entire design has been basted in place, sew around the edge with small, invisible stitches, taking care not to pull stitches too tightly since this puckers the material. To accomplish this, start with a very fine knot in your thread which is hidden under the seam of the appliqué piece. Bring your needle out on the very edge of the fold of the seam. Enter the background material at approximately the same place and come back up through the background and appliqué piece at about ¹/₁₆" from the first stitch. Enter the background material just under the edge of the appliqué piece, then come up through the background again the same distance under the fold of the appliqué to its edge. In this way the tiny stitches will be hidden.

Assembling the Quilt

After the blocks have been completed, experiment with arrangement by placing blocks on a large surface. When the best possible combination has been achieved, sew the blocks together. Interesting designs are often produced when four blocks are sewn together.

Borders and Bindings

A border produces the framework for a quilt design. In other instances it serves to increase the size of the quilt. Some patterns are best without an added border. The border is added after the blocks are joined and can include parts of the overall design or it can be decorated with fine quilting. After the quilting, excess batting and lining are trimmed off. A bias binding is added all around the edges to produce a neat finishing touch.

Linings and Fillings

The quilt lining may be of the same fabric as used for the top, or it may be of a blending or contrasting color. When 36" or 42" fabric is used, remove the selvedge and sew two or more lengths together to obtain the proper width. For a smooth, seamless lining, percale sheeting is an excellent choice. The filling should be of the finest cotton batting obtainable. Inferior products will produce inferior results.

Lay the lining flat, smoothing it out. The cotton batting is placed on top of the lining and smoothed out to eliminate the wrinkles. The top is placed over these two layers and all three layers are carefully basted together.

Basting the Layers Together

Starting at center of quilt, baste out to each side through the three layers. Then starting at center again, baste to each corner diagonally. Then baste all outer edges together.

Quilting Designs and How to Use Them

The care given to the quilting you are about to begin will make the difference between a beautiful hand-crafted article to use with pride or just another piece of bedding. Start at one end of the quilt and work through to the other end, keeping the fullness that develops ahead of the work. Use small, firm running stitches through all three layers, following the outline of the pattern. Fill in large sections with your choice of patterns. Remove pins as the work nears them.

Diagonal lines form beautiful diamond patterns, or you might choose a combination of circles. When you use large plain blocks alternated with pieced or appliquéd blocks, carefully trace the quilting pattern before starting, to assure a uniformly accurate design in each block. There are many quilting designs, but you can try your own hand at designing to produce a quilt that will truly be your own.

In quilting an appliquéd quilt, be sure you outline every appliqué piece. If the pieces are large, an additional row or two of quilting will fill the empty spaces. In quilting a pieced quilt, each piece should be outlined close to the seams—$1/16''$. This is very important to bring out the design of the quilt on the back as well as the front. No more than one square inch of the quilt should remain unquilted.

The closer the stitches, the better the quilting, and it takes many hours of practice to accomplish very fine results. The quilting should be done toward the center wherever it is possible. A really good quilter will do as many as 14 stitches to an inch.

Quilting on a Frame or Hoop

The most satisfactory results are obtained by using a quilting frame. If space is not available the quilter will use a hoop. Quilting is done in the same manner although the preparation of the quilt differs slightly.

Frame Method: Compact quilting frames are now available in needlework departments or through mail order houses. Modern frames are convenient to use and easy to handle. To mount the quilt, smooth the lining on a large, flat surface, seamed surface up. Next, unroll the cotton batting and gently spread over the lining as evenly as possible. Smooth the completed quilt top over the lining and batting and place sharp dressmaker pins through the three layers not more than 6″ apart or baste as described. With thumb tacks, attach one end of the three layers to one of the side rails of the quilting frame and roll the pinned quilt on this rail. After placing on the frame, unroll enough to reach the other rail and tack in place. You are ready to start quilting.

Hoop Method: Prepare your quilt in the same manner as for the frame. Make certain that the three layers are basted together, so that the quilt will not slip when moving the hoop. Start quilting at the center of the quilt and work to the outer edges. Pull the quilt taut in the hoop, moving any slight fullness towards the outside of the quilt. It may be necessary to cut the basting thread as your work progresses.

Chapter 10

Quilt Designs and Patterns

IN 1922 THE Ladies' Art Company of St. Louis, Missouri, published a booklet called *Quilt Pattern Book, Patchwork and Appliqué*. It contained over five hundred patterns that could be used for quilts and quilting. The designs on the following pages are reproduced from that booklet. They are easily converted into patterns of any size. The maximum price of a pattern in 1922 was 10¢ each or 3 for 25¢.

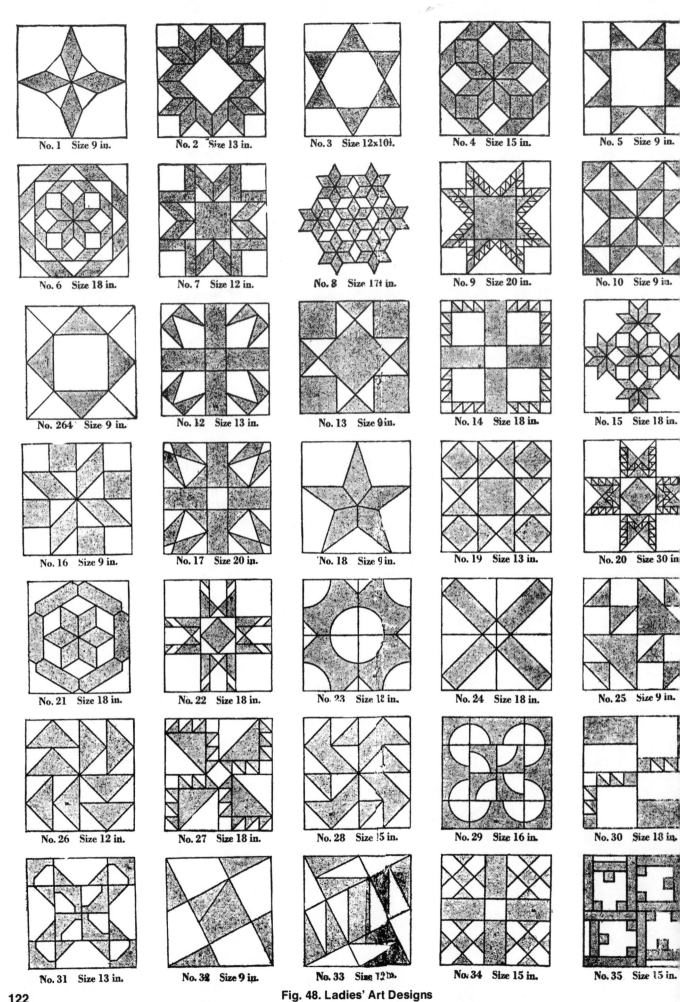

No. 1   Size 9 in.
No. 2   Size 13 in.
No. 3   Size 12x10½.
No. 4   Size 15 in.
No. 5   Size 9 in.
No. 6   Size 18 in.
No. 7   Size 12 in.
No. 8   Size 17½ in.
No. 9   Size 20 in.
No. 10   Size 9 in.
No. 264   Size 9 in.
No. 12   Size 13 in.
No. 13   Size 9 in.
No. 14   Size 18 in.
No. 15   Size 18 in.
No. 16   Size 9 in.
No. 17   Size 20 in.
No. 18   Size 9 in.
No. 19   Size 13 in.
No. 20   Size 30 in
No. 21   Size 18 in.
No. 22   Size 18 in.
No. 23   Size 12 in.
No. 24   Size 18 in.
No. 25   Size 9 in.
No. 26   Size 12 in.
No. 27   Size 18 in.
No. 28   Size 15 in.
No. 29   Size 16 in.
No. 30   Size 18 in.
No. 31   Size 13 in.
No. 32   Size 9 in.
No. 33   Size 12 in.
No. 34   Size 15 in.
No. 35   Size 15 in.

122   Fig. 48. Ladies' Art Designs

No. 36 Size 9 in.   No. 37 Size 9 in.   No. 38 Size 18 in.   No. 39 Size 15 in.   No. 40 Size 15½ in.

No. 41 Size 19 in.   No. 42 Size 9 in.   No. 43 Size 10x8.   No. 44 Size 18 in.   No. 46 Size 18 in.

No. 47 Size 12x10½.   No. 48 Size 15 in.   No. 49 Size 28x12½.   No. 50 Size 18 in.   No. 298 Size 9 in.

No. 55 Size 18 in.   No. 57 Size 9 in.   No. 58 Size 12 in.   No. 59 Size 10 in.   No. 60 Size 20 in.

No. 61 Size 18 in.   No. 62 Size 15 in.   No. 63 Size 18 in.   No. 64 Size 6x10½.   No. 66 Size 18 in.

No. 67 Size 24 in.   No. 68 Size 18 in.   No. 69 Size 12½ in.   No. 71 Size 9 in.   No. 74 Size 18 in.

No. 75 Size 24 in.   No. 76 Size 9 in.   No. 77 Size 12 in.   No. 78 Size 9 in.   No. 79 Size 15 in.

Fig. 48. Ladies' Art Designs *(cont.)*

123

No. 80   Size 15 in.
No. 81   Size 16 in.
No. 82   Size 18 in.
No. 83   Size 14 in.
No. 84   Size 15 in.

No. 85   Size 15 in.
No. 86   Size 15 in.
No. 87   Size 15 in.
No. 88   Size 12 in.
No. 89   Size 12 in.

No. 90   Size 12 in.
No. 91   Size 15 in.
No. 92   Size 18 in.
No. 94   Size 9 in.
No. 95   Size 12 in.

No. 96   Size 9 in.
No. 97   Size 15 in.
No. 98   Size 10x3¾.
No. 99   Size 24 in.
No. 100   Size 13 in.

No. 101   Size 13 in.
No. 102   Size 15 in.
No. 103   Size 15½ in.
No. 104   Size 13 in.
No. 105   Size 13 in.

No. 106   Size 13 in.
No. 107   Size 13 in.
No. 108   13½x12½.
No. 109   Size 13x11½.
No. 112   Size 9 in.

No. 114   Size 15 in.
No. 115   Size 8¾ in.
No. 117   Size 24 in.
No. 118   Size 15 in.
No. 119   Size 9 in.

Fig. 48. Ladies' Art Designs *(cont.)*

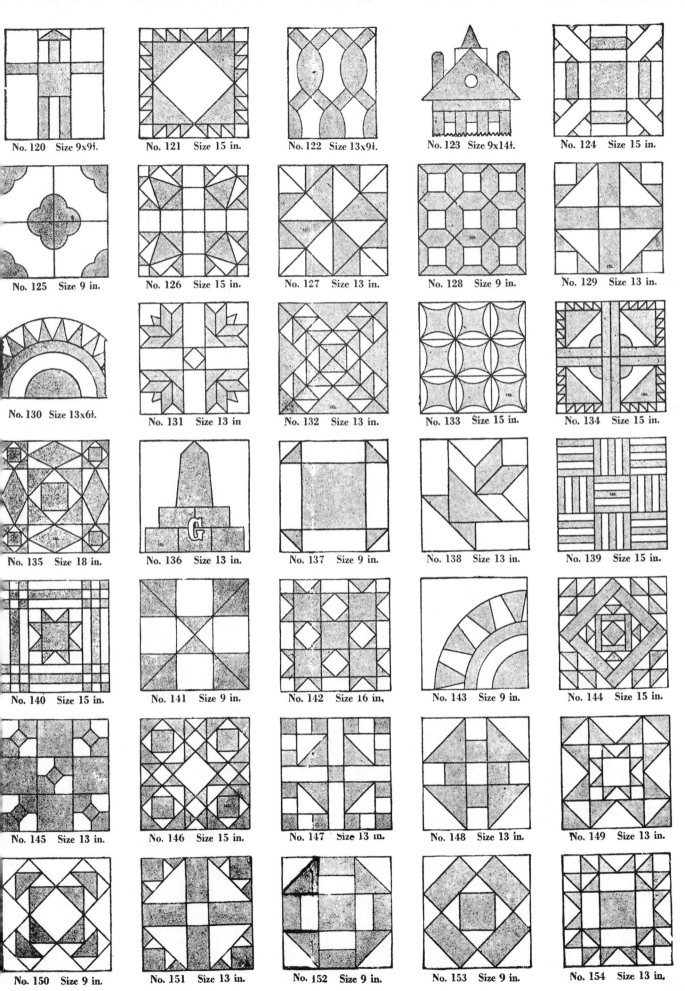

No. 120   Size 9x9½.

No. 121   Size 15 in.

No. 122   Size 13x9½.

No. 123   Size 9x14½.

No. 124   Size 15 in.

No. 125   Size 9 in.

No. 126   Size 15 in.

No. 127   Size 13 in.

No. 128   Size 9 in.

No. 129   Size 13 in.

No. 130   Size 13x6½.

No. 131   Size 13 in

No. 132   Size 13 in.

No. 133   Size 15 in.

No. 134   Size 15 in.

No. 135   Size 18 in.

No. 136   Size 13 in.

No. 137   Size 9 in.

No. 138   Size 13 in.

No. 139   Size 15 in.

No. 140   Size 15 in.

No. 141   Size 9 in.

No. 142   Size 16 in.

No. 143   Size 9 in.

No. 144   Size 15 in.

No. 145   Size 13 in.

No. 146   Size 15 in.

No. 147   Size 13 in.

No. 148   Size 13 in.

No. 149   Size 13 in.

No. 150   Size 9 in.

No. 151   Size 13 in.

No. 152   Size 9 in.

No. 153   Size 9 in.

No. 154   Size 13 in.

Fig. 48. Ladies' Art Designs (cont.)

125

No. 155   Size 13 in.   No. 156   Size 13 in.   No. 157   Size 9 in.   No. 158   Size 13 in.   No. 159   Size 13 in.

No. 160   Size 13 in.   No. 161   Size 13 in.   No. 162   Size 15 in.   No. 163   Size 13 in.   No. 164   Size 9 in.

No. 165   Size 13 in.   No. 166   Size 13 in.   No. 167   Size 39½ in.   No. 168   Size 12 in.   No. 169   Size 13 in.

No. 170   Size 10 in.   No. 171   Size 13 in.   No. 172   Size 13 in.   No. 173   Size 9 in.   No. 174   Size 13 in.

No. 175   Size 13 in.   No. 176   Size 13 in.   No. 177   Size 13 in.   No. 178   Size 9 in.   No. 179   Size 9 in.

No. 181   Size 9 in.   No. 182   Size 6x12½   No. 183   Size 13 in.   No. 185   Size 15 in.   No. 190   Size 18 in.

No. 191   Size 9 in.   No. 192   Size 9 in.   No. 193   Size 24x28   No. 194   Size 13 in.   No. 195   Size 9 in.

     Fig. 48. Ladies' Art Designs *(cont.)*

No. 196   Size 9 in.
No. 197   Size 13 in.
No. 198   Size 9 in.
No. 199.   Size 7 in.
No. 200   Size 9 in.

No. 201   Size 15 in.
No. 202   Size 13 in.
No. 203   Size 15 in.
No. 204   Size 9 in.
No. 205   Size 13 in.

No. 206   Size 9 in.
No. 207   Size 9 in.
No. 208   Size 9 in.
No. 209   Size 15 in.
No. 210   Size 13 in.

No. 211   Size 18 in.
No. 212   Size 15 in.
No. 213   Size 9 in.
No. 214   Size 13 in.
No. 215   Size 13 in.

No. 216   Size 13 in.
No. 217   Size 13 in.
No. 218   Size 9 in.
No. 219   Size 18 in.
No. 220   Size 13 in.

No. 221   Size 13 in.
No. 222   Size 18 in.
No. 223   Size 13 in.
No. 224   Size 13 in.
No. 225   Size 9 in.

No. 226   Size 15 in.
No. 227   Size 15 in.
No. 228   13x12½.
No. 229   Size 13 in.
No. 230   Size 18 in.

Fig. 48. Ladies' Art Designs (cont.)

127

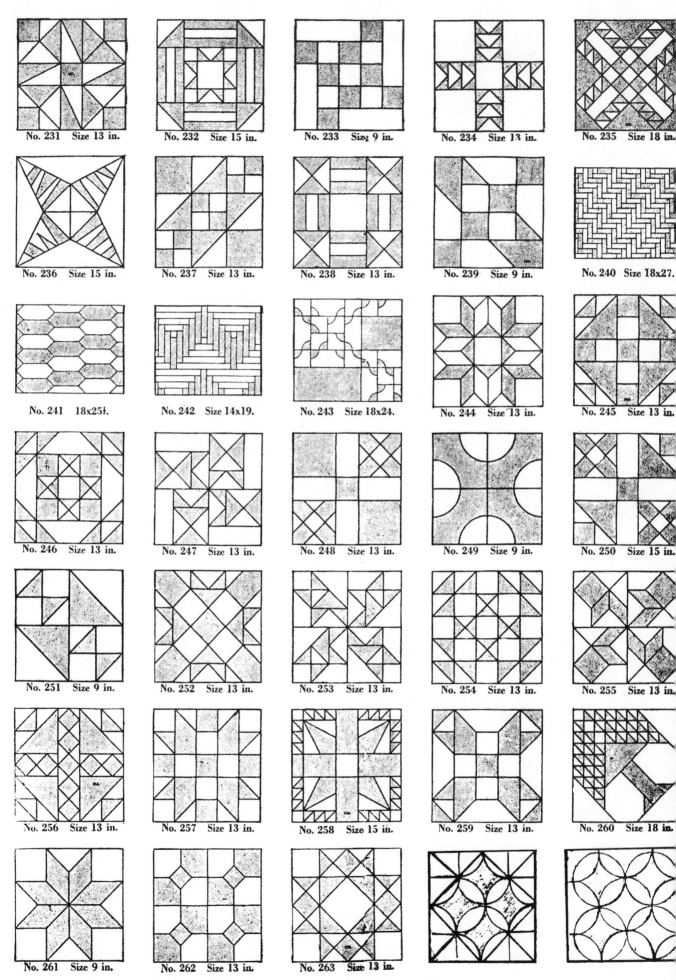

No. 231   Size 13 in.

No. 232   Size 15 in.

No. 233   Size 9 in.

No. 234   Size 13 in.

No. 235   Size 18 in.

No. 236   Size 15 in.

No. 237   Size 13 in.

No. 238   Size 13 in.

No. 239   Size 9 in.

No. 240   Size 18x27.

No. 241   18x25½.

No. 242   Size 14x19.

No. 243   Size 18x24.

No. 244   Size 13 in.

No. 245   Size 13 in.

No. 246   Size 13 in.

No. 247   Size 13 in.

No. 248   Size 13 in.

No. 249   Size 9 in.

No. 250   Size 15 in.

No. 251   Size 9 in.

No. 252   Size 13 in.

No. 253   Size 13 in.

No. 254   Size 13 in.

No. 255   Size 13 in.

No. 256   Size 13 in.

No. 257   Size 13 in.

No. 258   Size 15 in.

No. 259   Size 13 in.

No. 260   Size 18 in.

No. 261   Size 9 in.

No. 262   Size 13 in.

No. 263   Size 13 in.

Fig. 48. Ladies' Art Designs *(cont.)*

No. 266   Size 24 in.

No. 267   Size 18 in.

No. 268   Size 18 in.

No. 269   Size 15 in.

No. 270   Size 9 in.

No. 271   Size 13 in.

No. 272   Size 13 in.

No. 273   Size 15 in.

No. 274   Size 13 in.

No. 275   Size 13 in.

No. 276   Size 9 in.

No. 277   Size 9 in.

No. 278   Size 13 in.

No. 279   Size 9 in.

No. 280   Size 13 in.

No. 281   Size 15 in.

No. 282   Size 13 in.

No. 284   Size 15 in.

No. 285   Size 24 in.

No. 286   Size 18 in.

No. 287   Size 9 in.

No. 288   Size 18 in.

No. 289   Size 18 in.

No. 290   Size 24 in.

No. 291   Size 15 in.

No. 292   Size 15 in.

No. 293   24x22

No. 294   Size 24 in.

No. 295   Size 24 in.

No. 296   Size 9 in.

Cathedral patterns (see bottom two righthand diagrams on opposite page) are made by folding and refolding muslin squares into multilayers and sewing them so as to make diamonds, with or without a circle around each.

No. 301   Size 24 i.

No. 304   Size 13 in.

No. 305   Size 15 in.

Fig. 48. Ladies' Art Designs *(cont.)*

No. 343 Size 13 in.   No. 344 Size 13 in.   No. 345 Size 13 in.   No. 346 Size 13 in.   No. 347 Size 13 in.

No. 348 Size 13 in.   No. 349 Size 13 in.   No. 350 Size 13 in.   No. 351 Size 9 in.   No. 352 Size 9 in.

No. 353 13x11⅓   No. 354 Size 18 in.   No. 355 Size 18 in.   No. 356 Size 9 in.   No. 357 Size 15 in.

No. 358 Size 12 in.   No. 359 Size 18 in.   No. 360 Size 9 in.   No. 361 18x19⅓   No. 362 Size 9 in.

No. 363 Size 13 in.   No. 364 Size 13 in.   No. 365 Size 13 in.   No. 366 Size 9x7⅓   No. 367 Size 18 in.

No. 368 Size 12x7⅓   No. 369 Size 13 in.   No. 370 10x10⅓   No. 371 Size 18 in.   No. 372 Size 15 in.

No. 373 15x15⅓   No. 374 Size 27 in.   No. 375 Size 13 in.   No. 376 Size 13 in.   No. 377 Size 15 in.

130   **Fig. 48. Ladies' Art Designs** *(cont.)*

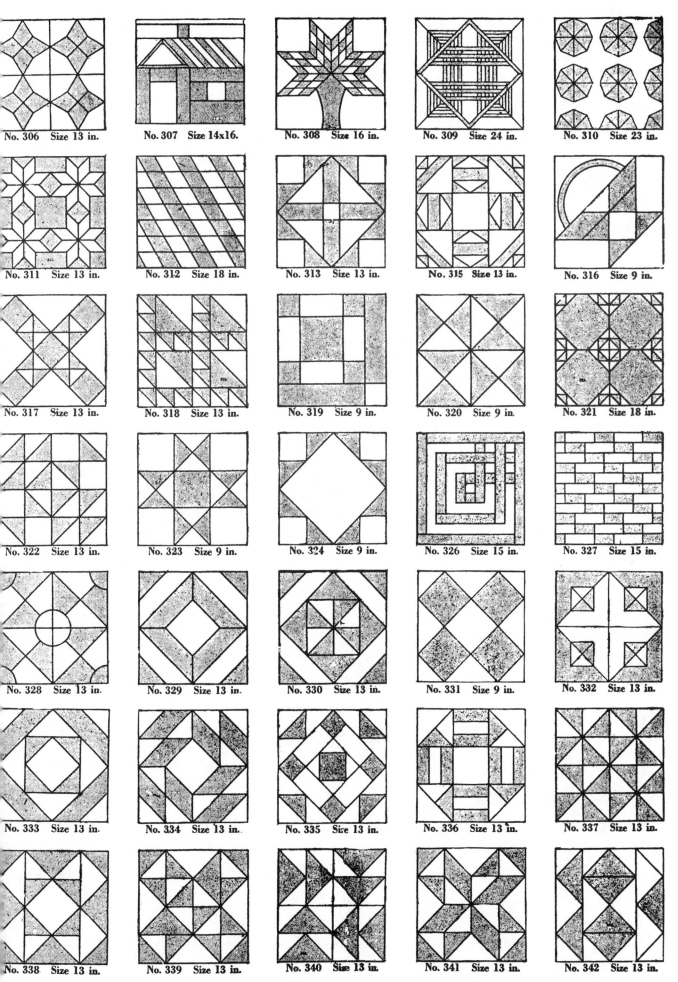

No. 306   Size 13 in.

No. 307   Size 14x16.

No. 308   Size 16 in.

No. 309   Size 24 in.

No. 310   Size 23 in.

No. 311   Size 13 in.

No. 312   Size 18 in.

No. 313   Size 13 in.

No. 315   Size 13 in.

No. 316   Size 9 in.

No. 317   Size 13 in.

No. 318   Size 13 in.

No. 319   Size 9 in.

No. 320   Size 9 in.

No. 321   Size 18 in.

No. 322   Size 13 in.

No. 323   Size 9 in.

No. 324   Size 9 in.

No. 326   Size 15 in.

No. 327   Size 15 in.

No. 328   Size 13 in.

No. 329   Size 13 in.

No. 330   Size 13 in.

No. 331   Size 9 in.

No. 332   Size 13 in.

No. 333   Size 13 in.

No. 334   Size 13 in.

No. 335   Size 13 in.

No. 336   Size 13 in.

No. 337   Size 13 in.

No. 338   Size 13 in.

No. 339   Size 13 in.

No. 340   Size 13 in.

No. 341   Size 13 in.

No. 342   Size 13 in.

Fig. 48. Ladies' Art Designs *(cont.)*

131

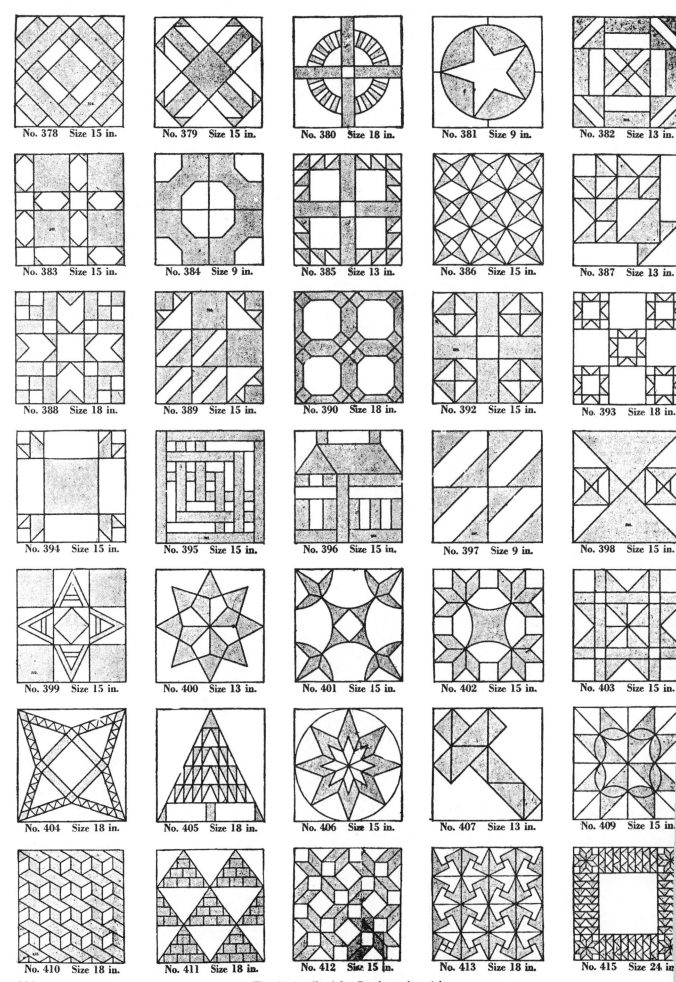

No. 378   Size 15 in.
No. 379   Size 15 in.
No. 380   Size 18 in.
No. 381   Size 9 in.
No. 382   Size 13 in.

No. 383   Size 15 in.
No. 384   Size 9 in.
No. 385   Size 13 in.
No. 386   Size 15 in.
No. 387   Size 13 in.

No. 388   Size 18 in.
No. 389   Size 15 in.
No. 390   Size 18 in.
No. 392   Size 15 in.
No. 393   Size 18 in.

No. 394   Size 15 in.
No. 395   Size 15 in.
No. 396   Size 15 in.
No. 397   Size 9 in.
No. 398   Size 15 in.

No. 399   Size 15 in.
No. 400   Size 13 in.
No. 401   Size 15 in.
No. 402   Size 15 in.
No. 403   Size 15 in.

No. 404   Size 18 in.
No. 405   Size 18 in.
No. 406   Size 15 in.
No. 407   Size 13 in.
No. 409   Size 15 in.

No. 410   Size 18 in.
No. 411   Size 18 in.
No. 412   Size 15 in.
No. 413   Size 18 in.
No. 415   Size 24 in.

132   Fig. 48. Ladies' Art Designs *(cont.)*

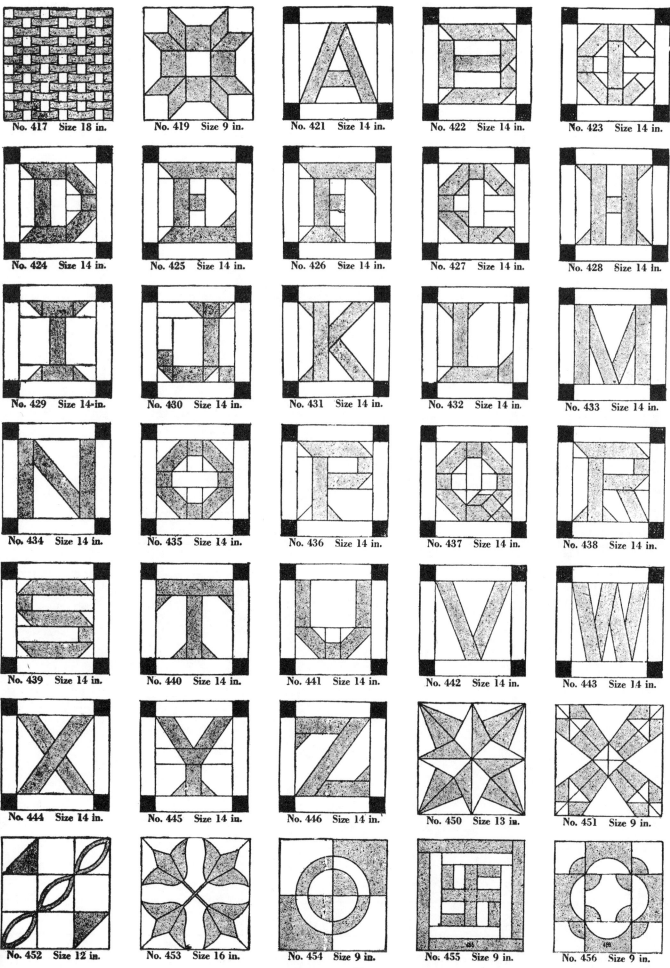

No. 417 Size 18 in. No. 419 Size 9 in. No. 421 Size 14 in. No. 422 Size 14 in. No. 423 Size 14 in.

No. 424 Size 14 in. No. 425 Size 14 in. No. 426 Size 14 in. No. 427 Size 14 in. No. 428 Size 14 in.

No. 429 Size 14 in. No. 430 Size 14 in. No. 431 Size 14 in. No. 432 Size 14 in. No. 433 Size 14 in.

No. 434 Size 14 in. No. 435 Size 14 in. No. 436 Size 14 in. No. 437 Size 14 in. No. 438 Size 14 in.

No. 439 Size 14 in. No. 440 Size 14 in. No. 441 Size 14 in. No. 442 Size 14 in. No. 443 Size 14 in.

No. 444 Size 14 in. No. 445 Size 14 in. No. 446 Size 14 in. No. 450 Size 13 in. No. 451 Size 9 in.

No. 452 Size 12 in. No. 453 Size 16 in. No. 454 Size 9 in. No. 455 Size 9 in. No. 456 Size 9 in.

Fig. 48. Ladies' Art Designs *(cont.)*

133

No. 457   Size 9 in.
No. 458   Size 9 in.
No. 460   Size 9 in.
No. 461   Size 12 in.
No. 462   Size 9 in.
No. 463   Size 18 in.
No. 464   Size 9 in.
No. 465   Size 9 in.
No. 466   Size 9 in.
No. 467   Size 12 in.
No. 468   Size 12 in.
No. 469   Size 12 in.
No. 470   Size 12 in.
No. 471   Size 12 in.
No. 472   Size 12 in.
No. 473   Size 12 in.
No. 474   Size 12 in.
No. 475   Size 12 in.
No. 476   Size 12 in.
No. 477   Size 9 in.
No. 478   Size 12 in.
No. 479   Size 12 in.
No. 480   Size 9 in.
No. 481   Size 12 in.
No. 482   Size 9 in.
No. 483   Size 9 in.
No. 484   Size 12 in.
No. 485   Size 9 in.
No. 486   Size 9 in.
No. 487   Size 12 in.
No. 488   Size 18 in.
No. 489   Size 12 in.
No. 490   Size 9 in.
No. 491   Size 9 in.
No. 492   Size 18 in.

Fig. 48. Ladies' Art Designs *(cont.)*

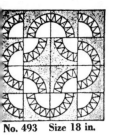

No. 493   Size 18 in.

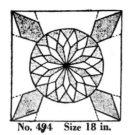

No. 494   Size 18 in.

No. 496   Size 12 in.

Applique Designs.

The following quilt blocks are designed for applique work. The method of making applique blocks is quite different than that followed in making pieced blocks. In applique work the design is formed by placing pieces of material cut in the various motifs of the design on a background of material, and securing the design to the background by means of buttonhole, outline, or other fine stitches. White muslin is generally used as a background, and suitable colored material for the design.

No. 51   Size 24 in.   No. 52   Size 11 in.   No. 53   Size 18 in.   No. 54   Size 15 in.   No. 56   Size 11½ in.

No. 65   Size 12x9½.   No. 70   Size 12½ in.   No. 72   Size 13 in.   No. 73   Size 16 in.   No. 93   Size 13 in.

No. 110   Size 9 in.   No. 111   Size 6½ in.   No. 113   Size 12 in.   No. 116   Size 13 in.   No. 180   Size 13 in.

No. 184   Size 13 in.   No. 186   Size 13 in.   No. 187   Size 12½ in.   No. 188   Size 7½ in.   No. 189   Size 13 in.

No. 283   Size 13 in.   No. 299   Size 15 in.   No. 300   Size 13 in.   No. 302   Size 13 in.   No. 303   Size 13 in.

Fig. 48. Ladies' Art Designs (cont.)

QUILTING DESIGNS.

Q 11. 17x22

Q 12. 17x22

Q 13. 17x22

Q 14. 17x22

Q 15. 17x22

Q 16. 15 in.

Q 17. 12 in.

Q 18. 13 in.

Q 19. 13 in.

Q 20. 16 in.

Q 21. 9 in.

Q 22. 10x13

Q 23. 22x8

Q 24. 9 in. sq., 7 in., bor.
12 in. sq., 10 in. bor.

Q 25. 32 in. wreath, 9 in. bor.

Q 26. 6 in. sq., 5 in. bor.
11 in. sq., 7 in. bor.

Q 27. 9 in. sq., 4 in. bor.
12 in. sq., 6 in. bor.

Q 28. 6 in. sq., 5 in. bor.
9 in. sq., 7 in. bor.

Q 29. 9 in. sq., 4 in. bor.
12 in. sq., 7 in. bor.

Fig. 48. Ladies' Art Designs (cont.)

Designs for
Etched Quilt Blocks

These taking perforated designs are especially suitable for etched quilt blocks. They are also suitable for many other purposes that will suggest themselves to the skilled needleworker.

137

Fig. 48. Ladies' Art Designs *(cont.)*

Fig. 48 Ladies' Art Designs *(cont.)*

If you find it difficult to adapt patterns (see pages 345, 346) from pictures, perhaps it would be desirable to get in touch with Heirloom Plastics, who provide hundreds of patterns for items in patchwork and appliqué. The following pages contain some of the featured designs.

Fig. 49. Heirloom Plastics Designs

PW41 Around the World
PW42 Always Friends
PW43 Baby Bunting
PW44 Child's Elephant Q.
PW45 Child's Pony Quilt
PW46 Crossroads
PW47 Cottage Tulips
PW48 Cat & Mice

A49 Iris
PW50 Drunkard's Path
PW51 Friendship Ring
PW52 Friendship Knot
PW53 Friendship Star
PW54 Flowing Ribbon
PW55 Falling Timbers
PW56 Goldfish

PW57 Glorified 9-Patch
PW58 Star & Cone
PW59 Heart's Desire
PW60 Heritage Quilt
PW61 Kaleidoscope
PW62 Lazy Daisy
PW63 Liberty Star
PW64 Lemon Star

PW65 Lucinda's Star
PW66 Love Ring
PW67 Merry-Go-Round
PW68 Milky Way
PW69 Morning Glory
A70 Mt. Vernon Wreath
PW71 Poinsettia
PW72 Pandora's Box

PW73 Pineapple
PW74 Philadelphia Pavements
PW75 Rob Peter to Pay Paul
PW76 Roman Stripe
PW77 Snow Crystals
PW78 Snow Crystal
PW79 Solomon's Puzzle
PW80 Streak of Lightning

A81 Shamrock
PW82 Flying Saucer
PW83 Wedding Ring
PW84 Wheel of Mystery
PW85 Worlds Without End
PW86 Windmill
PW87 Necktie
PW88 Spool

PW1
Arkansas
Snow Flake

PW2
Bouquet
in a Fan

PW3
Bachelor's
Puzzle

PW4
Corner
Posts

PW5
Crazy
Anne

PW6
City
Square

PW7
Chevron

PW8
Coffin
Star

PW9
Clamshell

PW10
Dresden
Plate

PW11
8-Pointed
Star

PW12
Formosa
Tea Leaf

PW13
Greek
Cross

PW14
Grandmoth-
er's Basket

PW15
Gretchen

PW16
Grape
Basket

PW17
Interlocked
Squares

PW18
Light &
Shadows

PW19
Morning
Star

PW20
Missouri
Star

PW21
Maple
Leaf

PW22
Nelson's
Victory

PW23
Old Mill
Wheel

PW24
Pontiac
Star

PW25
Purple
Cross

PW26
Pine
Tree

PW27
Rose
Dream

PW28
Silver
& Gold

PW29
Sailboats

PW30
Star of
Le Moyne

PW31
The Anvil

PW32
Tree Ever
lasting

PW33
Pilot's
Wheel

PW34
The Four
Winds

PW35
The Guid-
ing Star

A36
Butterfly

A37
Butterfly
& Flower

A38
Dutch
Tulip

A39
Rosebud

A40
Whirligig

Flock of Geese

Fly Foot

Fox & Geese

Variable Star

Hovering Birds

Clay's Choice

Brown Goose

Tea Leaf

Fig. 49. Heirloom Plastics Designs *(cont.)*

Sage Bud
B-100, (24"), 55¢

St. Gregory's Cross
GC-101, (12"), 55¢

Album
AL-102, (12"), 55¢

Steps to the Altar
SA-103, (12"), 55¢

Martha Washington Star
MW-104, (16"), 55¢

Cat's Cradle
C-105, (12"), 55¢

Barbara Frietchie Star
BF-106, (16"), 55¢

Square Deal
SD-107, (16"), 55¢

Water Glass
WG-108, (12"), 55¢

Spring Beauty
SB-109, (16"), 55¢

Hole in Barn Door
B-110, (12"), 55¢

Autograph Quilt
AQ-111, (16"), 55¢

Monkey Wrench
MW-112, (10"), 55¢

Puss in the Corner
PC-113, (12"), 55¢

Jackson's Star
JS-114, (16"), 55¢

Stepping Stones
S-115, (16"), 55¢

Hour Glass
HG-116, (16"), 55¢

Road to Oklahoma
RO-117, (16"), 55¢

Tail of Benjamin's Kite
TB-118, (12"), 55¢

Shoo Fly
SF-119, (12"), 55¢

Kansas Trouble
T-120, (16"), 55¢

Magnolia Bud
MB-121, (16"), 55¢

Jacob's Ladder
JL-122, (12"), 55¢

Prairie Queen
PQ-123, (12"), 55¢

Arabic Lattice
AR-124, (9"), 55¢

Fig. 49. Heirloom Plastics Designs *(cont.)*

PF105
Blazing Star

PW89, Grandmother's Cross

A90
Hawaiian Flow

PW92
Flowers in a Basket

A93
Rose of Sharon

PW94
Many Pointed Star

PW95
Grandma's Red & Wh

PW96
Double Irish Chain

PW97
California Star

A100
Prairie Rose

A98
Swag & Tassle
Border

A99
Tulip Border

PF104
Star & Cross

PF101
Diamond Star

PF103
Lone Star

PF102
8-Pointed Star

Fig. 49, Heirloom Plastics Designs (*cont.*)

Although these quilt designs are anywhere from fifty to one hundred years old, there might be a few that you would be interested in duplicating.

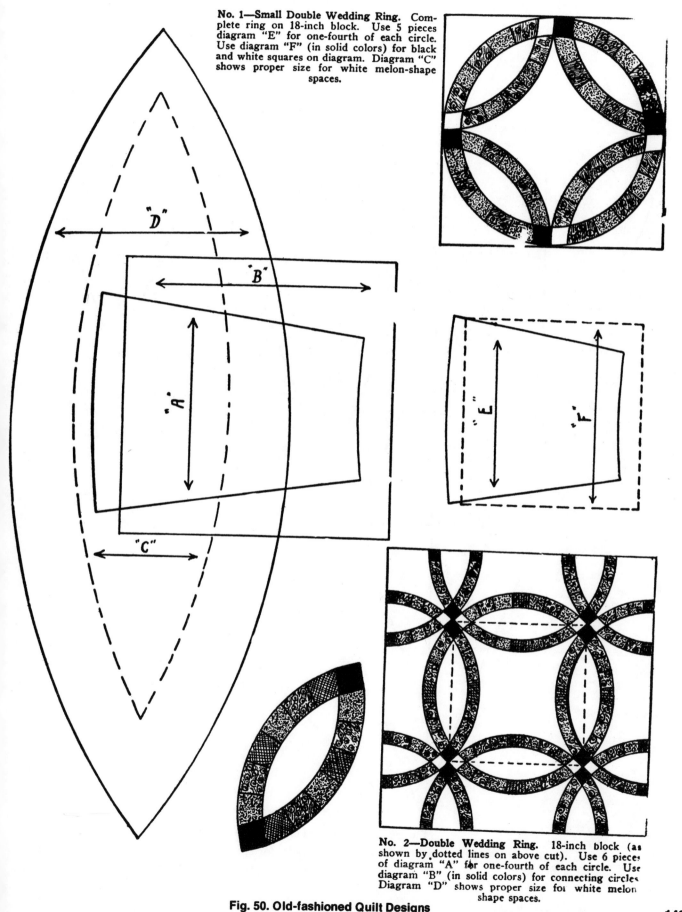

No. 1—Small Double Wedding Ring. Complete ring on 18-inch block. Use 5 pieces diagram "E" for one-fourth of each circle. Use diagram "F" (in solid colors) for black and white squares on diagram. Diagram "C" shows proper size for white melon-shape spaces.

No. 2—Double Wedding Ring. 18-inch block (as shown by dotted lines on above cut). Use 6 pieces of diagram "A" for one-fourth of each circle. Use diagram "B" (in solid colors) for connecting circles. Diagram "D" shows proper size for white melon shape spaces.

Fig. 50. Old-fashioned Quilt Designs

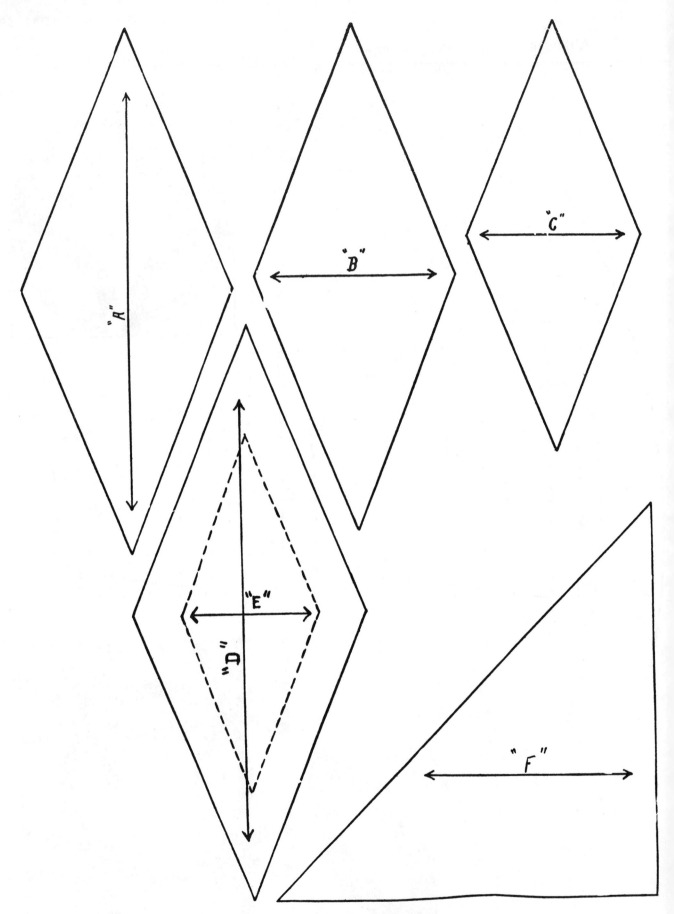

Fig. 50. Old-fashioned Quilt Designs *(cont.)*

Shapes for designs on page 145. Be sure to allow for seams, as all diagrams for patterns are finished size.

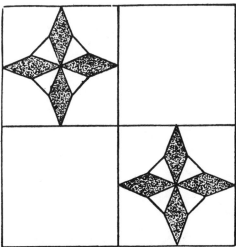

No. 3—Fancy Star. 12-inch block for each star. Use diagram "A" for diamonds. Use half of diagram "A" for triangles.

No. 4—Fancy Flowers. 18-inch block complete. Use diagram "B" for diamonds. Use 3⅛-inch square in center.

No. 5—Pot of Flowers. 18-inch block complete. Use diagram "B" for diamonds. Use diagram "F" for triangles. Use ⅞-inch strip for stems.

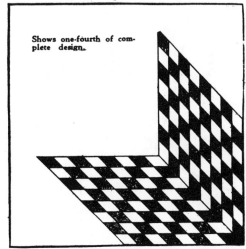

Shows one-fourth of complete design.

No. 6—Texas Star. Use diagram "E" for diamonds.

No. 7—Star with Diamonds. 18-inch block. Use diagram "C" for diamonds. Use 2⅝-inch squares.

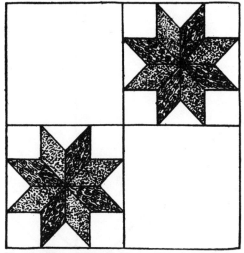

No. 8—Eight-Pointed Star. 12-inch block for each star. Use diagram "D" for diamonds.

Fig. 50 Old-fashioned Quilt Designs (cont.)

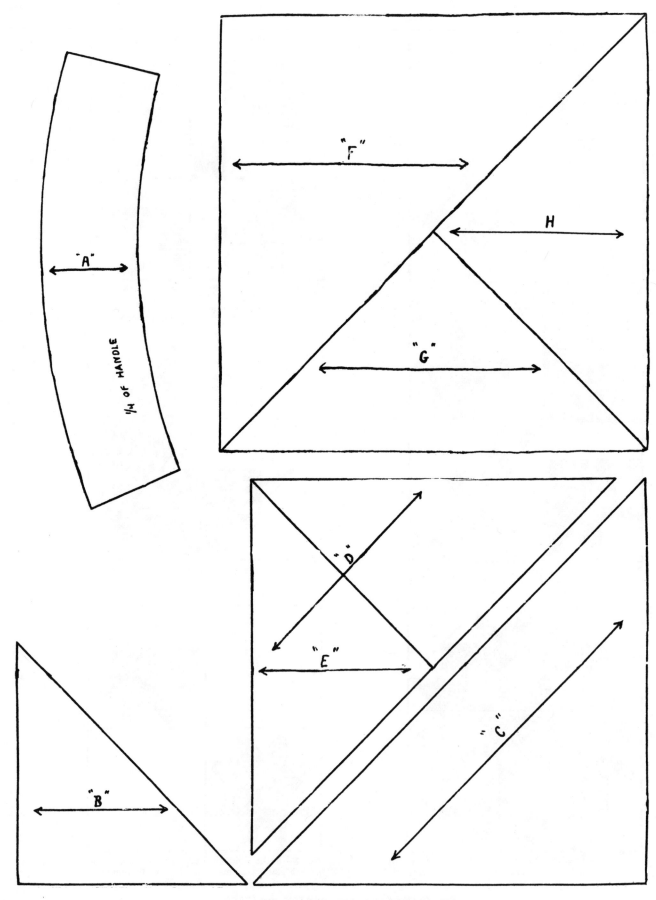

Fig. 50. Old-fashioned Quilt Designs (cont.)

Shapes for designs on page 147. Be sure to allow for seams, as all diagrams for patterns are finished size.

No. 9—Pinwheel. 18-inch block for design as shown. Use diagram "F" for triangles.

No. 10—Basket. 18-inch block. Use diagram "A" for one-fourth of handle. Use diagram "B" for triangles.

No. 11—Reverse X. 18-inch block for design as shown. Use diagram "G" for large triangles. Use diagram "H" for small triangles.

No. 12—Evening Star. 18-inch block. Use diagram "C" for points of star. Use 8¾-inch square for center.

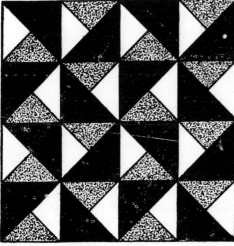

No. 13—Windmill. 18-inch block as shown. Use diagram "F" for large triangles. Use diagram "G" for small triangles.

No. 14—Swastika. 24-inch block or four 12-inch blocks. Use diagram "D" for large triangles. Use diagram "E" for small triangles.

Fig. 50. Old-fashioned Quilt Designs *(cont.)*

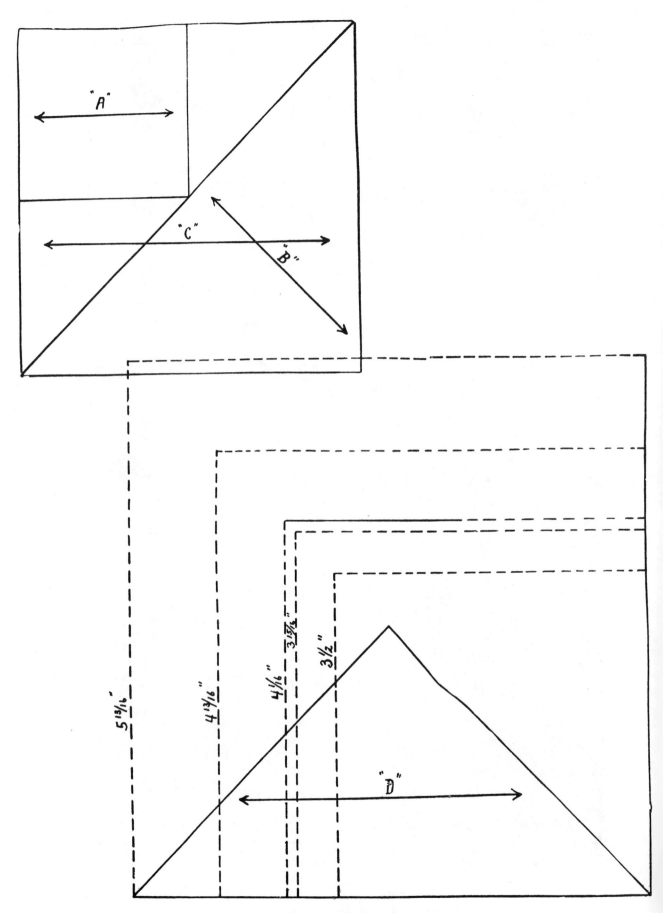

148   **Fig. 50. Old-fashioned Quilt Designs** *(cont.)*

Shapes for designs on page 149. Be sure to allow for seams, as all diagrams for patterns are finished size.

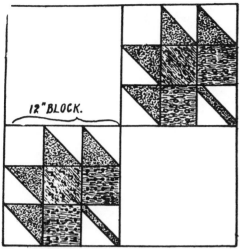

No. 15—Maple Leaf. 12-inch block for each leaf. Use diagram "B" for triangles. Use diagram "C" for squares. Use ⅝-inch strip for stem.

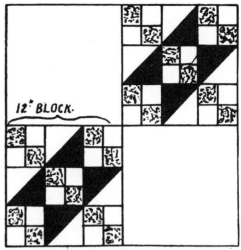

No. 16—Double Hour Glass. 12-inch block for each. Use diagram "A" for squares. Use diagram "B" for triangles.

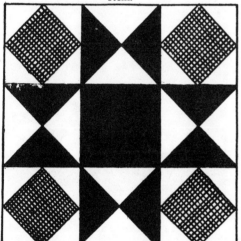

No. 17—Ornate Star—18-inch block. Use diagram "D" for triangles. Use 5⅛-inch square in center. Use 4⅛-inch squares in corners.

No. 18—Jack's Blocks. 18-inch block. Use 3½-inch squares.

No. 19—Eccentric Star. 12-inch block for each star. Use 4⅛-inch square for center. Use diagram "F" for white triangles.

No. 20—Mosaic. 18-inch block. Use 3⅛-inch squares.

Fig. 50. Old-fashioned Quilt Designs *(cont.)*

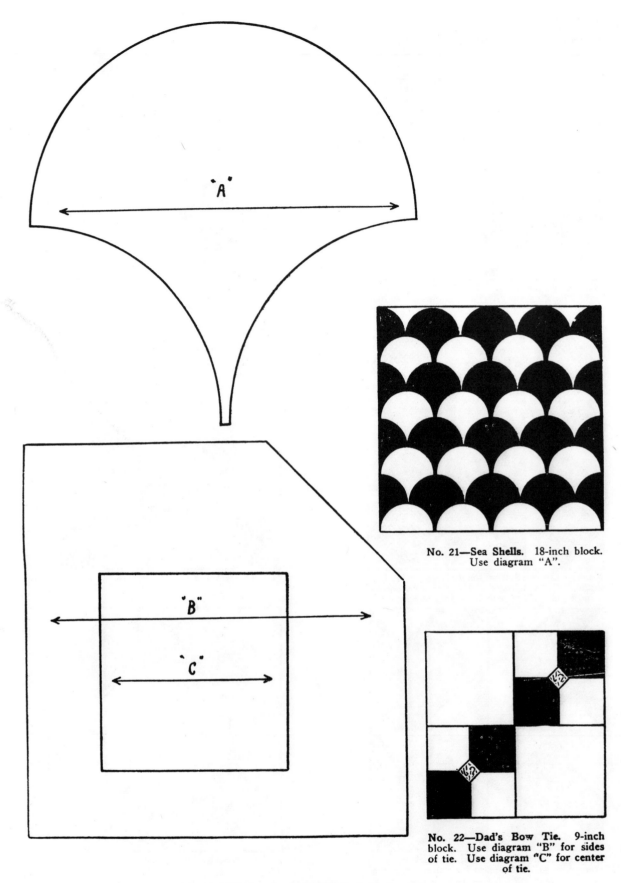

No. 21—Sea Shells. 18-inch block. Use diagram "A".

No. 22—Dad's Bow Tie. 9-inch block. Use diagram "B" for sides of tie. Use diagram "C" for center of tie.

Fig. 50. Old-fashioned Quilt Designs *(cont.)*

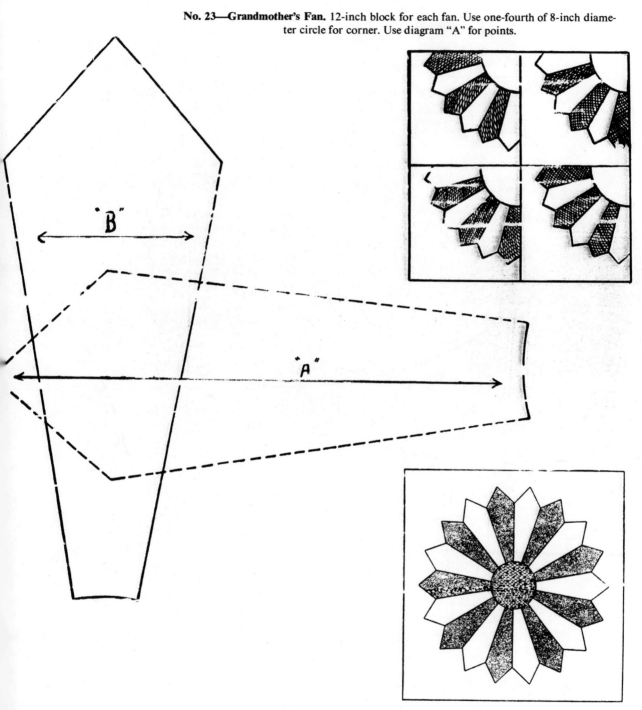

No. 23—Grandmother's Fan. 12-inch block for each fan. Use one-fourth of 8-inch diameter circle for corner. Use diagram "A" for points.

No. 24—Sun Flower. 18-inch block. Use 4-inch diameter circle for center. Use diagram "B" for petals.

Called Friendship Ring or Dresden Plate when ends of petals are rounded instead of pointed.

Fig. 50. Old-fashioned Quilt Designs *(cont.)*

No. 25—Cushion Design. 18-inch block as shown. Use diagram "A" for center. Use half of diagram "B" for sides.

No. 26—Grecian Star. 18-inch block. Use diagram "A" for center. Use diagrams "C" and "D" for parts of star.

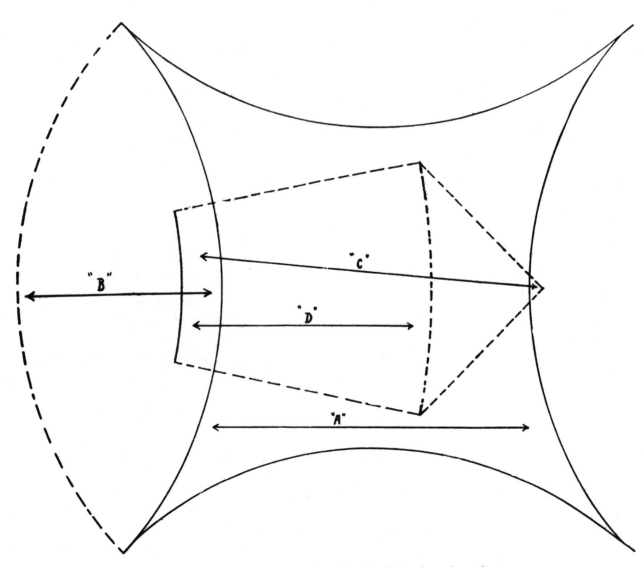

Fig. 50. Old-fashioned Quilt Designs *(cont.)*

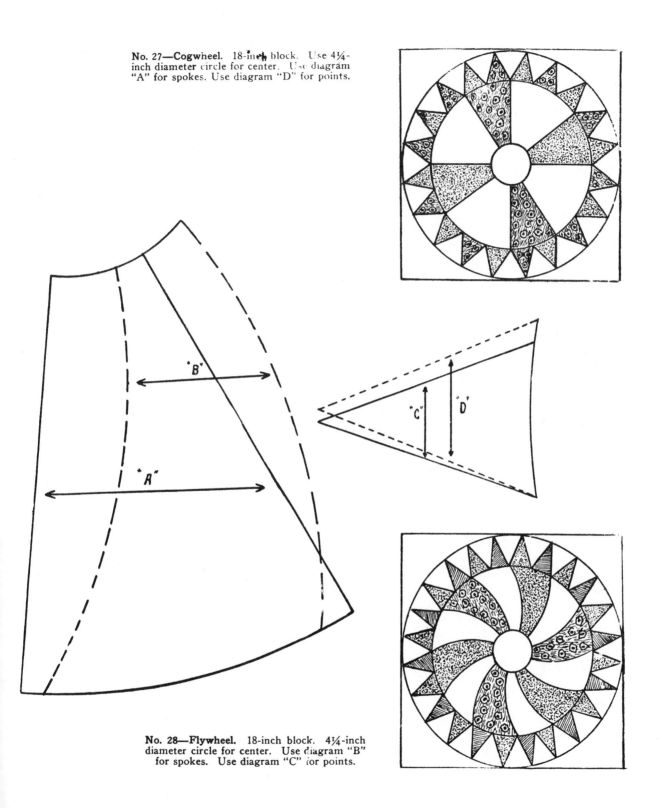

No. 27—**Cogwheel.** 18-inch block. Use 4¼-inch diameter circle for center. Use diagram "A" for spokes. Use diagram "D" for points.

No. 28—**Flywheel.** 18-inch block. 4¼-inch diameter circle for center. Use diagram "B" for spokes. Use diagram "C" for points.

Fig. 50. Old-fashioned Quilt Designs *(cont.)*

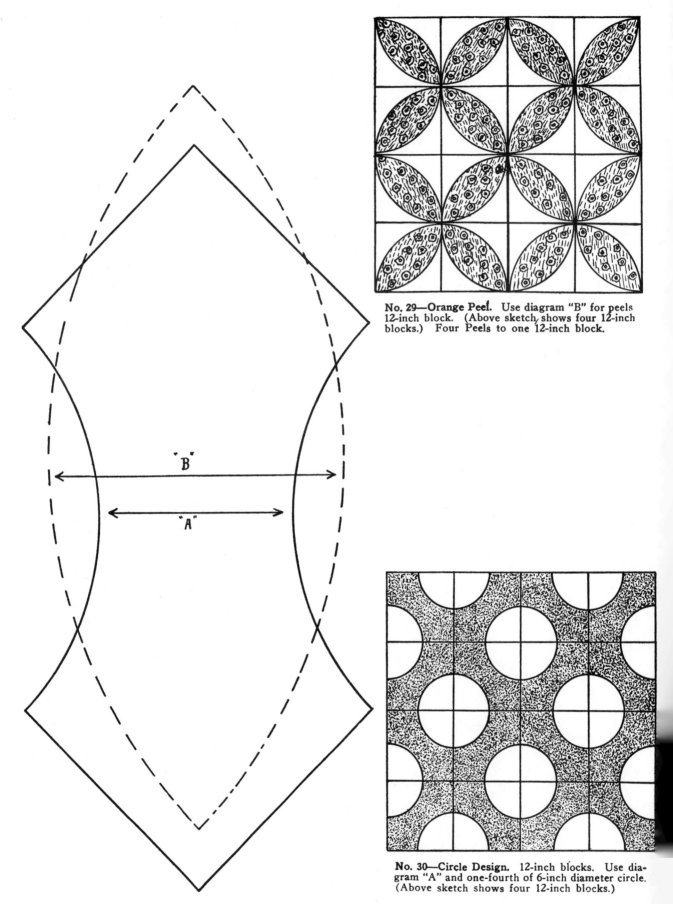

No. 29—Orange Peel. Use diagram "B" for peels 12-inch block. (Above sketch shows four 12-inch blocks.) Four Peels to one 12-inch block.

No. 30—Circle Design. 12-inch blocks. Use diagram "A" and one-fourth of 6-inch diameter circle. (Above sketch shows four 12-inch blocks.)

Fig. 50. Old-fashioned Quilt Designs *(cont.)*

154

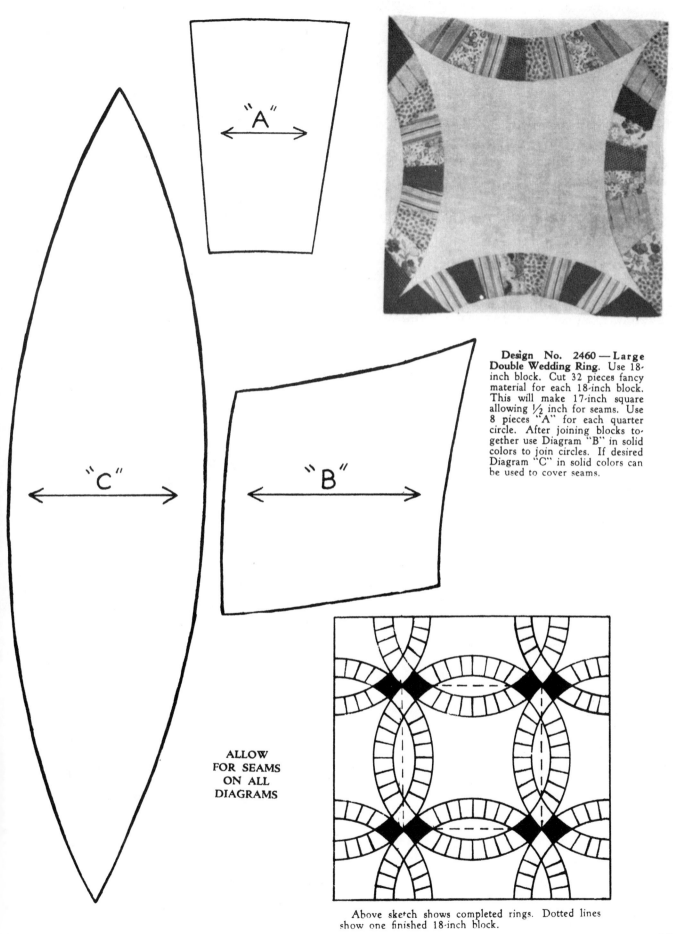

"A"

"C"

"B"

Design No. 2460 — Large Double Wedding Ring. Use 18-inch block. Cut 32 pieces fancy material for each 18-inch block. This will make 17-inch square allowing ½ inch for seams. Use 8 pieces "A" for each quarter circle. After joining blocks together use Diagram "B" in solid colors to join circles. If desired Diagram "C" in solid colors can be used to cover seams.

ALLOW
FOR SEAMS
ON ALL
DIAGRAMS

Above sketch shows completed rings. Dotted lines show one finished 18-inch block.

Fig. 50. Old-fashioned Quilt Designs *(cont.)*

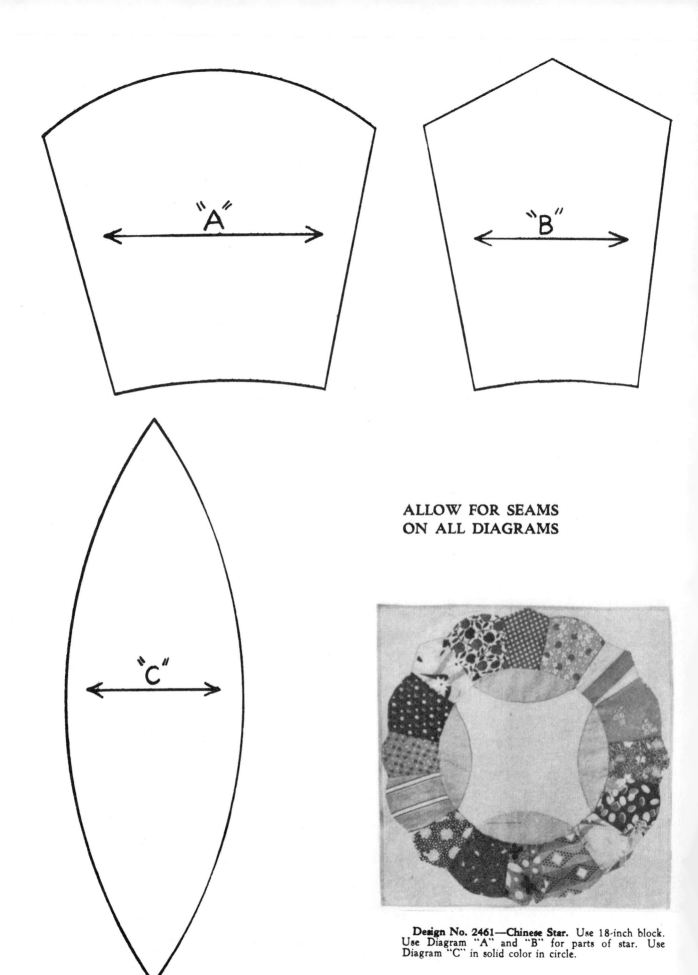

"A"

"B"

"C"

ALLOW FOR SEAMS
ON ALL DIAGRAMS

Design No. 2461—Chinese Star. Use 18-inch block.
Use Diagram "A" and "B" for parts of star. Use
Diagram "C" in solid color in circle.

Fig. 51. Grandmother's Designs

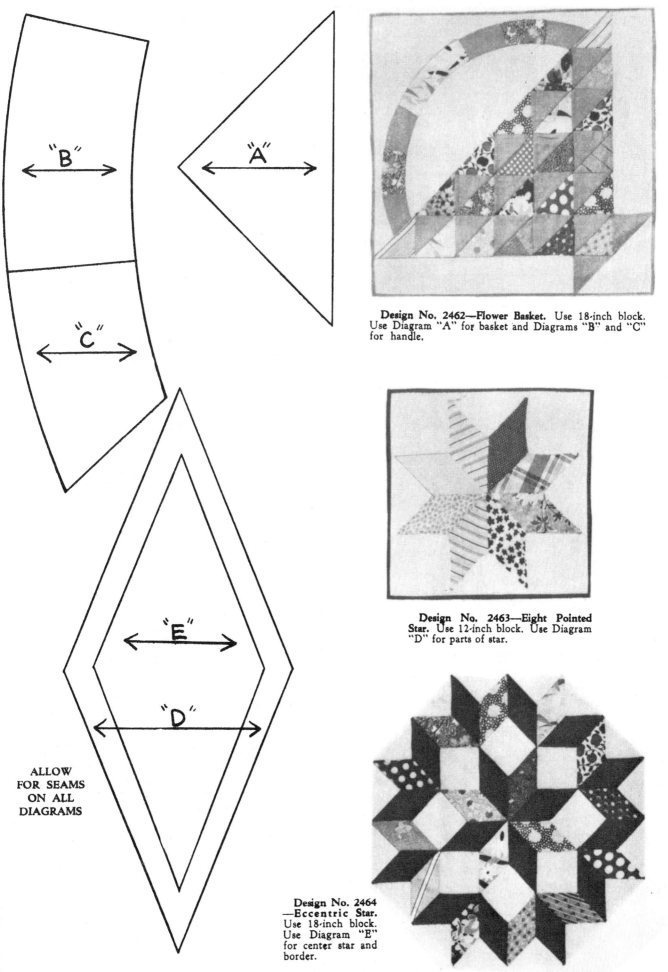

"B"

"A"

"C"

Design No. 2462—Flower Basket. Use 18-inch block. Use Diagram "A" for basket and Diagrams "B" and "C" for handle.

"E"

"D"

ALLOW
FOR SEAMS
ON ALL
DIAGRAMS

Design No. 2463—Eight Pointed Star. Use 12-inch block. Use Diagram "D" for parts of star.

Design No. 2464 —Eccentric Star. Use 18-inch block. Use Diagram "E" for center star and border.

Fig. 51. Grandmother's Designs *(cont.)*

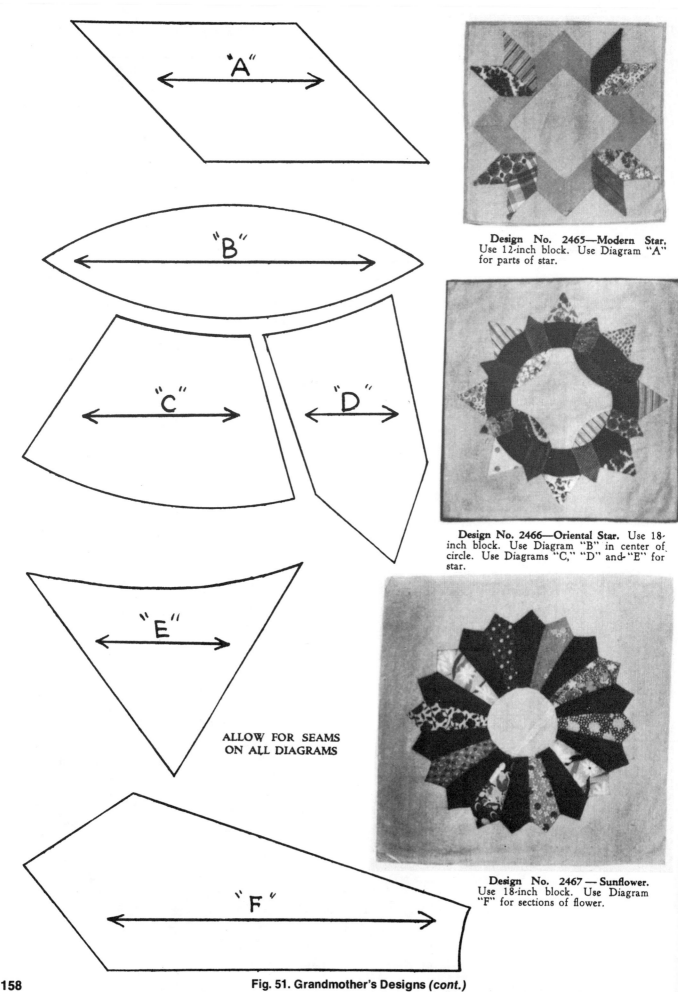

"A"

"B"

"C"

"D"

"E"

ALLOW FOR SEAMS
ON ALL DIAGRAMS

"F"

Design No. 2465—Modern Star.
Use 12-inch block. Use Diagram "A"
for parts of star.

Design No. 2466—Oriental Star. Use 18-inch block. Use Diagram "B" in center of circle. Use Diagrams "C," "D" and "E" for star.

Design No. 2467 — Sunflower.
Use 18-inch block. Use Diagram
"F" for sections of flower.

158   **Fig. 51. Grandmother's Designs (cont.)**

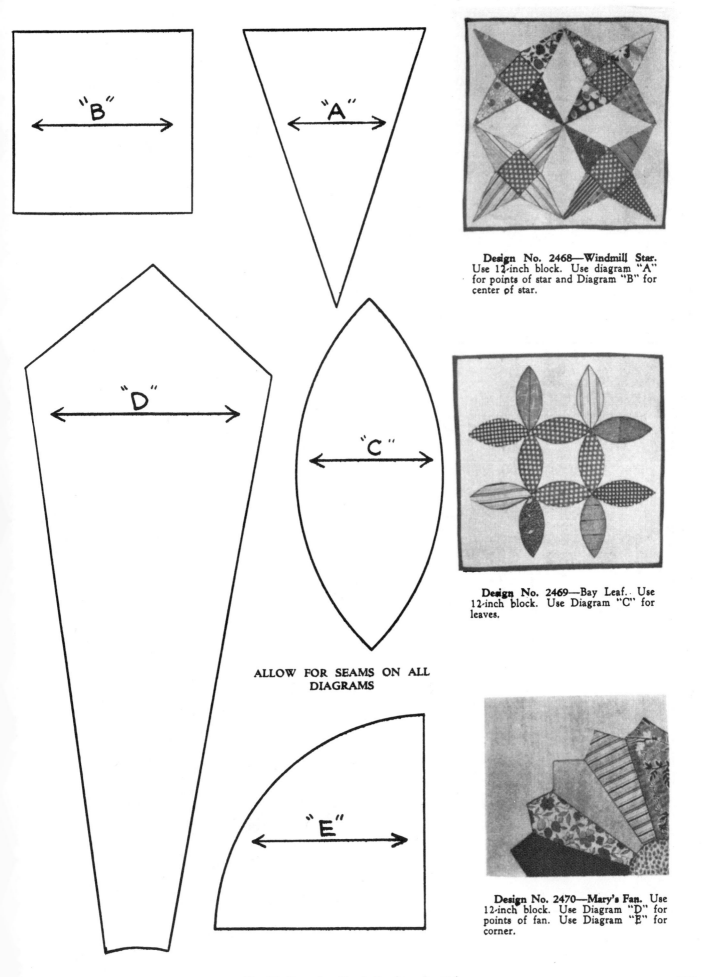

"B"

"A"

"D"

"C"

"E"

ALLOW FOR SEAMS ON ALL
DIAGRAMS

Design No. 2468—Windmill Star.
Use 12-inch block. Use diagram "A"
for points of star and Diagram "B" for
center of star.

Design No. 2469—Bay Leaf. Use
12-inch block. Use Diagram "C" for
leaves.

Design No. 2470—Mary's Fan. Use
12-inch block. Use Diagram "D" for
points of fan. Use Diagram "E" for
corner.

Fig. 51. Grandmother's Designs (cont.)

159

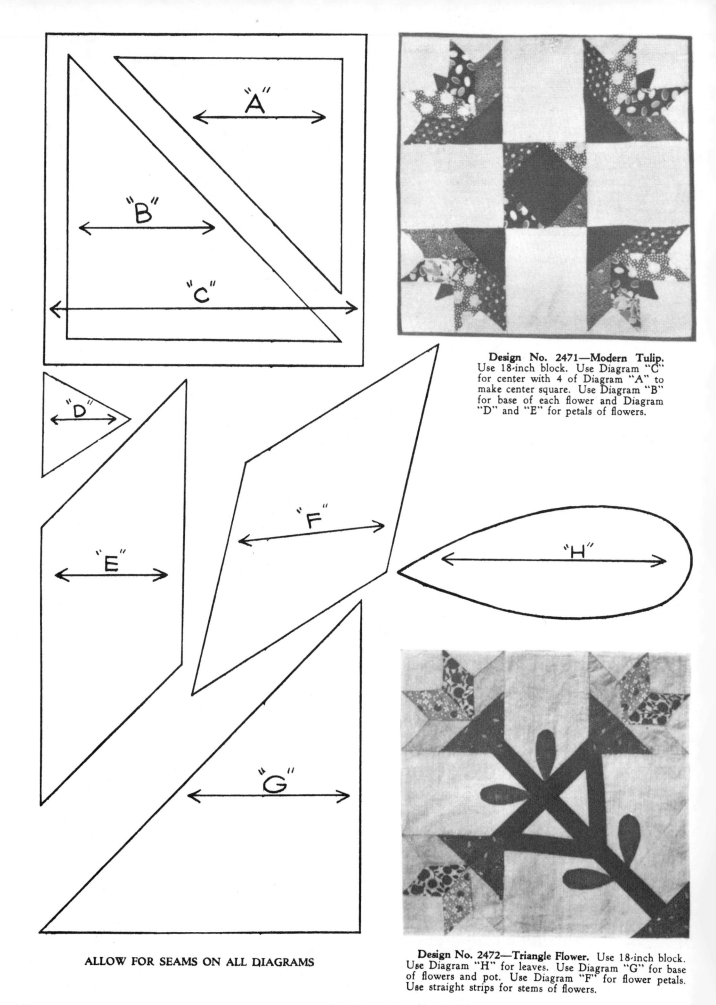

Design No. 2471—Modern Tulip.
Use 18-inch block. Use Diagram "C"
for center with 4 of Diagram "A" to
make center square. Use Diagram "B"
for base of each flower and Diagram
"D" and "E" for petals of flowers.

ALLOW FOR SEAMS ON ALL DIAGRAMS

Design No. 2472—Triangle Flower. Use 18-inch block.
Use Diagram "H" for leaves. Use Diagram "G" for base
of flowers and pot. Use Diagram "F" for flower petals.
Use straight strips for stems of flowers.

Fig. 51. Grandmother's Designs *(cont.)*

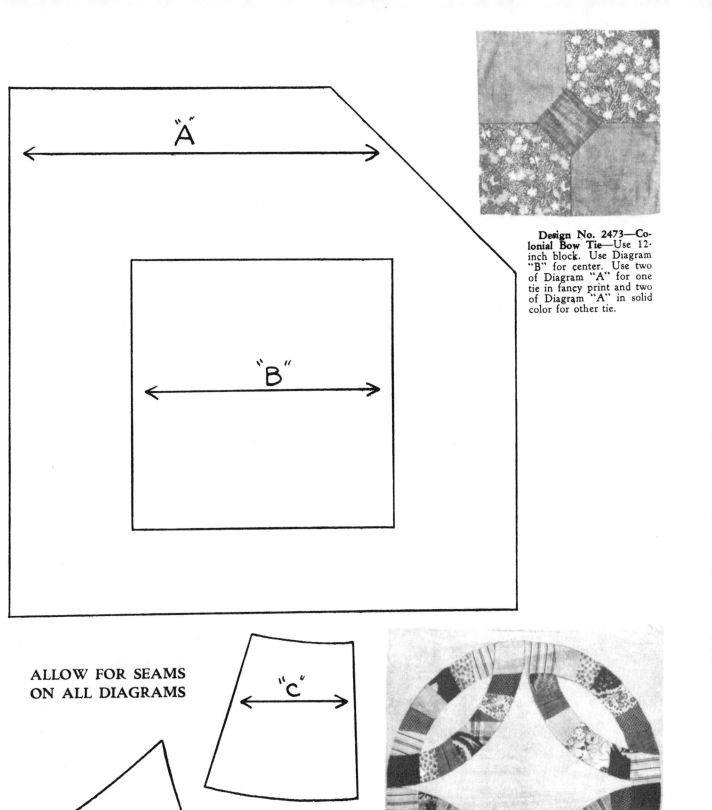

"A"

"B"

Design No. 2473—Colonial Bow Tie—Use 12-inch block. Use Diagram "B" for center. Use two of Diagram "A" for one tie in fancy print and two of Diagram "A" in solid color for other tie.

ALLOW FOR SEAMS
ON ALL DIAGRAMS

"C"

"D"

Design No. 2474.—Small Double Wedding Ring. Use 18-inch block. Use Diagram "C" for quarter circles. Use Diagram "D" for joining quarter circles.

Fig. 51. Grandmother's Designs *(cont.)*   161

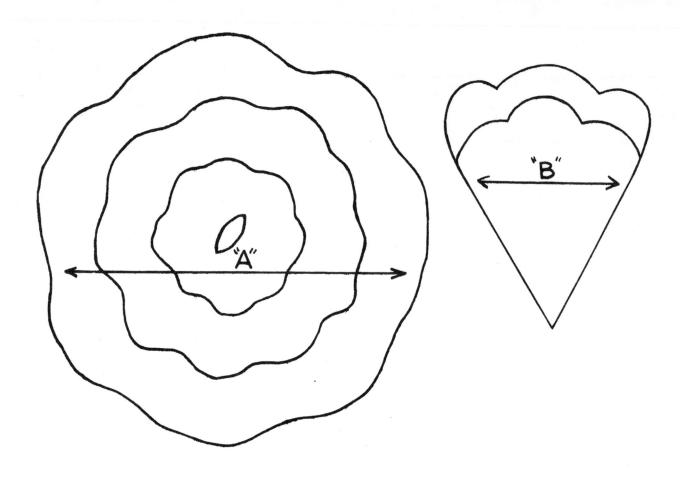

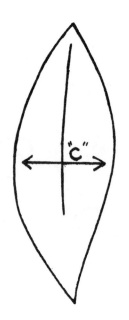

**ALLOW FOR SEAMS ON ALL
DIAGRAMS**

Design No. 2475—Rose Wreath. Use 18-inch block. Use Diagram "A" for flowers in solid pink. Applique with outline stitch in three shades of rose six strand floss. Use Diagram "B" for buds. Use Diagram "C" for leaves. Use bias pieces for stems.

Fig. 51. Grandmother's Designs *(cont.)*

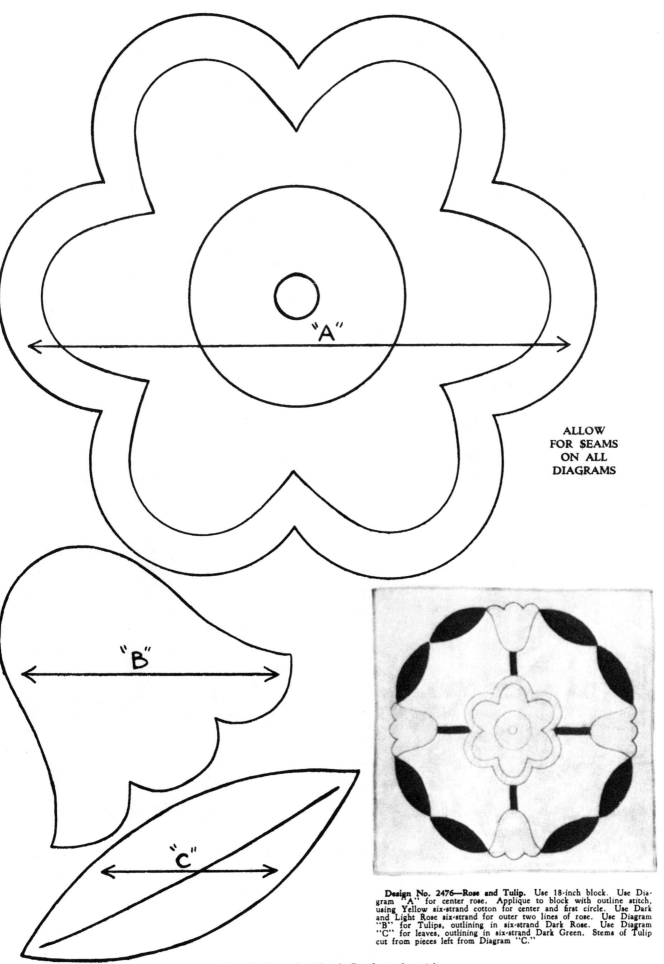

"A"

ALLOW
FOR SEAMS
ON ALL
DIAGRAMS

"B"

"C"

Design No. 2476—Rose and Tulip. Use 18-inch block. Use Diagram "A" for center rose. Applique to block with outline stitch, using Yellow six-strand cotton for center and first circle. Use Dark and Light Rose six-strand for outer two lines of rose. Use Diagram "B" for Tulips, outlining in six-strand Dark Rose. Use Diagram "C" for leaves, outlining in six-strand Dark Green. Stems of Tulip cut from pieces left from Diagram "C."

Fig. 51. Grandmother's Designs *(cont.)*

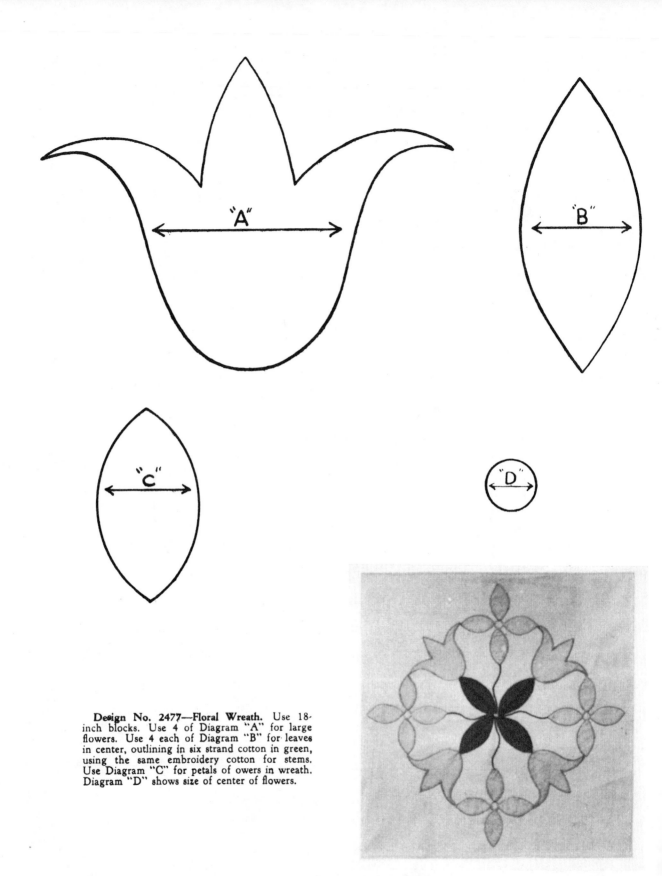

Design No. 2477—Floral Wreath. Use 18-inch blocks. Use 4 of Diagram "A" for large flowers. Use 4 each of Diagram "B" for leaves in center, outlining in six strand cotton in green, using the same embroidery cotton for stems. Use Diagram "C" for petals of owers in wreath. Diagram "D" shows size of center of flowers.

ALLOW FOR SEAMS ON ALL DIAGRAMS

Fig. 51. Grandmother's Designs *(cont.)*

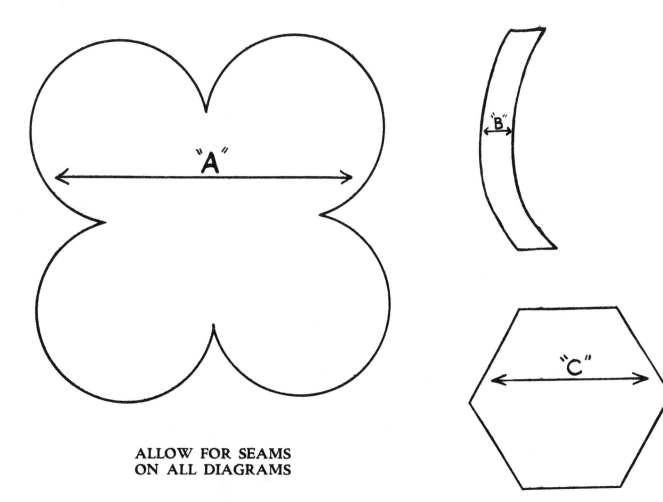

"A"

"B"

"C"

ALLOW FOR SEAMS
ON ALL DIAGRAMS

Design No. 2478—Good Luck Clover Leaf. Use 18-inch block. Use Diagram "A" for clover leaves. Applique to block with darker shade of six-strand cotton. Outline diamond in center with same green. Use Diagram "B" for stem of leaves.

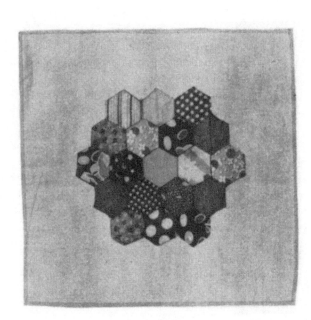

Design No. 2479—Grandmother's Flower Garden. Use 12-inch block. Use Diagram "C" to form motif as in illustration below. Applique finished piece to block.

Fig. 51. Grandmother's Designs *(cont.)*

Design No. 2481
Sunbonnet Girl Reading

Design No. 2480
Sunbonnet Girl Gardening

Design No. 2482
Sunbonnet Girl Sweeping

Design No. 2483
Sunbonnet Girl with Doll

Embroider with six-strand cotton. Fence in brown. Ground in darker brown. Girl's dress and stockings in light blue, arms and legs in light pink, flowers in light and dark rose, yellow and green. Applique sunbonnet in delft blue material with darker shade of blue thread.

Design No. 2485
Sunbonnet Girl Strolling

Design No. 2484
Sunbonnet Girl Sprinkling Flower

Be sure to allow for seams on all
Diagrams.

Fig. 51. Grandmother's Designs *(cont.)*

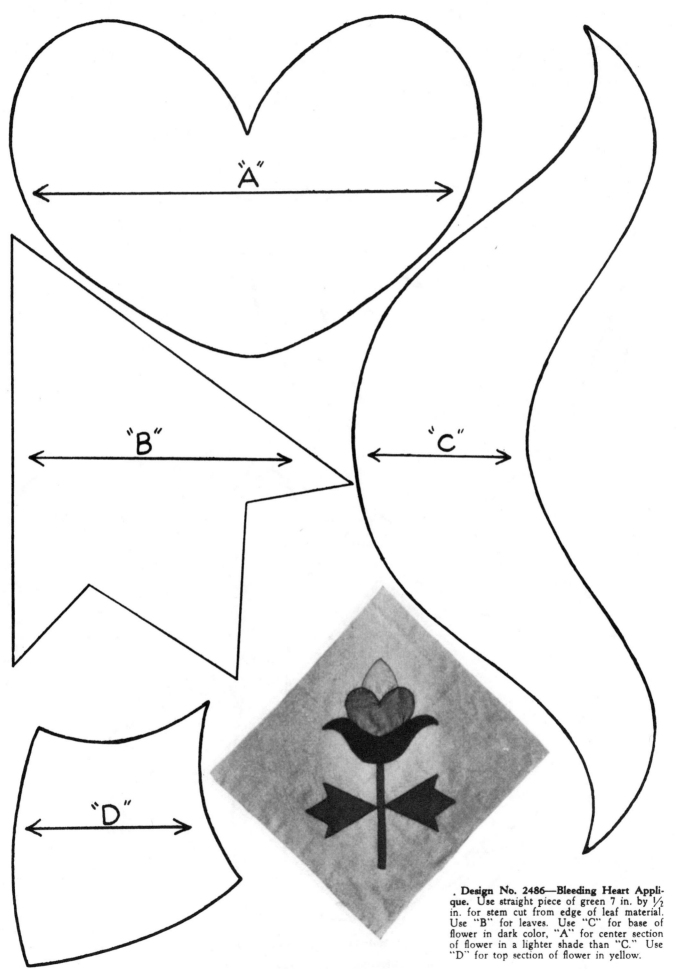

"A"

"B"

"C"

"D"

. **Design No. 2486—Bleeding Heart Applique.** Use straight piece of green 7 in. by ½ in. for stem cut from edge of leaf material. Use "B" for leaves. Use "C" for base of flower in dark color, "A" for center section of flower in a lighter shade than "C." Use "D" for top section of flower in yellow.

Fig. 51. Grandmother's Designs *(cont.)*

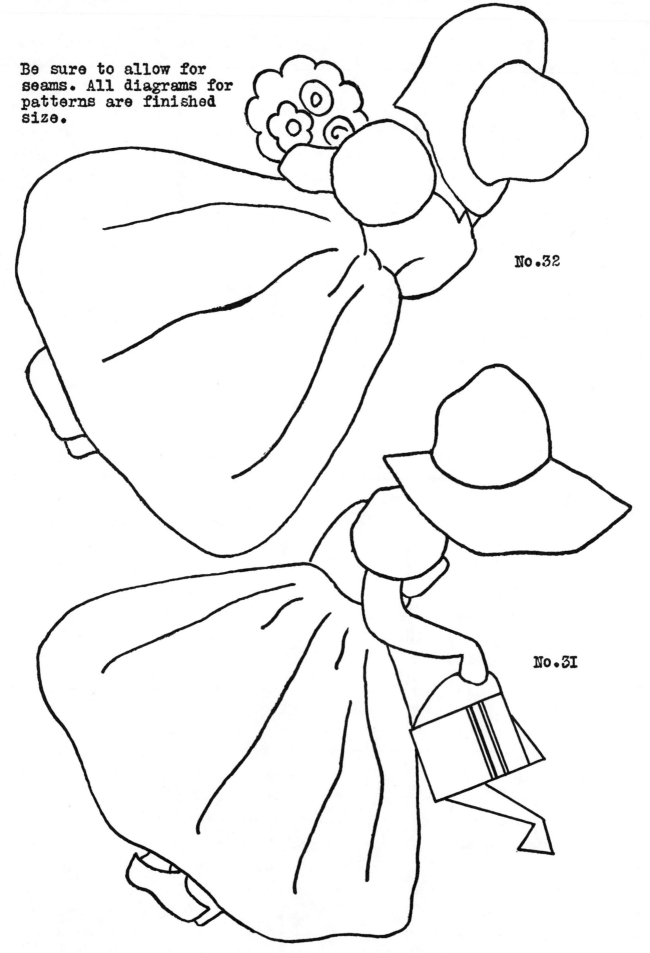

Be sure to allow for seams. All diagrams for patterns are finished size.

No.32

No.31

168   **Fig. 52. More Old-fashioned Quilt Designs**

Patterns for sun bonnet babies on page 170.

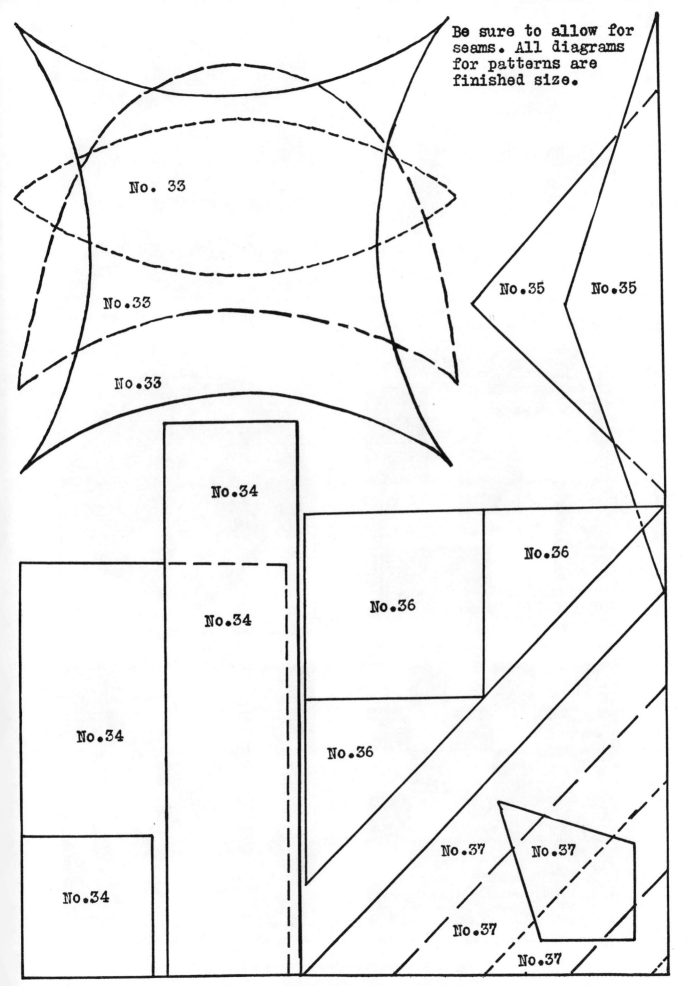

Be sure to allow for seams. All diagrams for patterns are finished size.

No. 33

No.33

No.33

No.35   No.35

No.34

No.34

No.34

No.36

No.36

No.36

No.34

No.37   No.37

No.37

No.37

Fig. 52. More Old-fashioned Quilt Designs *(cont.)*

Patterns for designs on page 170.

No. 31   **No. 32**
Sun Bonnet Babies. Applique. Use 12-inch blocks for each number.

No. 33—**Irish Chain.** Applique. 12-inch block.

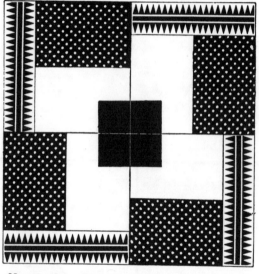

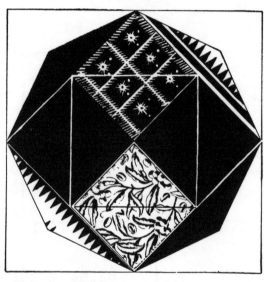

·No. 34—**Swastika.** 12-inch block.

No. 35—**Jewel.** 9-inch block.

No. 36—**Strawberry Basket.** 12-inch block.

No. 37—**Pineapples.** 12-inch block.

Fig. 52. More Old-fashioned Quilt Designs *(cont.)*

Patterns are on pages 168 and 169.

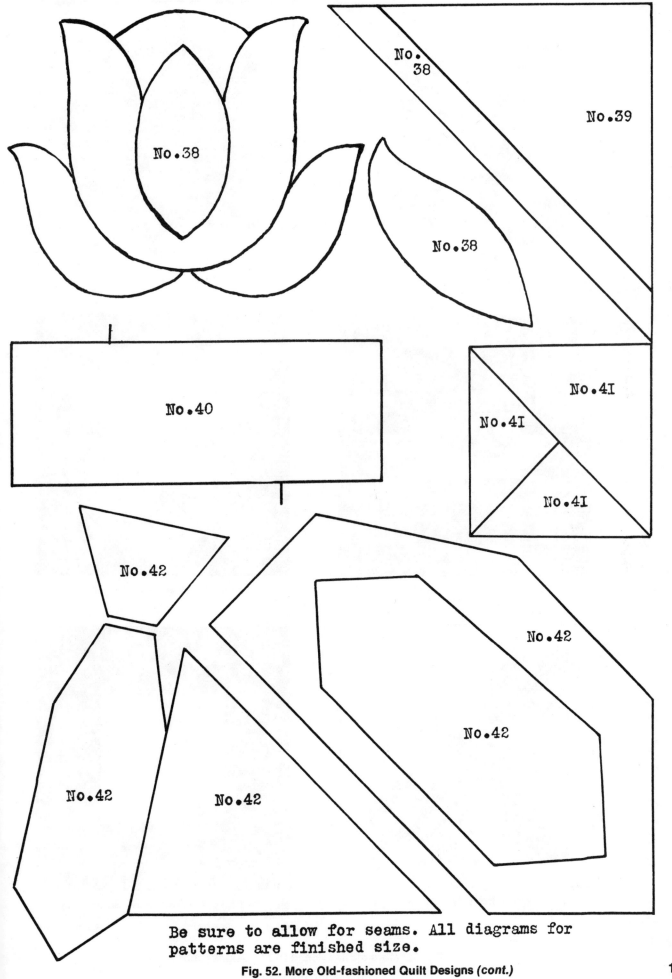

No. 38

No. 38

No. 38

No. 39

No. 40

No. 41

No. 41

No. 41

No. 42

No. 42

No. 42

No. 42

No. 42

Be sure to allow for seams. All diagrams for patterns are finished size.

Fig. 52. More Old-fashioned Quilt Designs *(cont.)*

Patterns for designs on page 172.

No. 38—Rare Old Tulip. Applique. 12-inch block. Stem ⅜-inch. Center stem 7 inches long.

No. 39—Pin Wheel. 9-inch Block.

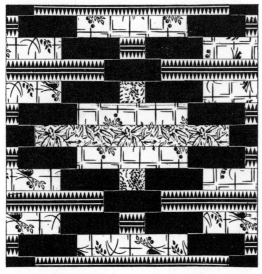

No. 40—Zigzag Blocks. 18-inch block. Continuous design.

No. 41—Arbor Window. 9-inch block.

No. 42—Egyptian Butterfly. Applique. 12-inch block.

No. 43—Crazy Patch—Hollow Square. 18-inch block. Center square 8½-inch. Requires no diagram. Sew scraps together on machine and cut out hollow square.

172

Fig. 52. More old-fashioned Quilt Designs *(cont.)*

Patterns are on page 171.

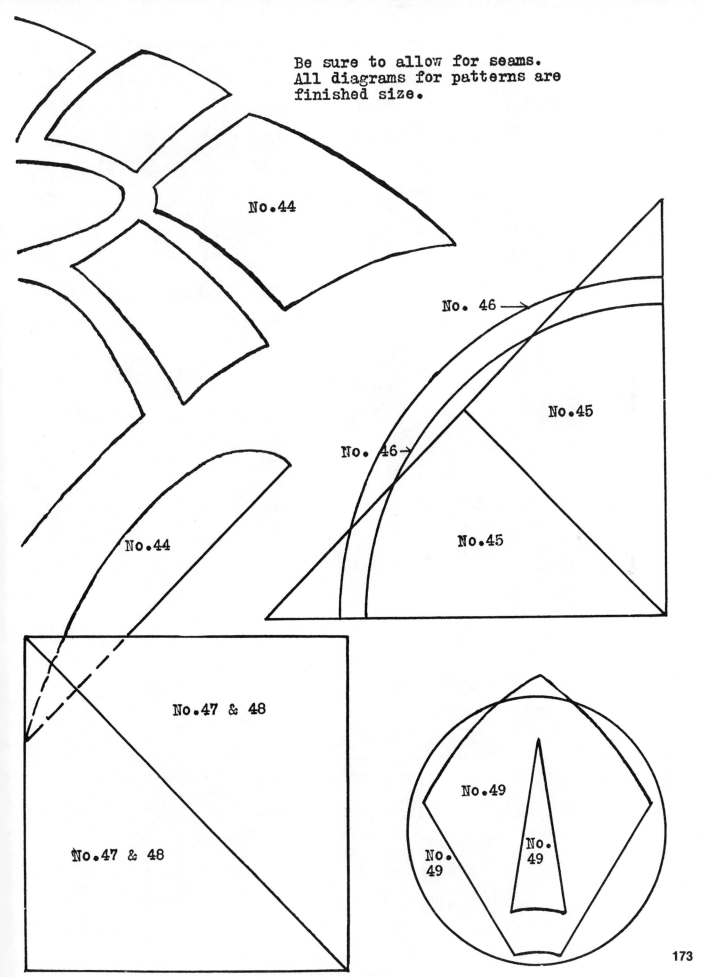

Be sure to allow for seams.
All diagrams for patterns are
finished size.

No.44

No.46 →

No.45

No. 46 →

No.45

No.44

No.47 & 48

No.47 & 48

No.49

No.
49

No.
49

Fig. 52. More Old-fashioned Quilt Designs *(cont.)*

Patterns for designs on page 174.

173

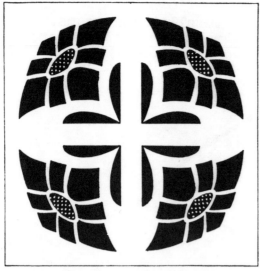

No. 44—Poinsettia. Applique. 18-inch block. Finished quilt shown on front cover.

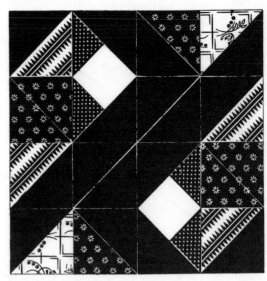

No. 45—Chinese Puzzle. 18-inch block. Continuous design.

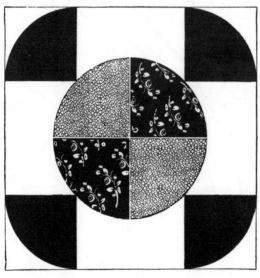

No. 46—Pilot Wheel. 12-inch block.

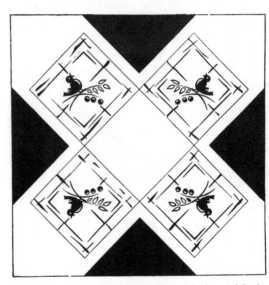

No. 47—Criss-Cross. 12-inch block. ½-inch strip between squares and triangles.

No. 48—Watermill. 12-inch block. ½-inch strip between squares and triangles.

No. 49—Star Flower. 9-inch block.

Fig. 52. More Old-fashioned Quilt Designs (cont.)

Patterns are on page 173.

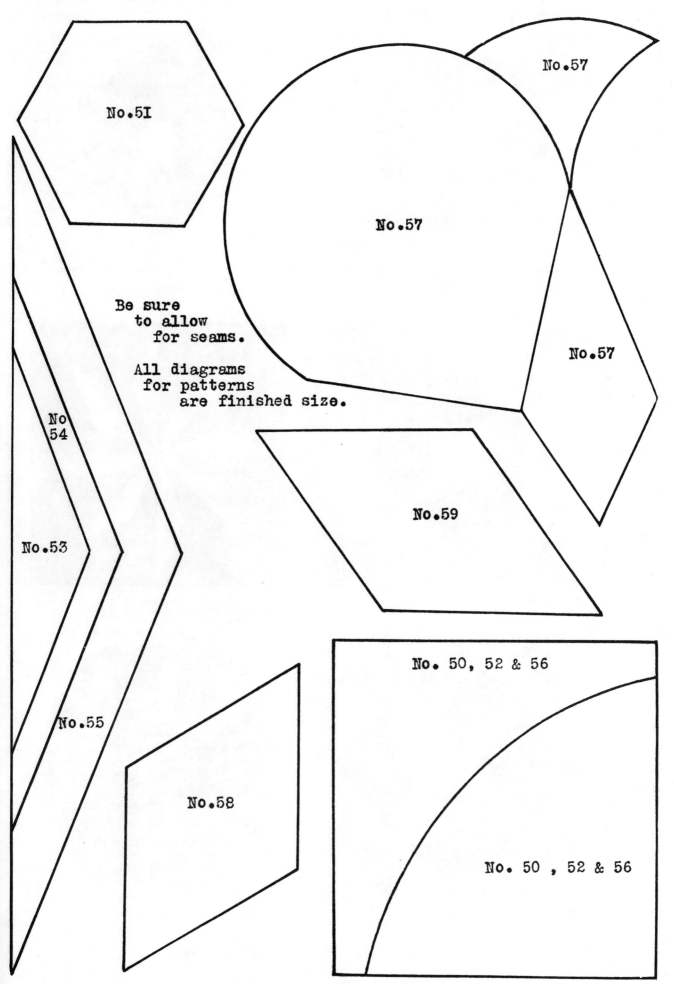

No.5I

No.57

No.57

No.57

Be sure
to allow
for seams.

All diagrams
for patterns
are finished size.

No
54

No.53

No.59

No.55

No. 50, 52 & 56

No.58

No. 50 , 52 & 56

Fig. 52. More Old-fashioned Quilt Designs *(cont.)*   175

Patterns for designs on pages 176 and 178.

No. 50—Cart Wheel. 12-inch block. Use 1½-inch strip in center.

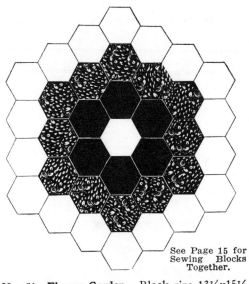

See Page 15 for Sewing Blocks Together.

No. 51—Flower Garden. Block size 13¾x15¼ inches. Outer row in solid color material.

No. 52—Window Squares. 12-inch block.

No. 53—9-inch. No. 54—12-inch. No. 55—18-inch—Star of the East.

No. 56—Broken Squares. 12-inch block. Use 1-inch strip in center.

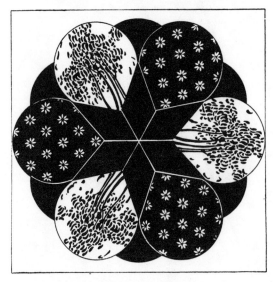

No. 57—Star and Planets. 12-inch block.

Fig. 52. More Old-fashioned Quilt Designs (*cont.*)

Patterns are on page 175.

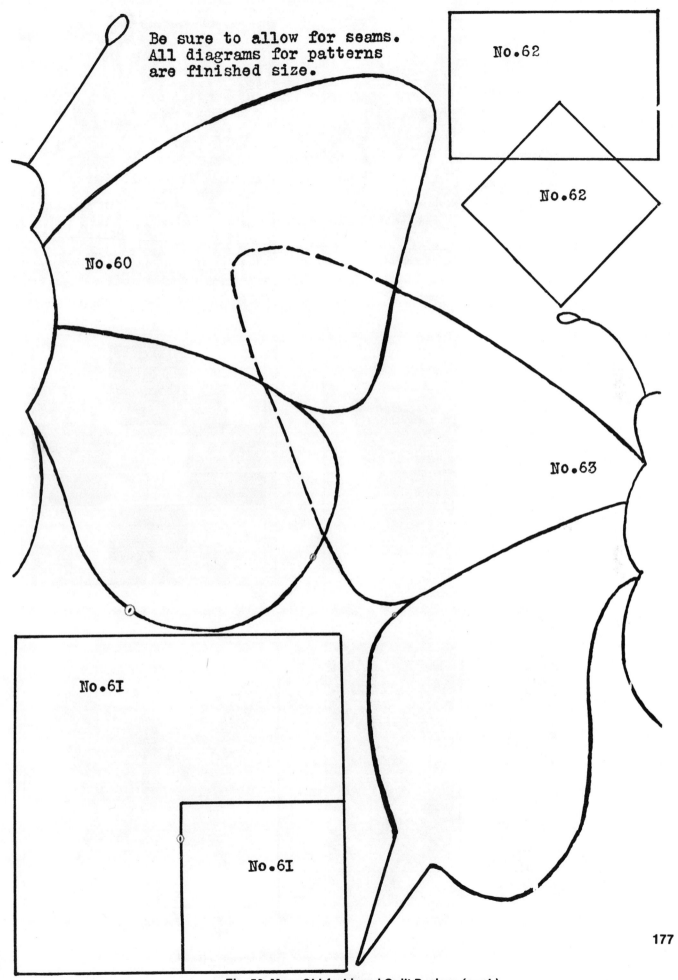

Be sure to allow for seams. All diagrams for patterns are finished size.

No.62

No.62

No.60

No.63

No.6I

No.6I

Fig. 52. More Old-fashioned Quilt Designs *(cont.)*

Patterns for designs on page 178.

No. 58—Block Puzzle. 9-inch block.

No. 59—Diamonds. 9-inch block. Continuous design.

No. 60—Plain Butterfly. Applique. 12-inch block.

No. 61—Pussy in the Corner. 12-inch block.

No. 62—Aunt Mary's Squares. 9-inch block. Continuous design.

No. 63—Fancy Butterfly. Applique. 12-inch block.

Fig. 52. More Old-fashioned Quilt Designs (cont.)

Patterns are on pages 175 and 177.

No. 65

No. 65

No. 65

No. 69

Be sure to allow
for seams.
All diagrams
for patterns
are finished
size.

No. 66

No.
67

No. 67

No. 64

Fig. 52. More Old-fashioned Quilt Designs *(cont.)*

Patterns for designs on page 180.

No. 64—Flower Tree. Applique. 9-inch block. ½-inch border around each block.

No. 65—Pot of Flowers. Applique. 9-inch block. Stems ⅜-inch. Longest stem 2½ inches.

No. 66—Royal Star. 9-inch block.

No. 67—Sunburst. Applique. 18-inch block. 6⅝-inch circle in center.

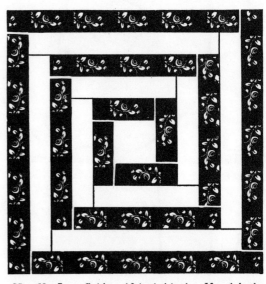

No. 68—Log Cabin. 12-inch block. Use 1-inch strips. Start with center 2-inch square. First four logs or row are 3 inches long. Second, 5 inches. Third, 7 inches. Fourth, 9 inches. Fifth, 11 inches. Allow for all seams on strips.

No. 69 — Crazy Patch Star. Size of cut star 10¼ inches. Sew pieces together with sewing machine, using any size scrap material, and cut out diamonds for star. Sew diamonds together to make star. Use solid color material for squares between stars. Use 2-inch strips for border.

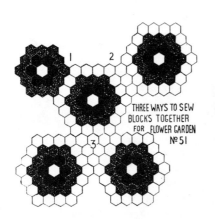

THREE WAYS TO SEW BLOCKS TOGETHER FOR FLOWER GARDEN № 51

180

Fig. 52. More Old-fashioned Quilt Designs (cont.)

Patterns are on page 179.

The Romance of the Circuit Rider
in
Patchwork

This entire set of patterns has been reproduced with the very kind permission of Nimble Needle Treasures, *1973 issues.*

Back in the days when ministers were fewer and religious faith stronger, the lean form of the Reverend G. C. Warvel astride his chestnut mare was a welcome silhouette against the winter sky. And no matter how severe the weather or how difficult the roads, this dauntless man of God came bringing his message of hope and cheer to his country parishioners assembled for worship in their crossroads churches.

For not merely to one, but to six communities did this good man minister in the course of his hundred-mile circuit in the Miami, Ohio, district. And until his coming, which occurred only eight times a year at each church, were deferred the marriages and memorial services of the entire countryside. So sound was his counsel, both on temporal and spiritual matters, and so powerful and constructive an influence did he exert in the lives of the people in this vast territory that even today his name and some interesting stories of his exploits may be found on the pages of Ohio history.

It was in sincere appreciation of his services that forty of the women of the United Brethren Church at Miami, Ohio, in 1862 presented the Reverend Warvel with this patchwork quilt. It is immensely interesting, not only because the varied patches represent each woman's ideas of beauty and symmetry but also because of the signatures of the makers with which each block is inscribed, in ink now so faded and blurred as to be almost undecipherable. The Danbys, the Pattersons, the Smiths, the Clevelands, and many other names prominent in Ohio development are all represented on the patches which make up this humble tribute to the character and deeds of a good man whose services were invaluable to this community.

The Circuit Rider's Quilt, as it is now called, is the property of the Chicago Art Institute in their treasured collection of typical examples of early American art and circuit craft.

Almost any one of the designs may be selected as a motif for a quilt. They can be used on blocks 11 inches square or larger.

Examples:

Mountain Daisy: Twenty 14-inch blocks, ten appliquéd and ten quilted ones, make a quilt 76 by 90 inches with 10-inch border.

Colonial Wreath: A simple leaf design is appliquéd onto ten 15-inch blocks and quilted on the joining blocks. With the appliquéd 9-inch border, finished size of 78 by 93 inches.

Sweet Clover: A graceful design of green leaves and pink buds. There are fifteen 12-inch blocks and a 9-inch appliquéd border. Finished size of the quilt is 78 by 90 inches.

Rambler Rose: Twelve 13-inch appliquéd blocks and twelve plain blocks (joined diagonally) are required for a quilt 74 by 95 inches. Diamond quilting is used on quilt and 10-inch border.

Cosmos: The eight-petaled blossoms can be made with four pink and four rose patches, pieced together, and then appliquéd onto a 13-inch block. Twelve blocks set together diagonally with twelve quilted blocks make a quilt 72 by 90 inches.

Spring Glory: Twelve 14-inch blocks are joined with quilted blocks and six-inch border. Finished size is 72 by 92 inches.

Fig. 53. The Circuit Rider's Quilt

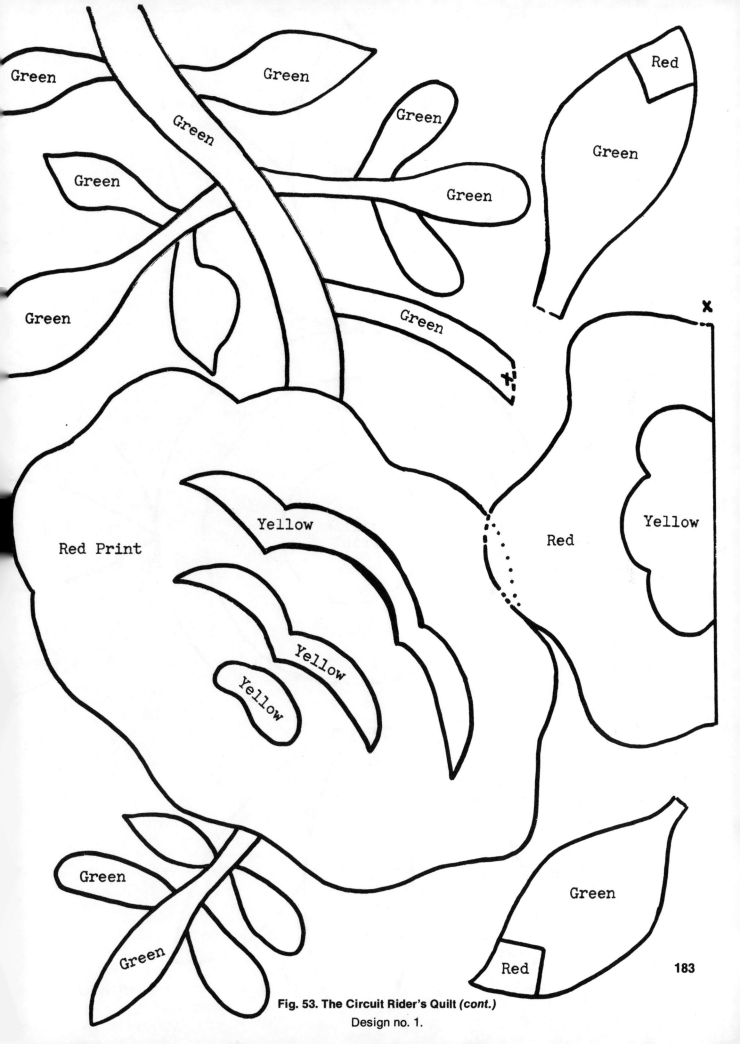

Fig. 53. The Circuit Rider's Quilt *(cont.)*
Design no. 1.

183

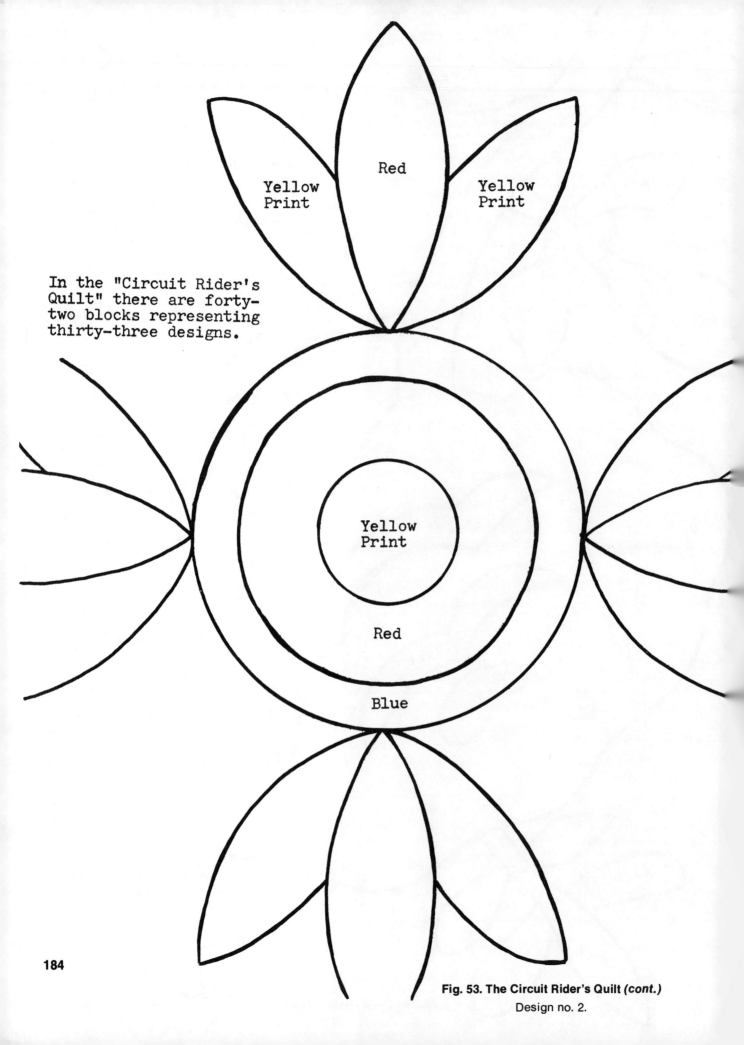

Yellow
Print

Red

Yellow
Print

In the "Circuit Rider's
Quilt" there are forty-
two blocks representing
thirty-three designs.

Yellow
Print

Red

Blue

Fig. 53. The Circuit Rider's Quilt *(cont.)*

Design no. 2.

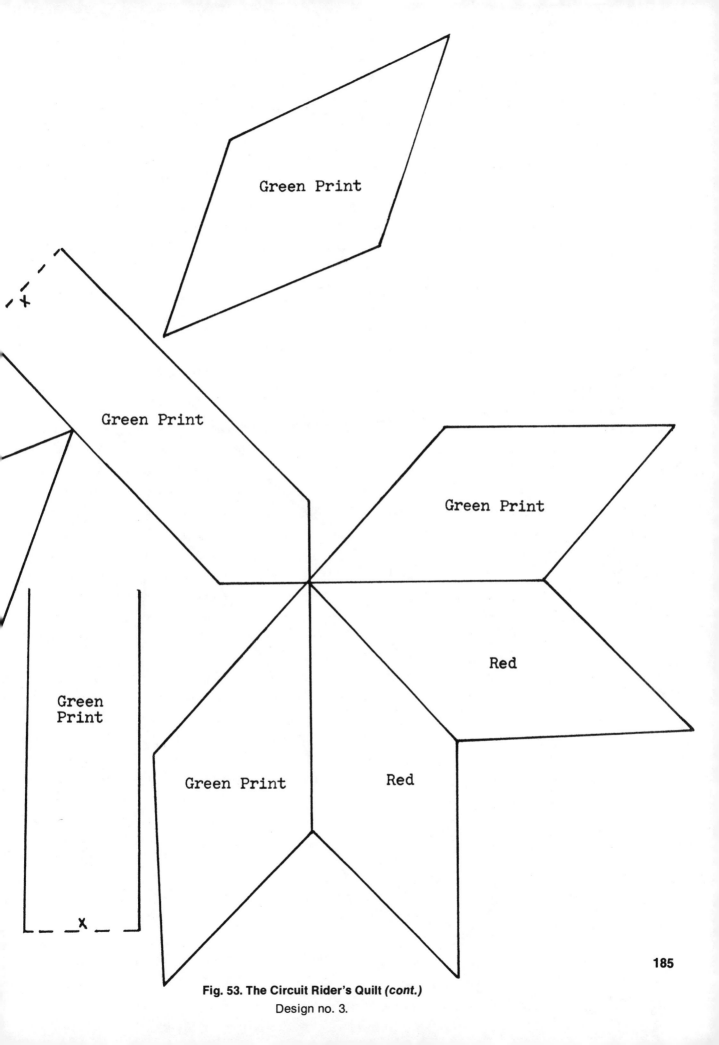

Green Print

Green Print

Green Print

Red

Green
Print

Green Print

Red

x

x

Fig. 53. The Circuit Rider's Quilt *(cont.)*
Design no. 3.

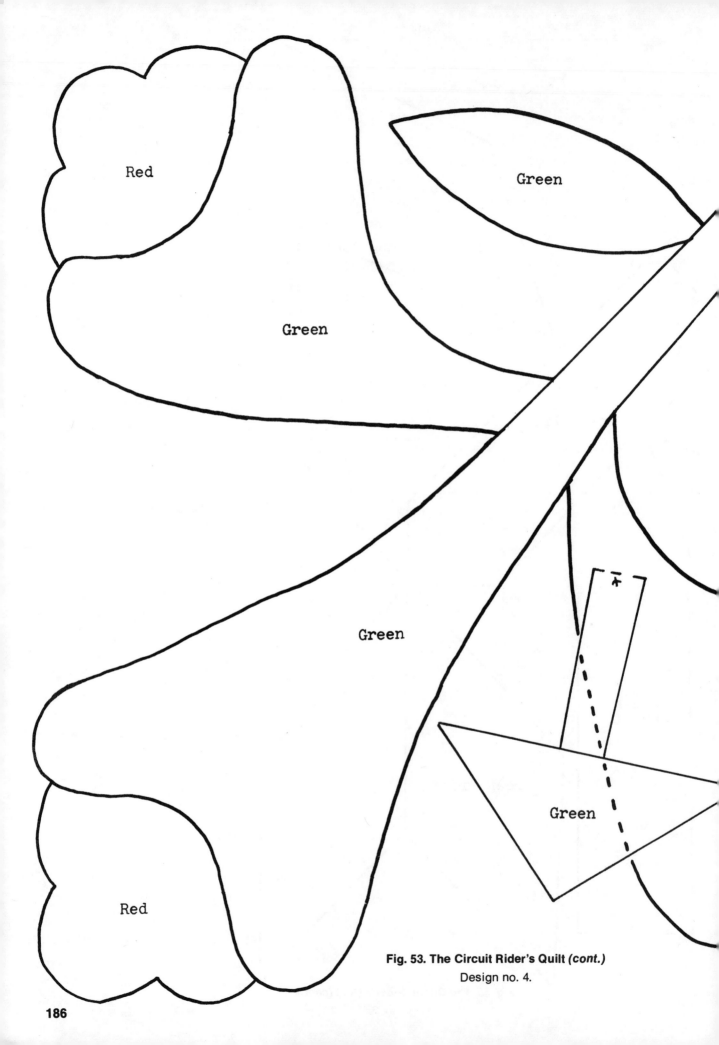

Red

Green

Green

Green

Red

Green

Fig. 53. The Circuit Rider's Quilt *(cont.)*

Design no. 4.

Fig. 53. The Circuit Rider's Quilt *(cont.)*
Design no. 5.

Red

Yellow

Green

Green

Red

Yellow

Fig. 53. The Circuit Rider's Quilt *(cont.)*
Design no. 6.

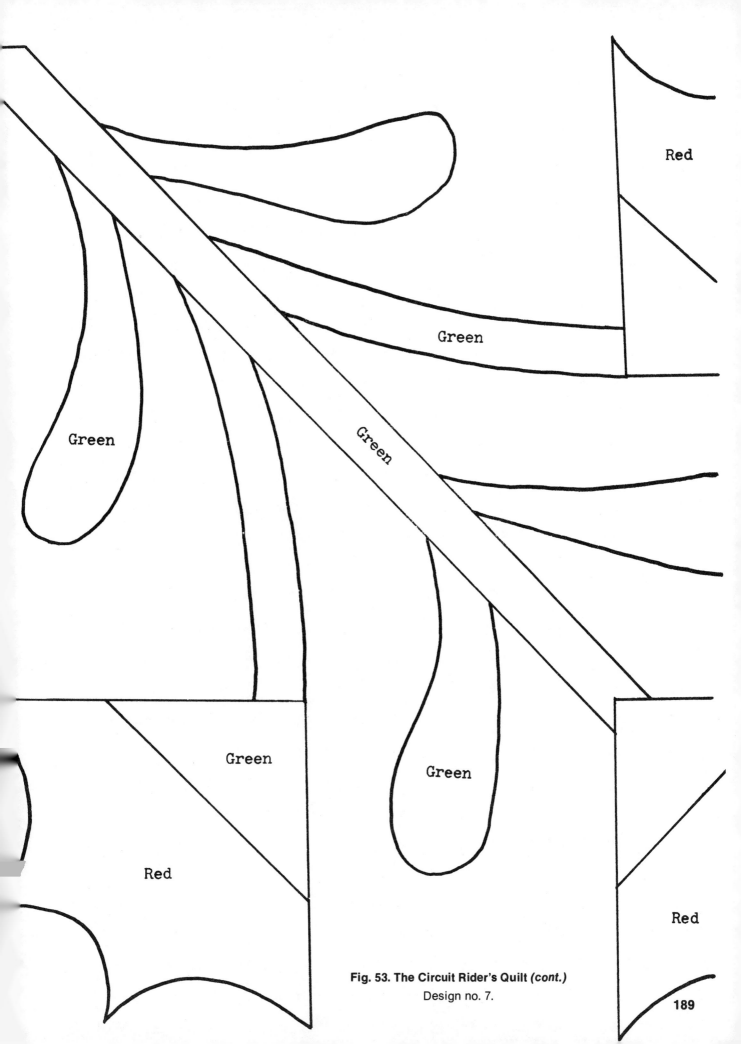

Fig. 53. The Circuit Rider's Quilt *(cont.)*
Design no. 7.

189

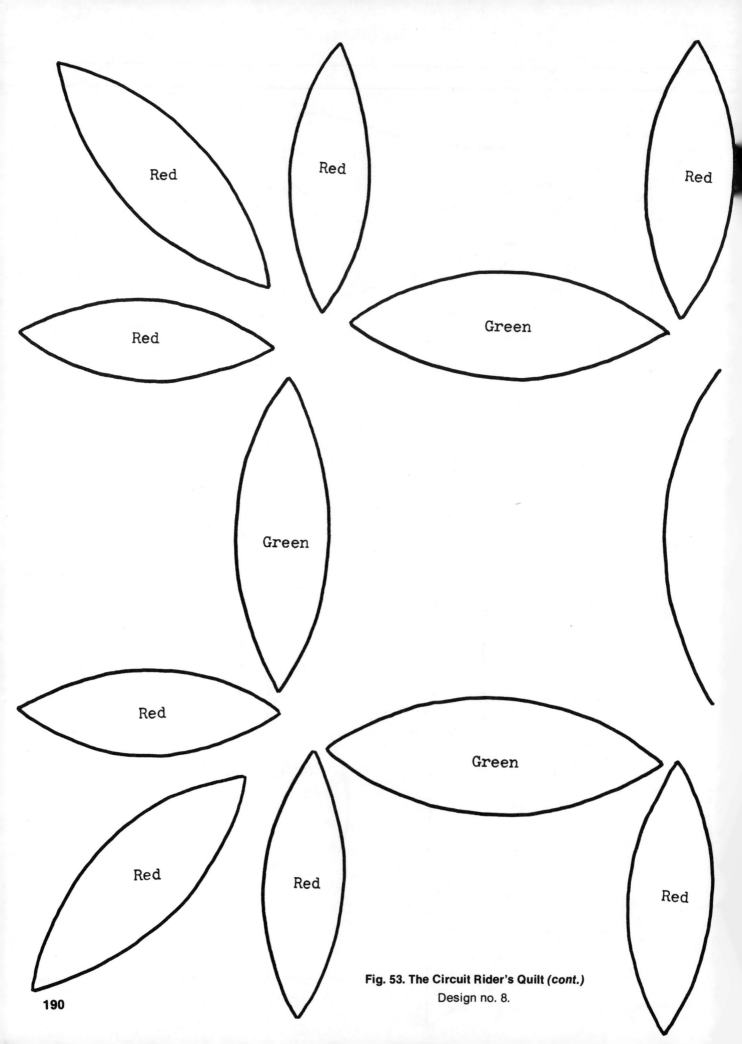

Fig. 53. The Circuit Rider's Quilt *(cont.)*
Design no. 8.

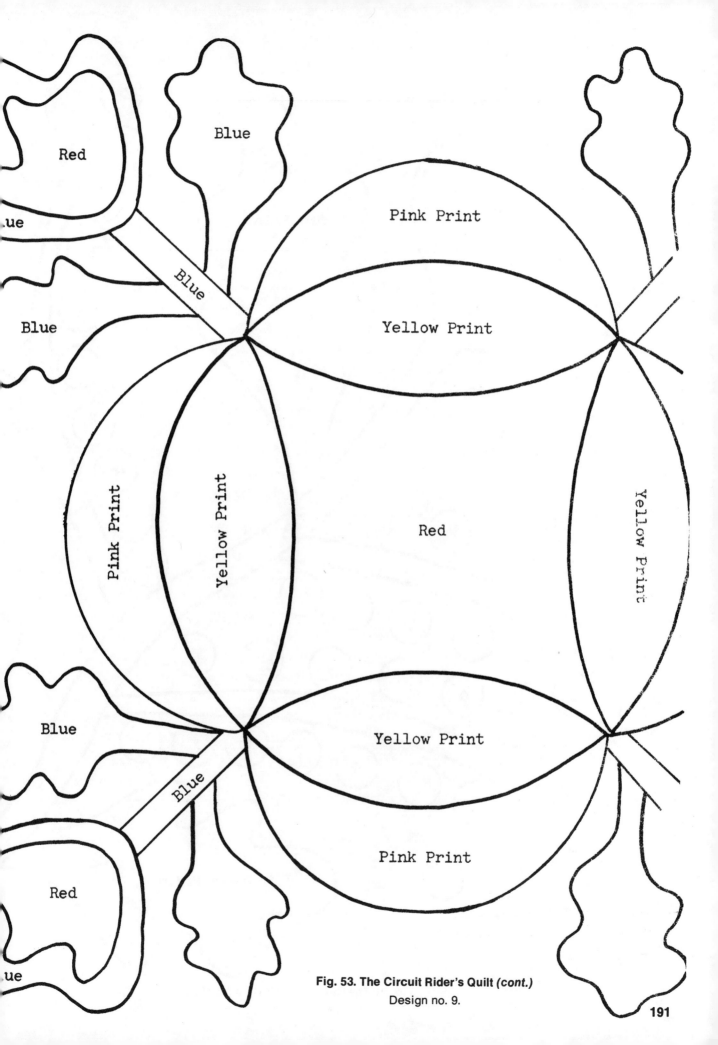

Fig. 53. The Circuit Rider's Quilt *(cont.)*
Design no. 9.

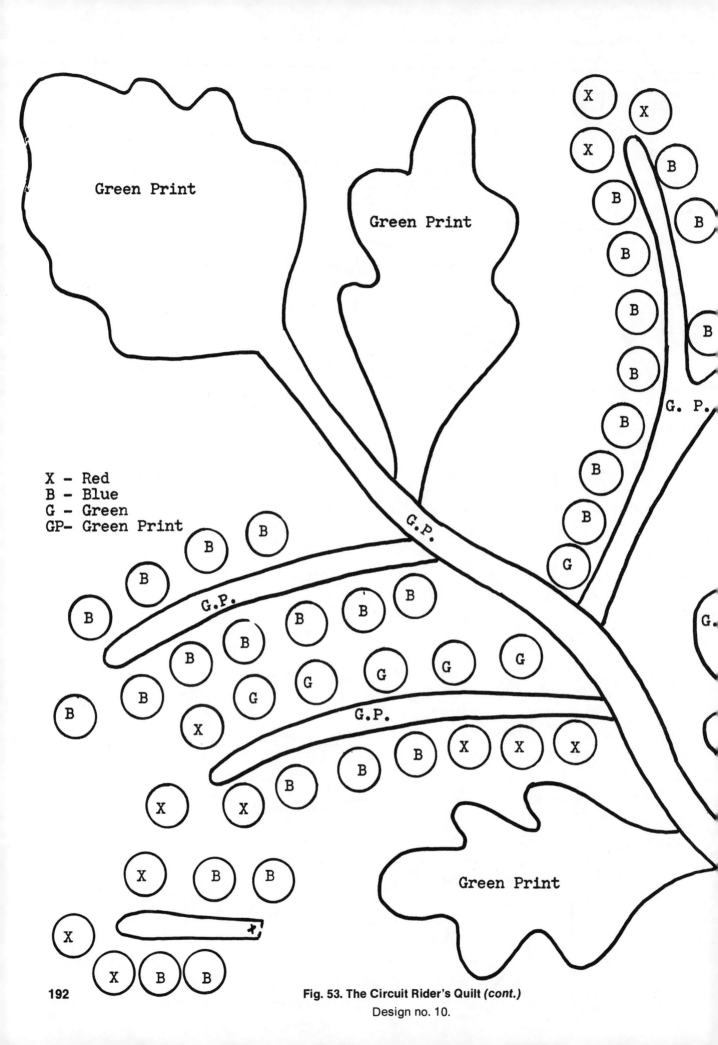

Green Print

Green Print

X – Red
B – Blue
G – Green
GP– Green Print

G. P.

G. P.

G. P.

G. P.

G.

G.

Green Print

Fig. 53. The Circuit Rider's Quilt *(cont.)*
Design no. 10.

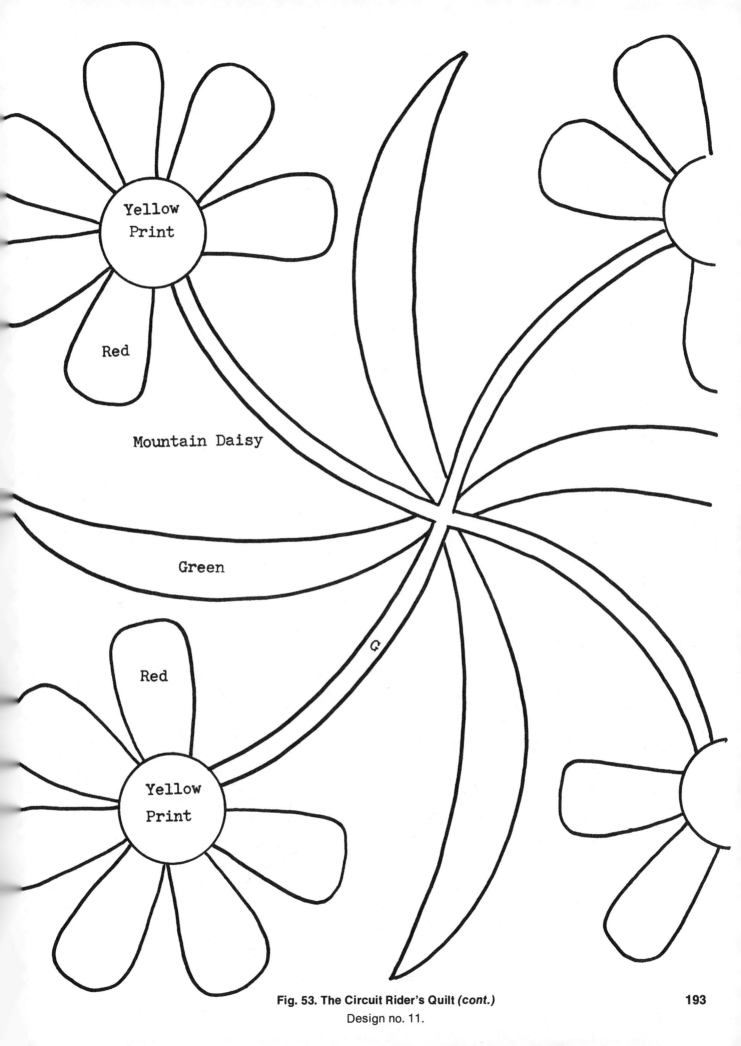

Yellow
Print

Red

Mountain Daisy

Green

Red

G

Yellow
Print

Fig. 53. The Circuit Rider's Quilt *(cont.)*   193
Design no. 11.

Colonial Wreath
Appliqued in Green Check

Fig. 53. The Circuit Rider's Quilt *(cont.)*
Design no. 12.

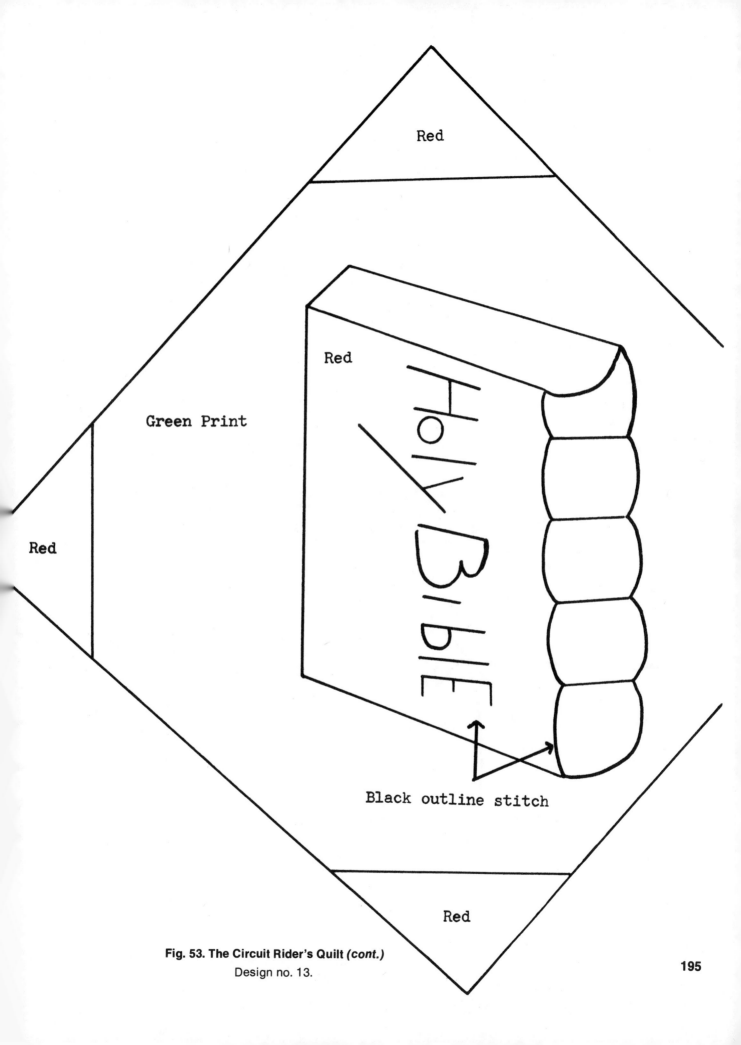

Red

Red

Green Print

Red

Holy BiblE

Black outline stitch

Red

Fig. 53. The Circuit Rider's Quilt *(cont.)*
Design no. 13.

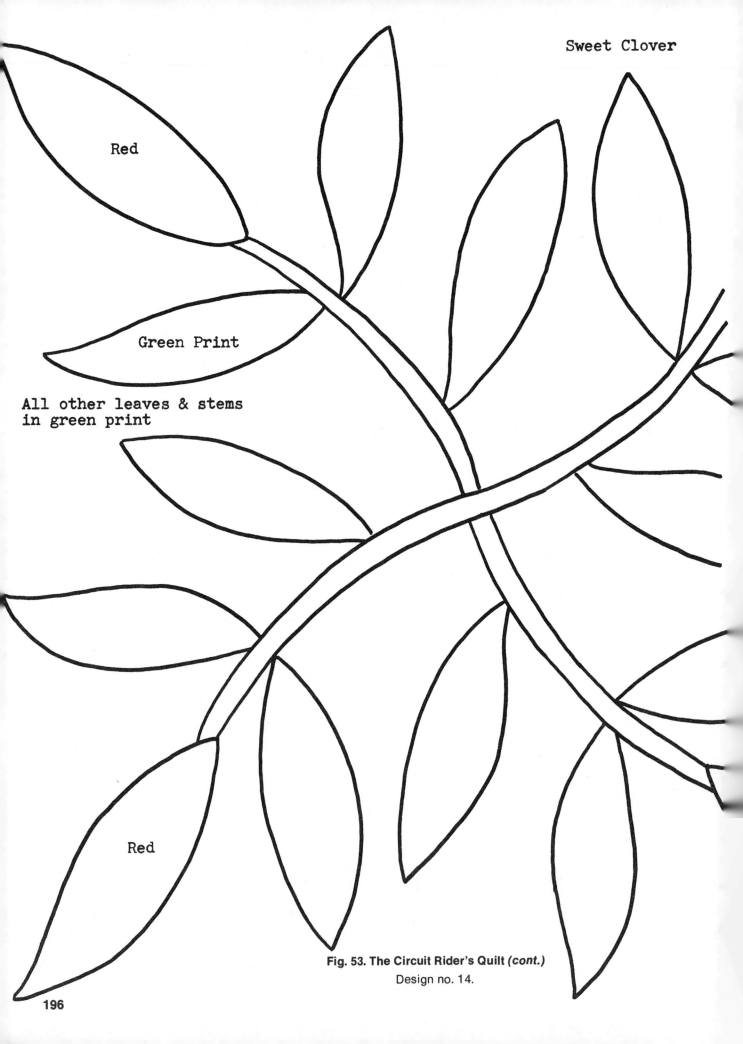

Sweet Clover

Red

Green Print

All other leaves & stems
in green print

Red

Fig. 53. The Circuit Rider's Quilt *(cont.)*

Design no. 14.

196

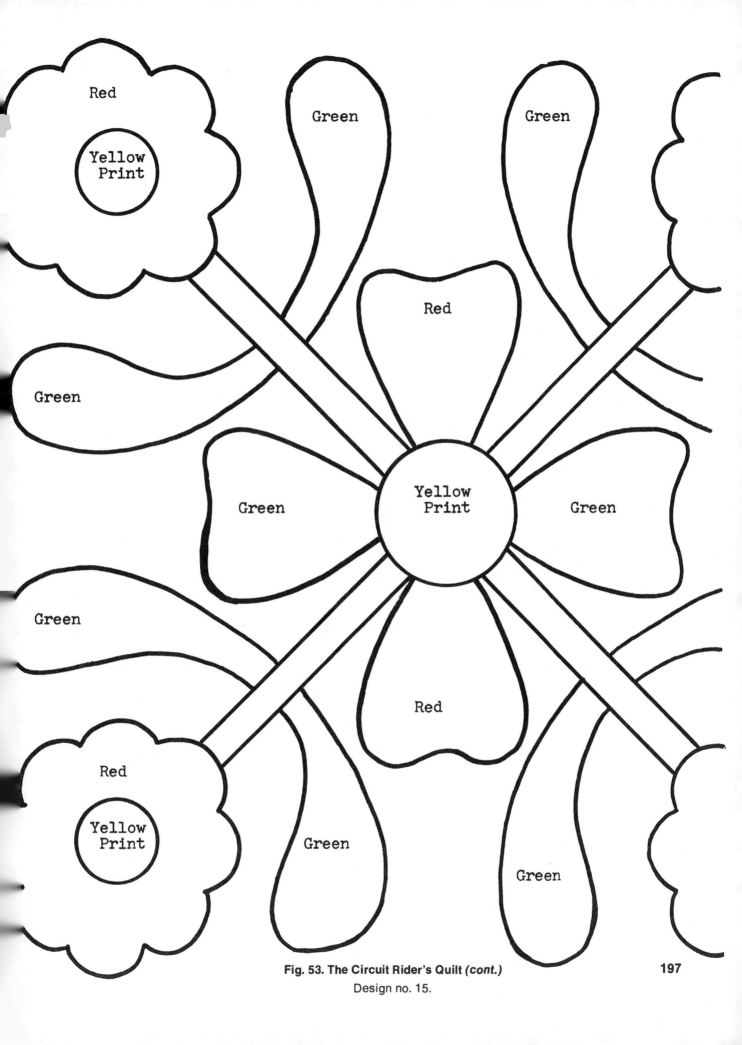

Fig. 53. The Circuit Rider's Quilt *(cont.)*

Design no. 15.

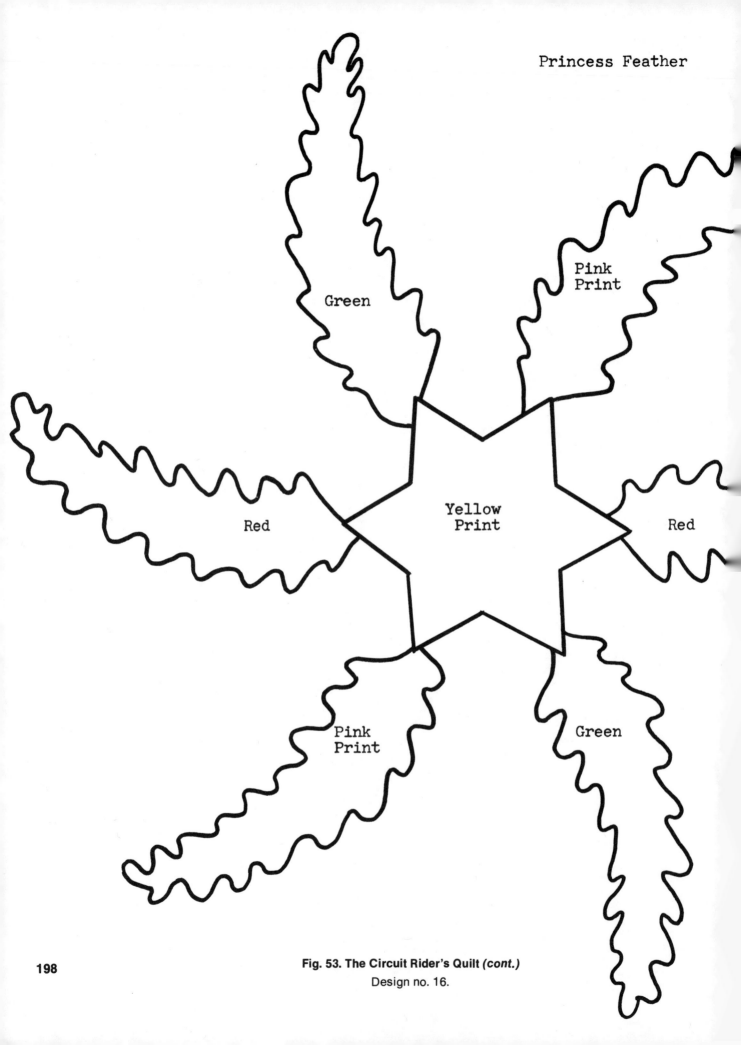

Princess Feather

Green

Pink Print

Red

Yellow Print

Red

Pink Print

Green

Fig. 53. The Circuit Rider's Quilt (cont.)

Design no. 16.

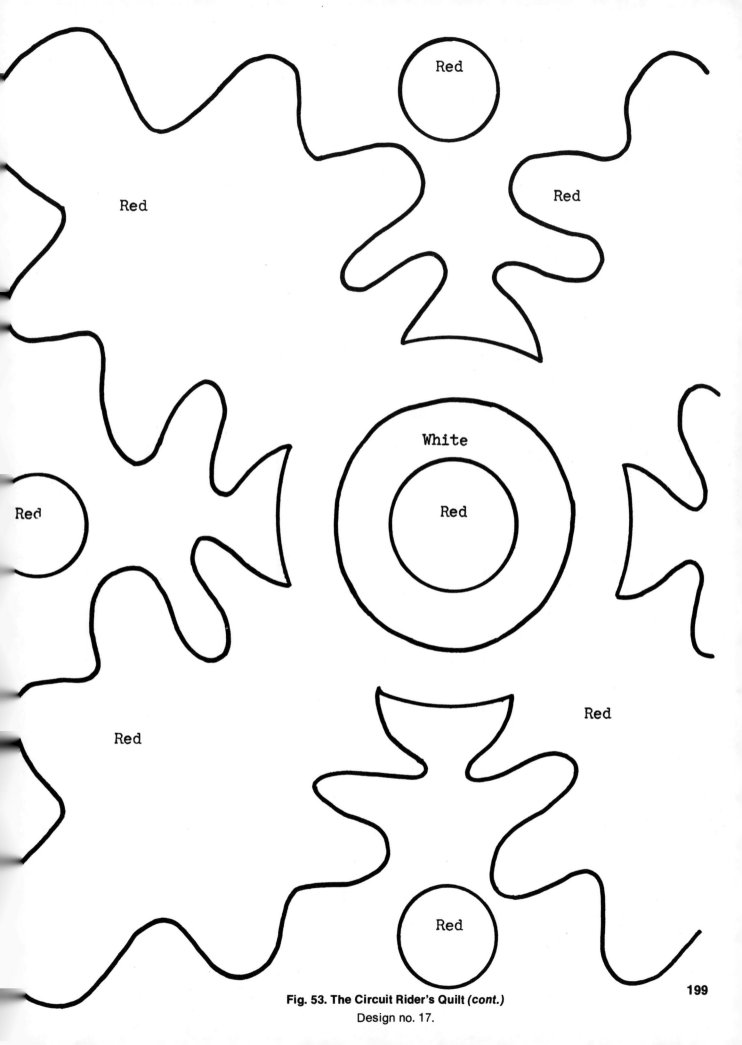

Fig. 53. The Circuit Rider's Quilt *(cont.)*

Design no. 17.

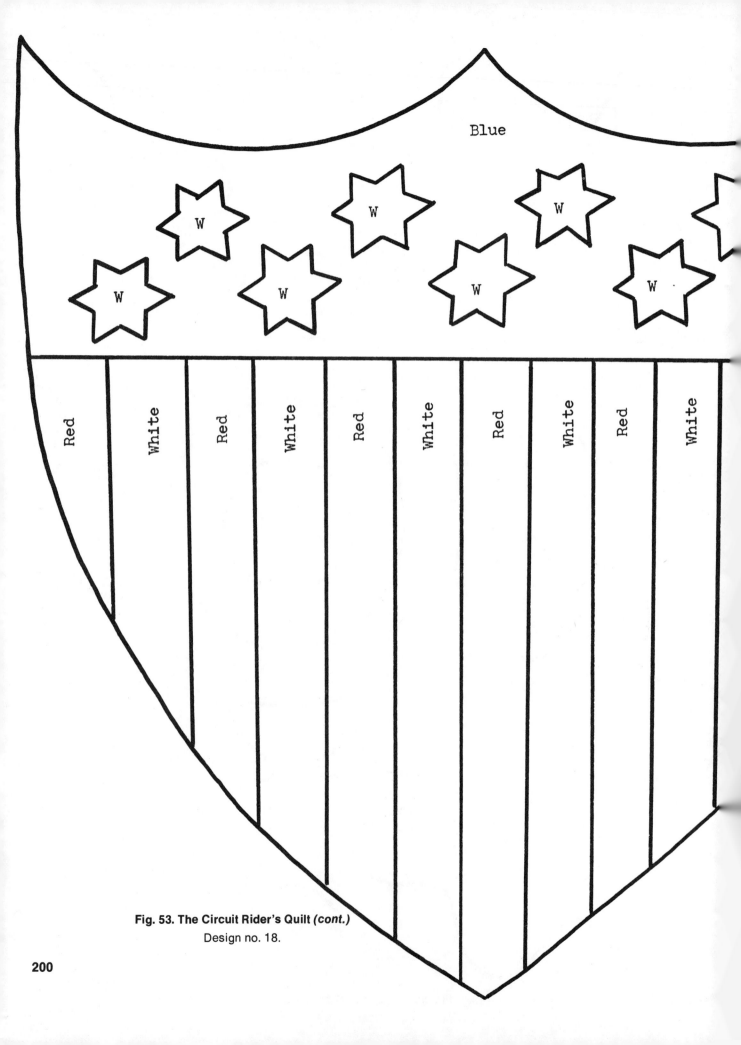

Blue

W W W

W W W W

Red | White | Red | White | Red | White | Red | White | Red | White

Fig. 53. The Circuit Rider's Quilt *(cont.)*

Design no. 18.

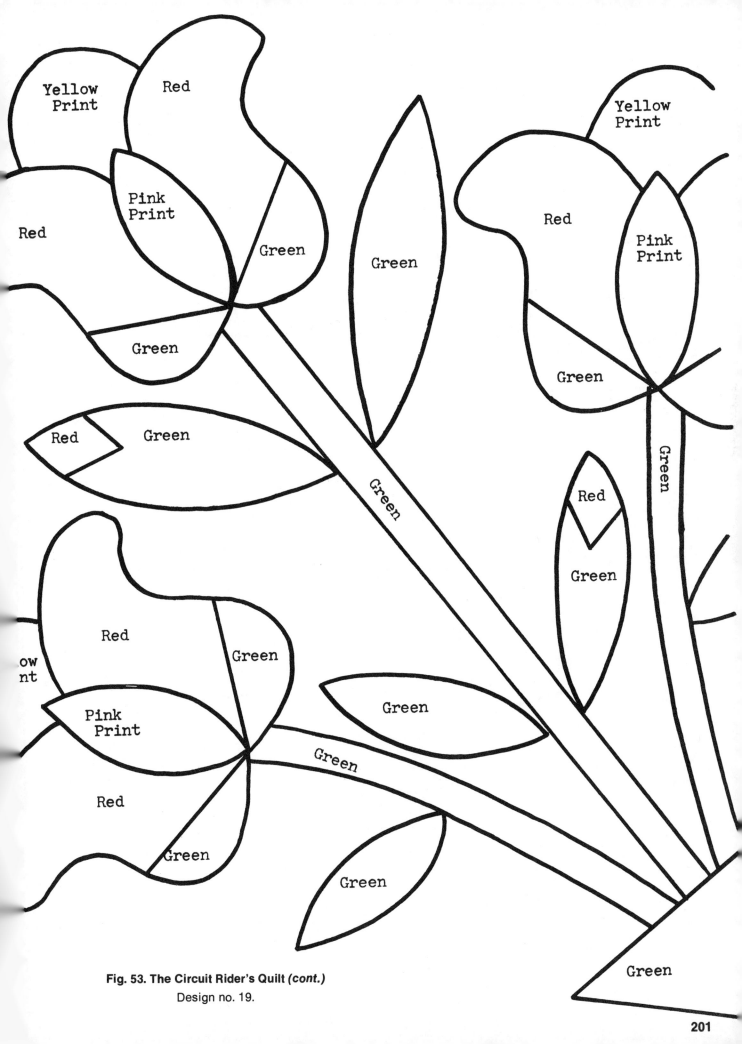

Fig. 53. The Circuit Rider's Quilt *(cont.)*
Design no. 19.

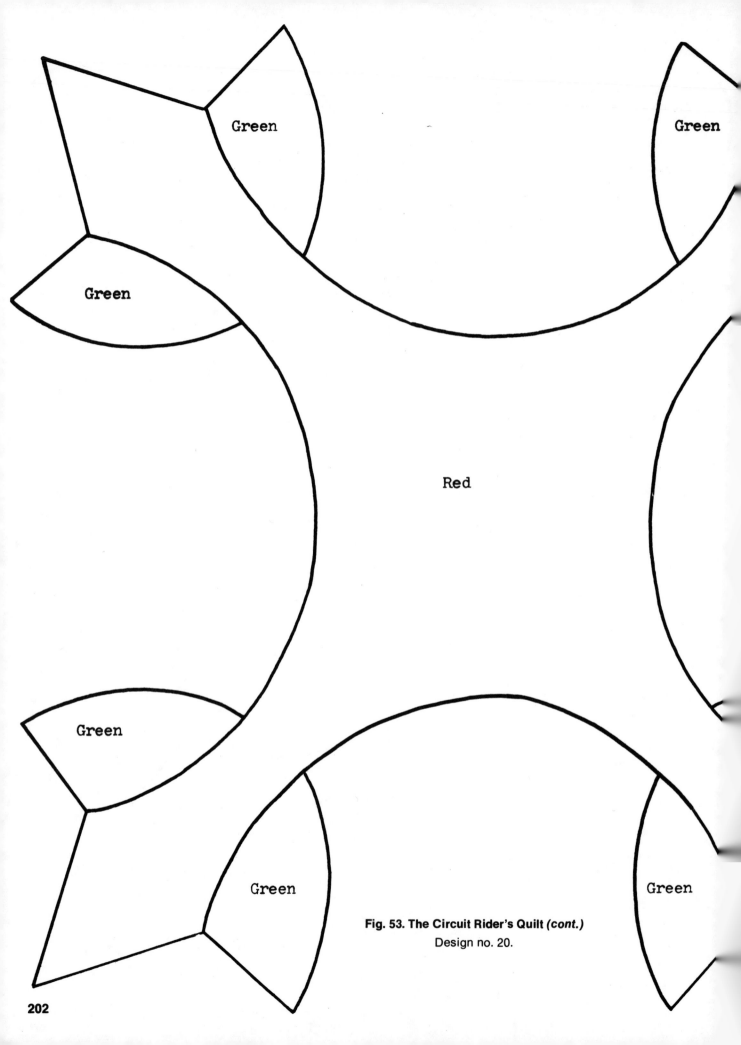

Green

Green

Green

Green

Red

Green

Green

Green

Fig. 53. The Circuit Rider's Quilt *(cont.)*
Design no. 20.

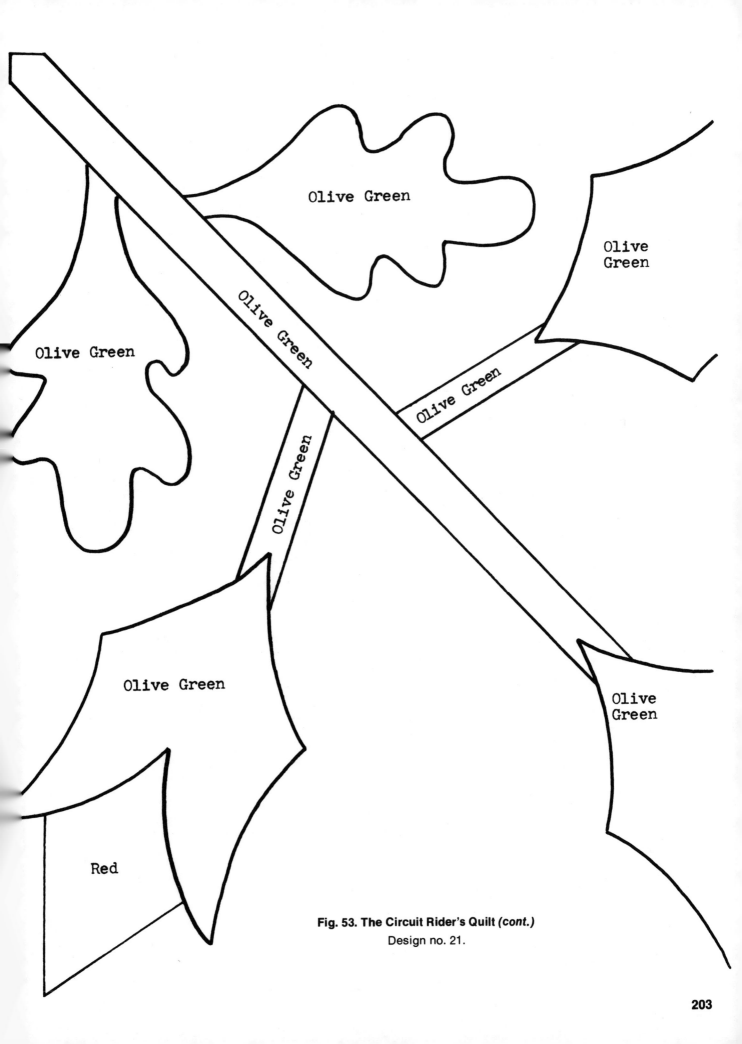

Olive Green

Olive Green

Olive Green

Olive Green

Olive Green

Olive Green

Olive Green

Red

Fig. 53. The Circuit Rider's Quilt *(cont.)*

Design no. 21.

Fig. 53. The Circuit Rider's Quilt *(cont.)*
Design no. 22.

Fig. 53. The Circuit Rider's Quilt *(cont.)*
Design no. 23.

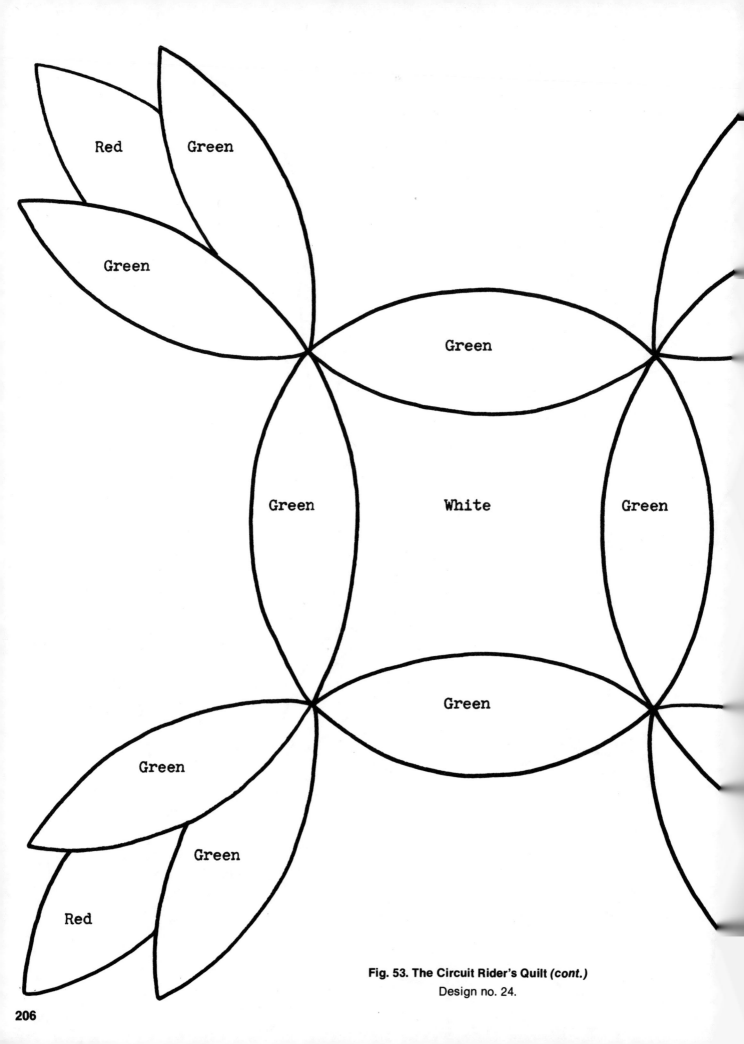

Fig. 53. The Circuit Rider's Quilt *(cont.)*
Design no. 24.

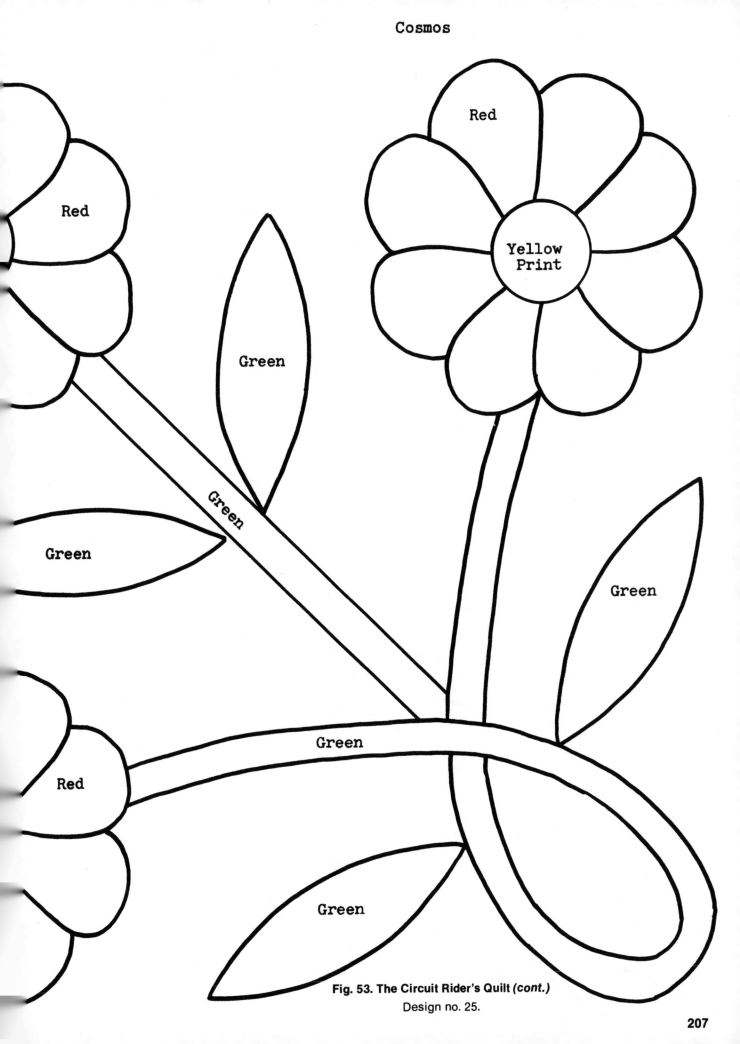

Fig. 53. The Circuit Rider's Quilt *(cont.)*
Design no. 25.

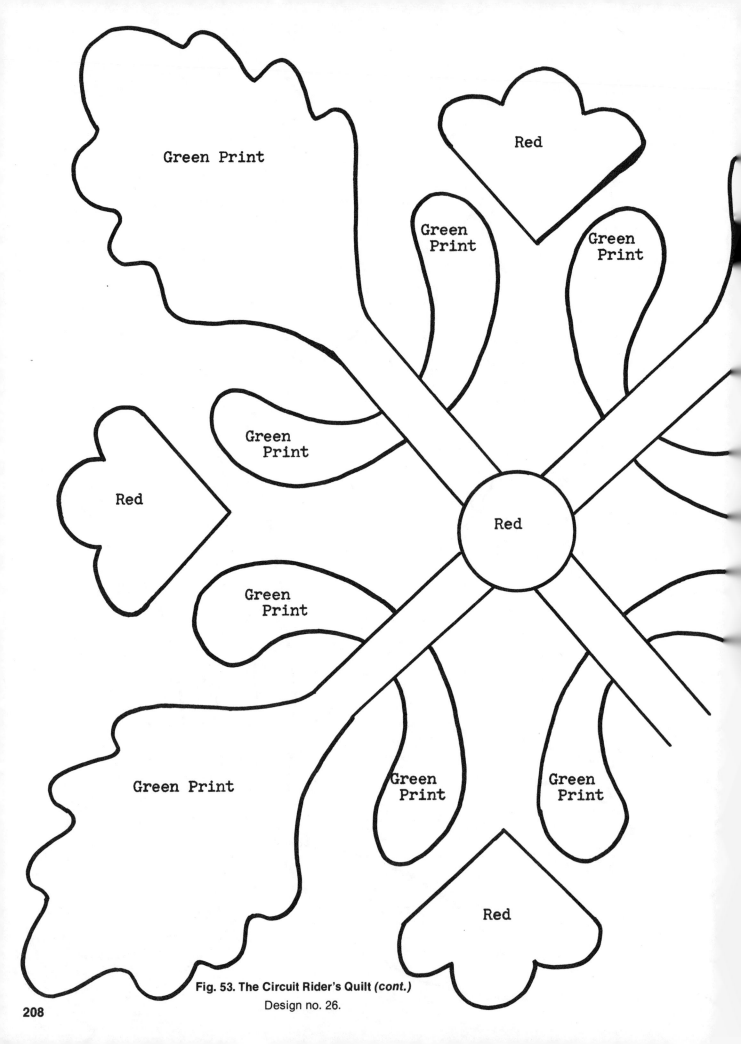

Fig. 53. The Circuit Rider's Quilt *(cont.)*

Design no. 26.

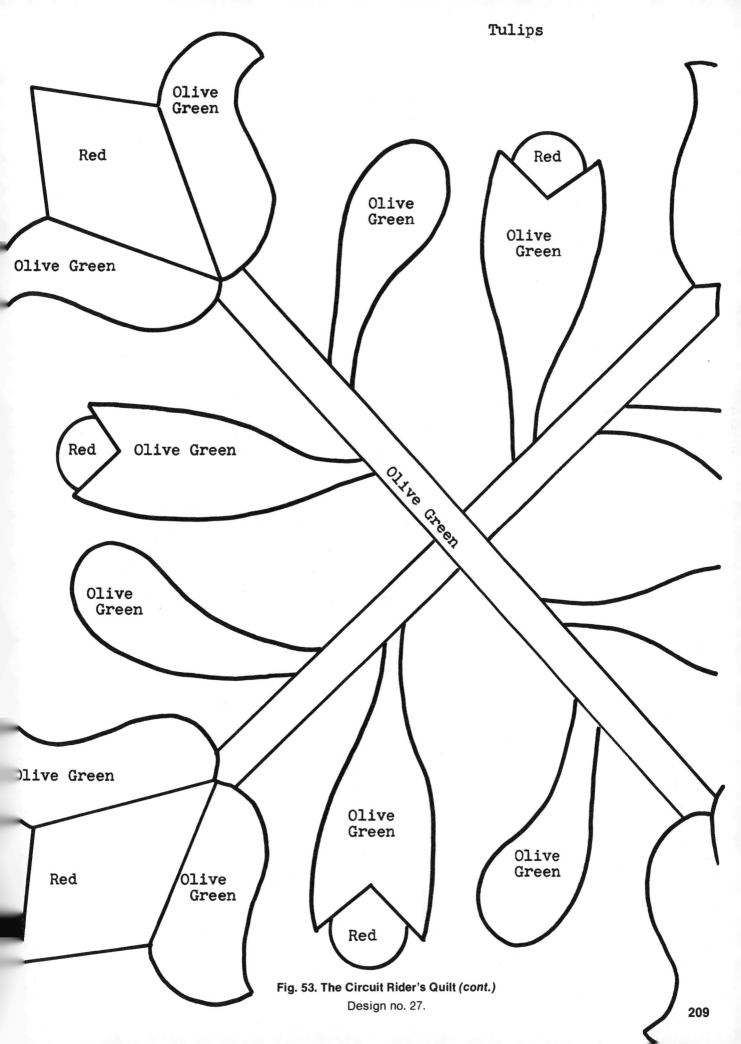

Fig. 53. The Circuit Rider's Quilt *(cont.)*

Design no. 27.

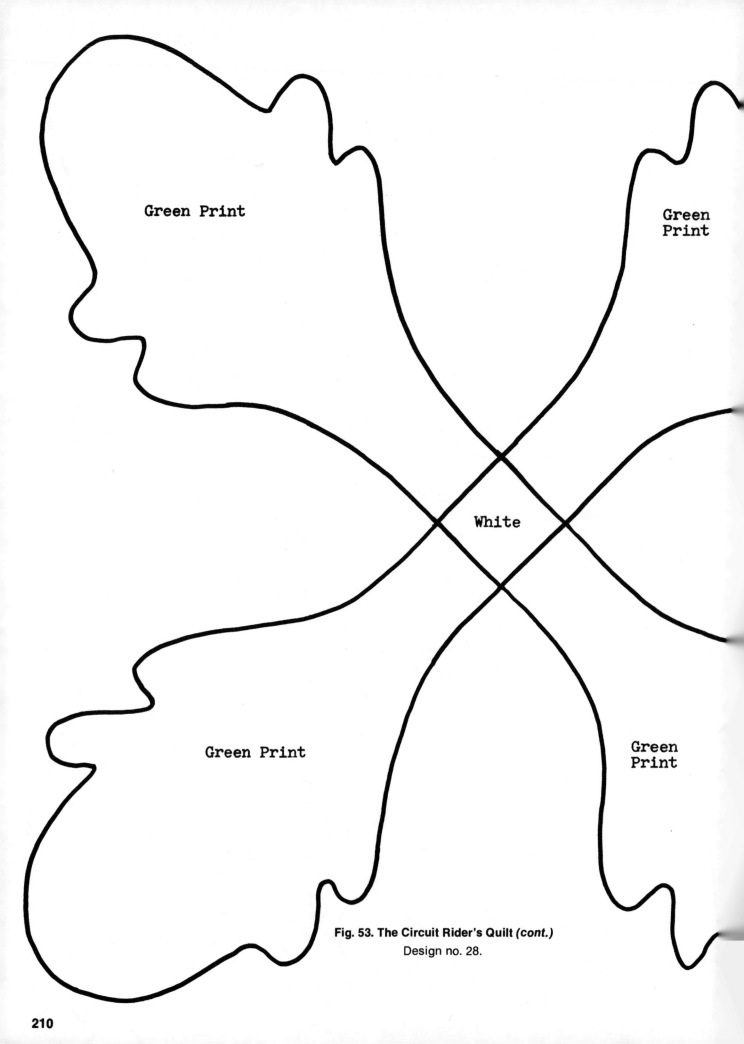

Green Print

Green Print

White

Green Print

Green Print

Fig. 53. The Circuit Rider's Quilt *(cont.)*
Design no. 28.

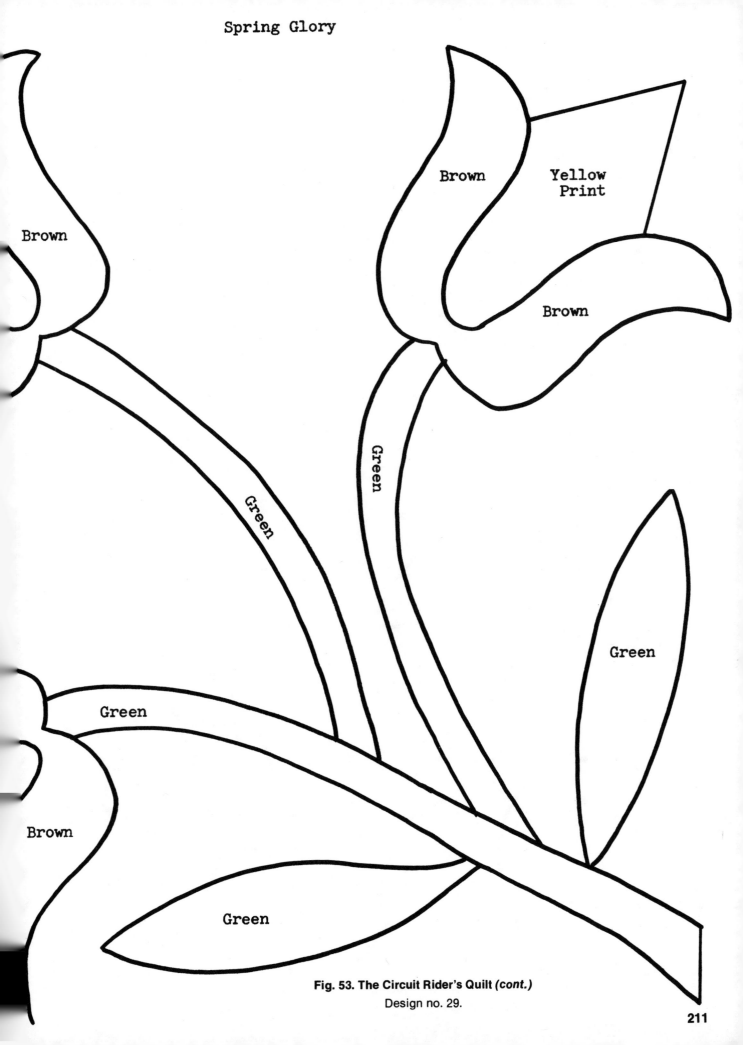

Spring Glory

Brown

Brown

Yellow
Print

Brown

Green

Green

Green

Green

Brown

Green

Fig. 53. The Circuit Rider's Quilt *(cont.)*
Design no. 29.

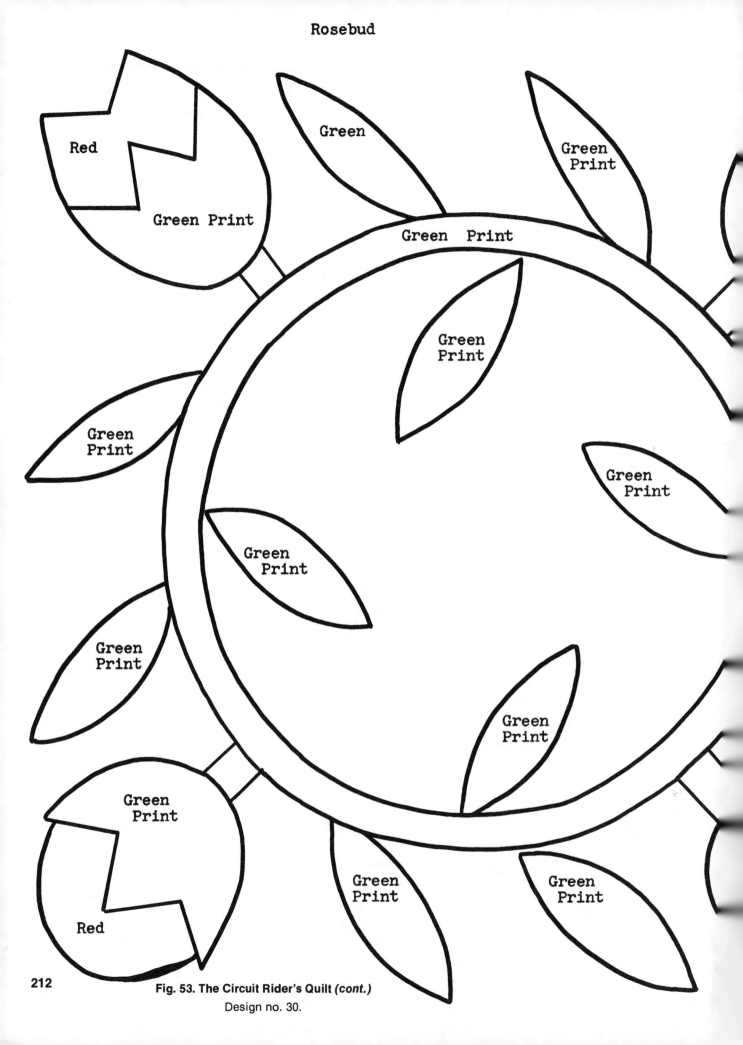

Fig. 53. The Circuit Rider's Quilt *(cont.)*
Design no. 30.

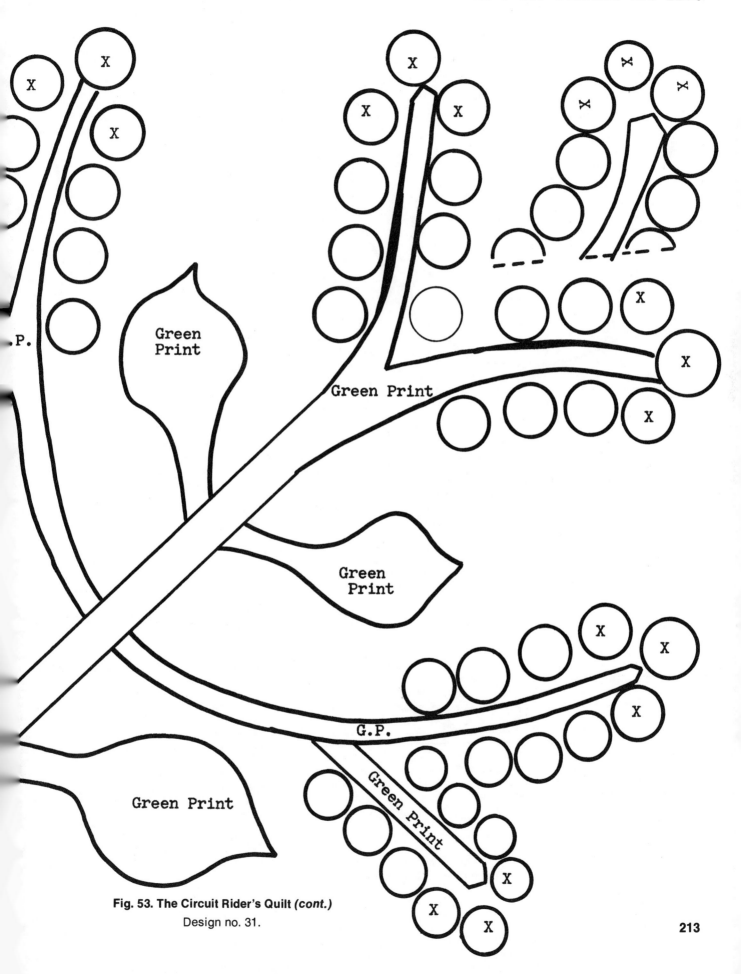

X--Red
All other berries are Blue

Fig. 53. The Circuit Rider's Quilt *(cont.)*
Design no. 31.

213

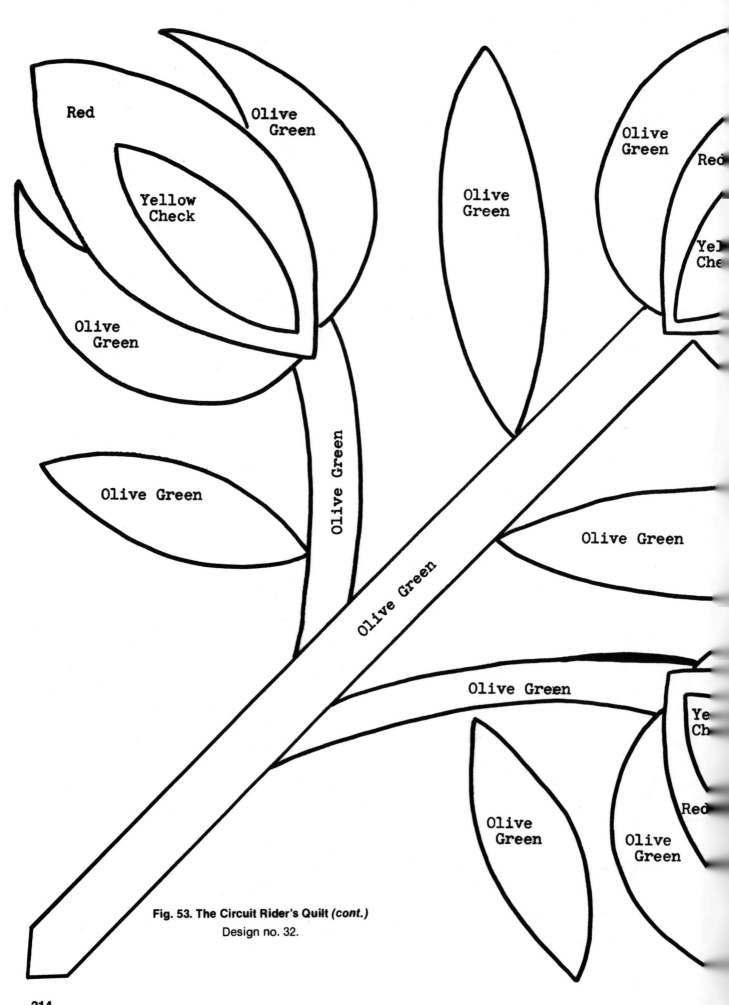

Fig. 53. The Circuit Rider's Quilt *(cont.)*
Design no. 32.

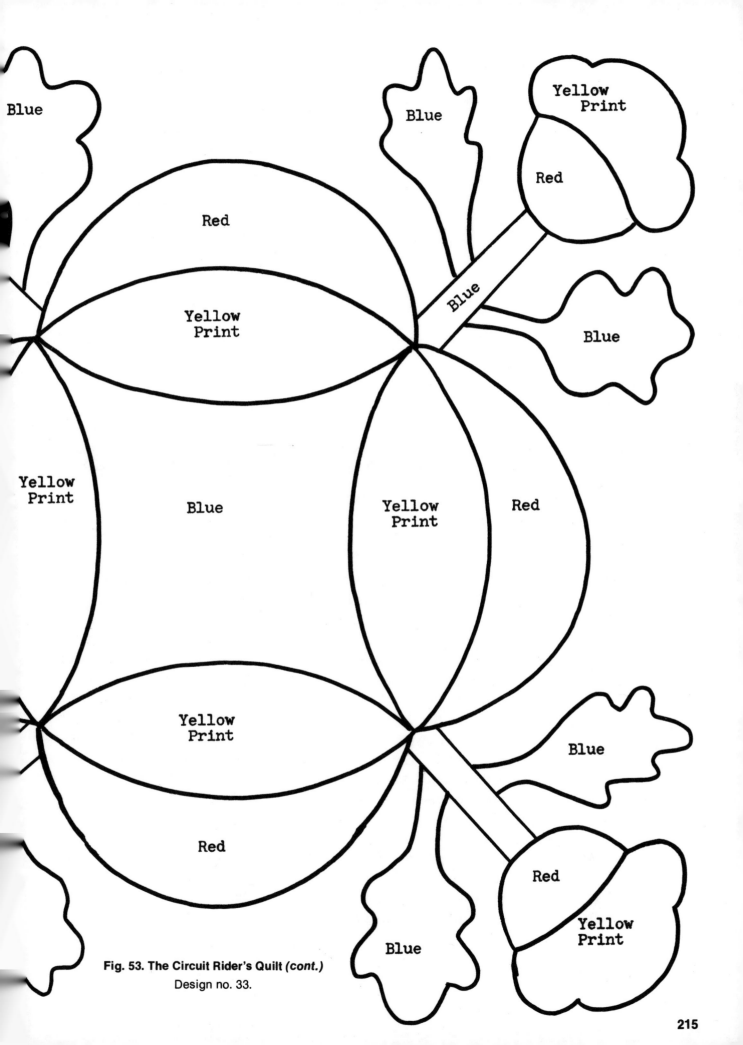

Blue

Blue

Yellow Print

Red

Red

Yellow Print

Blue

Blue

Yellow Print

Blue

Yellow Print

Red

Blue

Red

Blue

Red

Yellow Print

Fig. 53. The Circuit Rider's Quilt *(cont.)*
Design no. 33.

Chapter 11

Hawaiian Quilts

WHEN THE FIRST New England missionaries landed in what was known as the Sandwich Islands, they introduced, along with religion, the needle and thread. Hawaiian garments before 1820 were tied instead of sewn. The women who were the chiefs were enormous in size, and wore wrap-arounds below the waist and nothing above. The Hawaiians had no woven fabrics. Instead, they used tapa made from the inner bark of the mulberry tree, pounded and "felted" until it was the size needed for a garment or a bedcover.

Three days after the four royal Hawaiian women came aboard the ship "Thaddeus" at Hakala, Hawaii, the ladies of the First American Board of Missions conducted a sewing circle. The missionary women wore Mother Hubbard dresses, which were greatly admired by the Hawaiian royal women. The New Englanders made such an outfit for the queen, who went ashore dressed in it. Soon all the native women wanted the same garment as their queen. So the muumuu came into existence.

Since the muumuus were cut full, all the cloth was used and there were no leftovers for the scrapbag. However, even so, quilting was introduced to the islands. Tapa coverlets were not washable, so the introduction of American fabrics for covers was welcome. The ladies of the royal household were the first to learn quilting, but in a short time stitchery was taught to all in the missionary schools.

The first quilts were simple blocks of patchwork, but soon the beautiful countryside furnished ideas for designs. It was inevitable that the native women would soon discard the simple patterns of their New England teachers. The Hawaiian women were accustomed to making their own designs on their tapa coverlets, so these designs were soon transferred to their quilts.

Quilts made in America were geometrical in design, utilizing circles, stars, squares, and triangles, but the Hawaiian women created patterns of leaves and flowers with their scissors. Usually two colors were used (or white and another color) and the design was cut out of one large piece of material. The design was large enough to cover the entire spread, as a rule. The result of this type of free-wheeling cutting looked like the cut-paper work that most of us did in our kindergarten days.

Many women used breadfruit, pineapple, and poinsettias for designs. Designs patterned after the sugar cane and coconut were not accepted. The designs became very intricate and original.

Today's Hawaiian quilts use a single large applique. The quilting is "contour" quilting with the lines of stitching about half an inch apart following the lines of the design until all the space is filled. This creates the rippled effect which simulates the blue waters of the surrounding Pacific Ocean.

Taboos grew up surrounding the making of a quilt. For example, it was *kapu* (forbidden) for anyone but the quilt owner to sit on it while the design was being basted to it. Each quilt maker was responsible for her own design, and she gave a special name to each one. It was *kapu* to steal another's design. Of course, this did not mean that it never happened.

Quilts were never put out to air with the design showing, for fear patterns might be stolen by other women who would then pass off as their own. The Hawaiian women believed it very bad manners to appropriate without permission, a design created by someone else. However, if caught, they ran the risk of having their misdeeds embarrassingly and loudly proclaimed to the world in song form at the next *luau* gathering.

The quilt was attached at both ends to poles of the quilting frames and rolled onto them. The quilters then worked from the center outward. In the old days the quilting frames were made in two heights, a high one for the missionaries, who sat on chairs, and a low one for the Hawaiians, who sat on the ground.

Some designs are heirlooms, passed from one generation to the next. Names such as Silver Sword of Haleakala, Coconut, and Pineapple, and the Queen's Vase are traditional. Some designs are so precious to their owners that as soon as the quilt is finished the design is destroyed.

It is usually drawn on a folded triangle of paper, then cut out, although a few women prefer to cut the design directly out of the material. The paper pattern is then placed on a folded eight-by-eight piece of cotton fabric in a color contrasting to the background material of the quilt. When it is cut out and unfolded, the pattern repeats itself in a design radiating from the center.

The design is then basted onto the background material, after which hundreds of tiny stitches are used to attach it permanently. This is where the quilt maker shows her real skill.

Later the decorated top sheet is joined to the padding in the middle and the bottom sheet, after which it is ready for the quilting.

Today it is the practice for one person to do the quilting in order to ensure uniform stitching; some women have even attempted to update the methods by attaching their patterns to the background material by machine stitching. Traditional quilters, however, will refuse to quilt such a coverlet, considering it a direct betrayal of their customs. [EDITOR'S NOTE: Some of the material in this chapter has come from *Nimble Needle Treasures*.]

Part III

Quilts Today

Chapter 12

Quilting Today

QUILTING CLASSES ARE now springing up everywhere—in colleges, adult education centers, high schools, stores, churches, private homes, and shopping malls. There are magazines exclusively devoted to the subject and articles about it appear in women's magazines.

To make a quilt today, one becomes aware of certain changes from traditional modes of work and design. Originally quilts were a means of utilizing precious scraps of fabric. Each quilt was the result of the inventiveness of the quilt maker, limited by the materials available to her.

Today our reasons for making quilts transcend practical considerations. We wish to personalize and individualize articles in daily use. Too many items used today are mass-produced and so are identical with those used by many people; they are completely impersonal. But we enjoy things we make ourselves. A quilt offers the opportunity of producing something of personal value, practical and aesthetic at the same time. Many women who have been doing other types of needlework are now turning to quilting.

Down through the years the surviving quilts have become pictures of the past. Antique quilts are now being collected and exhibited. The total beauty of a quilt is seen when it is on a wall. However, today's quilters want the quilt for warmth as much as for beauty.

Many of today's women are reverting in some ways to the "old-fashioned" woman who makes things for herself. Quilting and patchwork are part of these "old-fashioned" trends. The fact that the old quilt is now one of the most desirable of collectibles to be found and that the price of an old quilt is rapidly spiraling also has caused the resurgence of interest.

State and county fairs are exhibiting quilts and holding blue-ribbon contests for new quilts. Women are beginning to believe that perhaps their quilts will soon become collectors' items. The quilt maker of today is recapturing the spirit and essence of early American quilting; she is turning back to the old designs. Today's woman often makes a block at a time, since she has no specified time limit to hurry her along, as her forebears had when quilt-making was necessary for utilitarian purposes.

Occupational therapy, research studies, and case histories all seem to agree that those who do quilting or other types of needlework or various arts and crafts live longer and enjoy life more than those who do not. Programs for the elderly are particularly helpful. At the Jewish Home for the Aged in Philadelphia, quilts and other items made by the residents are offered for sale at the gift shop or in the Elder Craftsmen Shop. This program, and others like it, provide the sick and elderly with a small income and an increased will to live. Not only do they find pleasure in working but they develop more self-confidence. The New York City Lighthouse for the Blind also has many quilted items on sale.

There are a number of co-operative groups working on quilts and related items. In the more depressed areas of the United States this type of enterprise supplements a very meager income in many cases.

Of the numerous groups and individuals interested in quilting today, a random sampling will show that they are both the young and those not so young.

Mountain Artisans

Mountain Artisans had its beginning when a low-income marketing co-operative in West Virginia requested marketing assistance from the Arts and Crafts section of the West Virginia Department of Commerce. The Arts and Crafts staff met with this co-operative's members and board, and were shown many examples of fine workmanship in quilts, personal clothing, and small items for the home—all well executed but not marketable. For one thing, the quilters themselves were limited by geography. And marketability of many of the things being made was a real problem. However, the women were willing to apply their skills to new products.

Thus the idea of the patchwork hostess skirt was born in West Virginia in 1968. The skirts and the fabric by the yard were delivered to a few stores around the country, and there was an immediate request for more skirts and thirty yards of fabric. The artisans were ill-equipped to handle matters of marketing, design, and purchase of material. A group of citizens who had been following and working with the project met with the Department of Commerce and formed Mountain Artisans as a nonprofit corporation. Participants were of all ages and economic brackets, united in a genuine interest in the survival of hand skills and in new economic opportunities for rural areas.

West Virginia artists donated designs for the first sample lines, while various individuals donated money to finance the initial operations.

Mountain Artisans learned that banks do not make loans on orders, but only against solid assets, and that many standard lending institutions do not lend to nonprofit corporations. There were many volunteers. A board member's husband (Jay Rockefeller) loaned space within his office building. First orders were filled and a small line of credit was extended by a bank in Charleston, West Virginia.

In August 1969 Mountain Artisans received from the Office of Economic Opportunity a grant that covered staff salaries, a Charleston, West Virginia, office, a small amount for marketing, and expenditures for production development and travel expense. The second sample line was developed and orders began coming in.

Today Mountain Artisans has fifteen co-operatives in seven different counties. About one hundred and fifty women work in the co-operative and each makes an average of between $1,000 and $1,500 a year, which is supplementary income. Sharon Percy Rockefeller, a board member, stated that the purpose of the Mountain Artisans was to help the women of the co-operative economically without disrupting their lives.

Dorothy Weatherford designs all products, including the adaptation of tradition patterns. Individual groups that make the products are paid for the number of hours needed to produce an item, plus an additional amount if they deliver on time.

The staff, board, and all the workers of Mountain Artisans are making this project a success.

The following four plates illustrate some of the items that are being distributed by Mountain Artisans.

The Freedom Quilting Bee

The Freedom Quilting Bee of Alberta, Alabama, was begun in 1966. It is a people's co-operative composed of black women whose artistry in patchwork quilting has become widely known. There are about fifty women in the co-operative, all from small farms in the area.

The women turned to quilting to supplement family incomes which averaged about $800 a year not long ago.

Their quilts, bright and bold in color, have been exhibited through the Smithsonian Institution Folk Life Festivals.

They make quilts, pillow tops, and pot holders, as well as dashikis.

The photographs on page 229 show two bold-color quilts and women working at a quilting frame.

Kutztown Folk Festival

In 1949 the first annual Pennsylvania Dutch Folk Festival was held in Kutztown, and since then every year around the Fourth of July the Festival has taken place. It is sponsored by the Pennsylvania Folklife Society to demonstrate and display the lore and folkways of the Pennsylvania Dutch and to collect, study, and publish information about the Dutch country and Pennsylvania through the publication of *Pennsylvania Folklife* magazine. The proceeds of these activities are used for scholarships and general educational purposes at Ursinus College, Collegeville, Pennsylvania.

Each year the Folk Festival has grown in size. In 1965 the Society started a quilting contest "to revive and preserve this nostalgic needlework, once an important part of early American folklife."

In rural Pennsylvania, especially in the "plain" Dutch areas, the art of quiltmaking has never died. Individuals, men as well as women, and small groups carry on the practice as a revenue-producing activity.

It is interesting that while the Festival, along with all other worldly events, is out of bounds for the strict "plain Dutch" sects, Amish and Mennonite women do enter their choice works of arts through the kindness of "worldly Dutch" neighbors. They never attend the Festival, or see their quilts on display, but there is an understanding between the "plain Dutch" seamstress and her friends: if her quilt wins a prize, she will collect the money.

Each year there are over 1,000 entries, from every section of the Dutch Country, as well as from the Deep South and from New England states. Pieced, appliquéd, and embroidered quilts are exhibited and some in the antique category. There are star patterns, gay pinwheels, hand-of-friendship designs, the Prince's Feather, and bright calico "flowers," to name just a few.

Entries are accepted both from individuals and from organizations. The judging is based on uniqueness of design, color, and needlework, appropriateness of materials used, craftsmanship, originality, beauty, attractiveness, and adaptation of customs and traditions of the Pennsylvania Dutch folk culture.

In the same building with the quilts an old-fashioned quilting bee is held, when expert quilters from Pennsylvania Dutch areas demonstrate their native skills. Women work all day around a large frame. As in the old days, the quilting proceeds from the outside toward the center, and the edges of the quilts are rolled under as they are completed. Four or five women work on each side of the quilt while visitors watch. The women compete in making the tiniest stitches.

Fig. 54. Pieced Quilt—*Courtesy of Mountain Artisans*

Fig. 55. Giant Puff in Earth Tones—*Courtesy of Mountain Artisans*

Fig. 56. Up, Up, and Away—*Courtesy of Mountain Artisans*

Fig. 57. Maxi Puff—*Courtesy of Mountain Artisans*

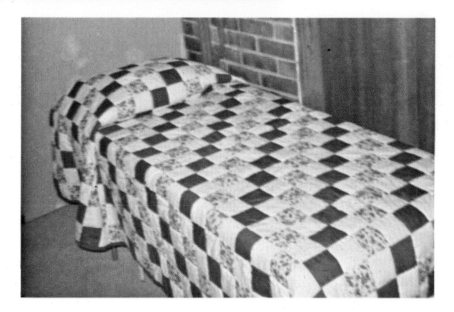

Fig. 58. Work Done by the
Freedom Quilting Bee

Fig. 59. Work Done by Lynne Spiegel

Fig. 60. *Top left and right:* Work by Mrs. Callie Everett. *Bottom left:* Work by Golda Bullion. *Bottom right:* Work by Mrs. George W. Hesson.

Fig. 61. Premium Quilt—*Courtesy of Mrs. Robert Reed*

Fig. 62. Kutztown Folk Festival

Mrs. Lydia Meeske

Mrs. Lydia Meeske, of Pocahontas, Iowa, seventy-nine years old, has made a quilt that is very unusual and probably one of a kind, since it has been made of fair ribbons (it is shown on page 234). It is a future heirloom for the family and may well be in a museum someday.

Mrs. Meeske used light aqua satin and arranged her red, white, and blue ribbons in a sunburst effect with a star for the center. There are nine blocks with twelve red, white, and blue ribbons in each block, for a total of one hundred and eight ribbons. Mrs. Meeske has hand-quilted it, and the long ecru cord fringe adds to the beauty. She had ribbons left over after completing the quilt, so she made a sofa pillow of those remaining. The ribbons used by Mrs. Meeske, incidentally, were those she won at various times.

She has a good background for quilting, for her mother made quilts, many of which are still in the family.

Fig. 63. Mrs. Lydia Meeske

Delina Fournier Labonte

Delina Fournier Labonte has spent nearly all of her eighty-three years in Holyoke, Massachusetts. Delina (or Maggie, as most people know her) has the bounce and enthusiasm of a teen-ager. Widowed after only a few years of marriage, Maggie has worked hard all her life to provide for the nieces and nephews whom she helped to raise.

Since she retired from active employment, Maggie spends most of her time and energy making quilts, which have numbered over forty since 1961.

Her favorite patterns are Sunbonnet Girl and Grandmother's Fan. One of her favorite coverlets was made for a king-size bed for which she had to assemble 2,800 one-inch squares, working from the center outward in a complicated pattern.

Maggie likes to keep up with her favorite TV shows and has devised a system for quilting while she watches. She times her rows of stitches by the half hour to match her programs. To Maggie Labonte quilting is a way of expressing her joy in living.

Lynne Spiegel

The joys of quilting are not just for the mature woman. There are many young people doing quilting today. Lynne Spiegel of Massachusetts is one of the examples of the young people in the business today.

During a spring vacation from college in 1970, Lynne visited friends in Oklahoma, where she saw some quilts being made by the Indians. Upon her return to

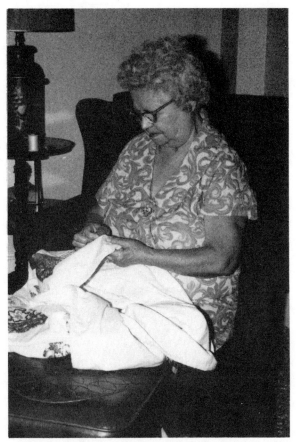

Fig. 64. Mrs. Delina Fournier Labonte

school, Lynne decided to make a quilt herself and persuaded Erica Reitmeyer to work with her. After making a few quilts, the girls were suddenly deluged with orders. Today they operate a thriving business in Boston, supplying quilts to the Design Research Boutique and to private customers.

Lynne and Erica make richly colored "modern" quilts from scraps of vivid Scandinavian fabrics pieced together in bold patterns.

Several of the quilts that the girls have made are shown on page 230. Lynne Spiegel is the young lady on the right.

Callie Everett

On page 231 are two quilts that were made in 1936 by Callie Everett of New Hope, Arkansas, for her daughter, who was kind enough to allow me to use the photographs. The colors are still bright and the quilts in constant use.

Golda Bullion

Golda Bullion, of Elkins, W. Va., calls her quilt shown on page 231 Nine-Patch and Nosegay. Her comment concerning this quilt is, "This has been a wedding present delight."

Mrs. George W. Hesson

Mrs. George W. Hesson, of Letart, West Virginia, is seventy-nine years young. She has been making quilts for many years. When she enumerates the various ones she has made, it seems as if she has gone through the roster of patterns previously listed. Her favorite is the Eight-Point Star, shown on page 231. She says that to make the quilt prettier she quilts it around each star petal.

Ruby Barrow

Mrs. Ruby Barrow, of Conroe, Texas, likes to use old-time patterns for her quilts. She has been kind enough to allow the author the use of photographs of several of her quilts, along with some comments that may prove useful to the reader.

No. 1: Mrs. Barrow calls it Ruby's Star, although she thinks that it is also known as Spider Web. It is a pattern that is first made on paper, as her grandmother did it. Each wedge has several strips. It is four blocks wide and five blocks long.

Fig. 65. Ruby's Star

No. 2: The Single Wedding Ring. Although Mrs. Barrow pieced this one, she says that an aunt made the same quilt before 1900 and called it The Single Wedding Ring. It also has been called Crown of Thorns.

Fig. 66. The Single Wedding Ring

No. 3: Mrs. Barrow calls this quilt her Odd Fellow quilt. Every block is the same size but of a different design of material. There are no two pieces of material alike. Each block is finished with a briar stitch.

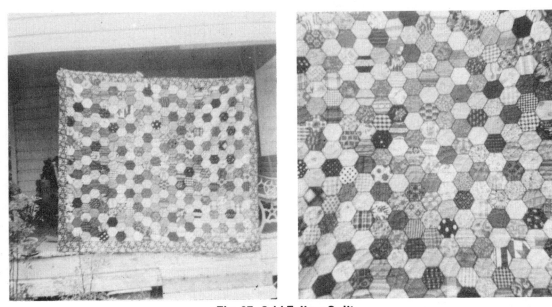

Fig. 67. Odd Fellow Quilt

No. 4: The Flower Garden. This quilt is set together with yellow. Mrs. Barrow did not use half blocks but filled these rows in with yellow, as in the patch around the flowers.

Fig. 68. The Flower Garden

No. 5: Log Cabin. Mrs. Barrow said that her grandmother made a similar quilt which she called Sunshine and Shadows.

Fig. 69. Log Cabin

No. 6: There is no name for this quilt. Mrs. Barrow joined the blocks with a small striped material. The manner in which they are cut makes the quilt look as if it were woven together.

Fig. 70. No-Name Quilt

Chapter 13

Things To Make

PATCHWORK, APPLIQUÉ, AND quilting are not used only for the making of quilts. The list of items that can be quilted is long; only a few will be discussed here—from a patchwork tablecover of 1870 to a patchwork picture frame of the 1970's.

Patchwork Table Cover

In 1870 *Treasures in Needlework,* by Mrs. Warren and Mrs. Pullan, featured instructions for a patchwork table cover:

" The table cover now submitted to the readers of the *Treasures* may be taken as an admirable specimen of patchwork, at once harmonious in design and effective in execution; and patchwork being still popular with a large number of ladies, it may serve to give them an idea, by the aid of which they may convert to useful account spare pieces of cloth, velvet, &c.

The materials necessary for its formation are braid of various widths and hues, purse-silk of different shades, bright coloured cloth, yellow or crimson fringe, and the design shapes, in tin or mill-board.

The size of the cloth will necessarily vary with the table to be covered but an ordinary square table will require one six foot square.

The centre-piece should be six inches in diameter, and of a bright mulberry colour; immediately surrounding this is the fillet, of white or bright blue, with the motto, buckle, pendant, &c., worked in silk; then succeeds the second circle of the centre, composed of eight pieces of the same coloured cloth as the central piece; next comes the second band, of bright scarlet, in four compartments, and then the wedge-shaped pieces.

The outer circle of wedge pieces is composed of twenty-four pieces of various colours; and for the guidance of those who may not have an idea of the arrangement of them, respecting their colours, we subjoin the following, to be placed in the order they are given—cobalt, green, scarlet, yellow, drab, white, cobalt, &c., &c.

It should be observed, that the colours should be placed diametrically opposite one another; that is to say, cobalt should face cobalt, green face green, &c., &c., by these means a uniformity of design will be preserved.

These wedge-shaped pieces should be eight inches long, and every alternate one braided, as in the figure, but each piece having a different pattern; thus there will be twelve plain and twelve braided.

The ground should be eleven inches deep, from the apex of the wedge-shaped pieces to the edge of the border pieces, composed of four separate portions, and of a bright mulberry, drab, or blue.

The corner pieces may be omitted, if thought proper, but it is economical to construct them in the semblance of a group of flowers, as in the annexed, because the portions of the cloth remaining from the cuttings of the other shapes can now be appropriated; thus the remnants of blue will form corollas, the green the calyxes and leaves, requiring only the additional aid of a chain stitch in silk to form the veinings of the leaves, stamens, &c.

Or the attached design will give a finish to the corners, and, from the peculiarity of its form, be greatly in keeping with the other parts of the table-cover. It may be constructed from such parts as will necessarily remain after cutting out the wedge-shaped pieces. By some persons this cornerpiece may be preferred, as in closer unison with the central design.

The border pieces are fifty-six in number, and partake of the same colours as the outer circle. They should be four and a half inches wide, and five inches long, and all braided with a different pattern on each side of the border; thus there will be fourteen different patterns required—thirteen for the consecutive pieces, and one for each corner piece.

Our engraver has thrown in various designs, some of which may be impractical, but will aid the mind in designing various embellishments to these squares.

The fringe may be crimson or bright yellow, according to taste.

The crest.—It will improve the effect of the cloth, if the crest is cut out in white cloth, and sewed on; after which such parts as require it may be either worked in silk, or touched up with coloured marking-inks.

The braiding.—Much of the beauty of the patterns will depend upon the arrangement of colours, as the greater the contrast the more beautiful the effect.

The cobalt grounds should have scarlet braid patterns.

The green, yellow braid.

The scarlet, yellow or purple.

The yellow, blue or crimson.

The drab, yellow.

The white, mulberry or green;

so that the *tout ensemble* may present a most beautiful grouping of colours, with a uniformity of design.

The lining may be of light blue, salmon, or mulberry, stitched to such point of the work as shall not interfere with the pattern. In this we would recommend the adoption of such stitching as the design lays down, so that it may serve the double purpose of strength and beauty.

In conclusion, we may mention that the addition of a tassel to each corner would give a more decided finish to the cloth, and assist in making it hang well, especially if loaded with a bullet.   "

Penguin Pillow

The original instructions of the early 1900's read as follows:

"Penguins are familiar and a bit beloved by all. So we have done a pair in appliqué to ornament the top of a small cushion. First the black flappers are applied, then the white shirt front and the bill and then the tailed dress coat, all the patches being neatly felled over one another. (Felled means over stitched.)

"The only decorative stitchery on this design is a short black line in tiny back-stitches lengthwise the center of the bill and an eye ringed and centered with pale yellow. The edge is finished with white rickrack braid set between front and back."

The penguins can be used as an appliqué for practically anything you desire. A crib quilt made of nine-inch squares of white with either blue or pink alternating squares would be attractive. The penguins should be in the white squares and made of solid pink or blue where the black would ordinarily be, while the shirt front would be of pink or blue gingham or small calico print to match the coat. The lining and border of the quilt would be of pink or blue too.

The penguins could also be used to decorate aprons, dresses, place mats, napkins, and tablecloths. They would be interesting if used as an appliqué on both sides of a felt or canvas tote bag.

Recollect and Remember, the Counterpane Twins

Making a "memory" quilt or coverlet can be loads of fun. The coverlet keeps alive the family lore in bits of gingham and print from sister's frocks, brother's shirts, and baby's rompers.

Fig. 71. Penguins for Appliqué

Coverlets of the brother and sister blocks are attractive for nursery beds. Nine-inch squares of unbleached muslin with the figure may be alternated with plain muslin squares or prints. If plain blocks are used, seam the squares together on the right side and cover these seams with bias fold of an appropriate color, sewed on flat, thus making a lining unnecessary.

For a single bed a quilt or coverlet with blocks of this size should be made seven blocks wide by eight long. Appliqué pieces for the figures should be cut out one quarter of an inch beyond the outlines, turned in, basted to the unbleached blocks, and blind stitched in place. Arms and feet are outlined with two strands of black floss.

Such counterpanes are quaint when Recollect and Remember are dressed in old-fashioned, bright, oil print calicoes, if one is more interested in decoration than sentiment. Alternating plain muslin blocks and bright red bias fold is most effective with the gay calico appliqué.

Fig. 72. A Counterpane Twin for Appliqué

Fig. 73. The Other Counterpane Twin for Appliqué

Holland Hanging in Felt Appliqué

The following instructions were printed in the 1890's.

"   Holland calls forth images of quaint and picturesque surroundings; dykes and windmills, men and boys in baggy trousers and tight little coats with enormous gold or silver buttons, women and girls in voluminous skirts and marvelous caps that tell what district they come from; of tulips and 'klompen.' It recalls dog-drawn milk-carts, neat little houses and the picturesque details for which the little country has long been famous.

Felt appliqué seems the ideal medium to portray the Dutch scene. It is easy to handle and satisfactory to work with so that it recommends itself for those reasons as much as for its time- and labor-saving qualities.

The first step, to keep the work as simple and systematic as possible, consists in cutting out the parts of which the picture is to be built [see pages 248-249]. You will find it a help to provide yourself with envelopes into which to slip the cut-out spots of the design; the windmill, the cottages, and their fences, each separately if you prefer, the three figures, each by itself, the dog, the cart, and the tulips in the foreground.

For the cutting, use sharp scissors. So much of the success of felt appliqué depends on clean-cut edges that we cannot too strongly stress the need for sharp tools that will make clean smooth incisions. You will note the eye of the figures, the folds in the boy's clothing, the ear- and leg-outlines of the dog, and the edges of the windmill sails. These are not stitches, of course, but little cuts in the fabric, some of them quite narrow—more slashes—but important to the effect. For these, a pair of sharp-pointed embroidery scissors, or a pair of small, sharp cuticle-scissors, or even a strong sharp penknife will be helpful. Cut always on the lines of the individual spots, and remember to allow extra fabric at the edge of a spot which is to be overlapped by another.

By far the most satisfactory way to attach the spots is to hem them on, using stitches so small as to be almost invisible on the right side and rather long underneath. Felt is kind to stitches, for it lets them sink unobtrusively into its texture, and when the sewing stitches are well spaced, they are not in the least obvious. Self-color thread should be used for hemming, and black or white for blindstitching, since the stitch will not show at all along the edge if this stitch is used. Sewed on, the spots cannot be pulled off by inquisitive little fingers. In sewing on the spots, be sure to sew down the edges of slashes also, and openings where there seems any likelihood of edges roughing up.

Minute single-stitches of sewing-cotton are used to make the girl's nostrils, and the two red yarn single-stitches used for the boy's lips. The girls' mouths, however, are mites of red felt, and all the rosy cheeks are little orange discs, which help to give the little figures a singularly toylike appearance. The windows of the cottages and the black portions of the girls' costumes are merely background 'showing through.'

Spots are sure to 'come right' if applied in the following order, which takes due account of successive overlappings. Start with the windmill on the dyke, first placing the water, then the sails of the mill, and lastly the mill itself. Now put on the white fence-spots—all of them. Next apply the house at the left, brown wall first, then green door and orange shutters, now the green gable, the orange eave-line, the window-frame and the roof of which the chimneypot is a part. Start building the second cottage with its pink-tan wall and upper story, add the brown window-frames, the brown door, the blue lintel above it, the eave-line and the other rooflines. And lo, the houses are built.

Now for the figures. Begin with the orange milk-cans, and follow these with the brown cart-sides. Next add what is seen of the wheel. Apply the boy's socks, then his shoes, then his trousers. Leave the top of the latter unstitched at the waistline in back and at the pocket-slash till the blouse is applied when the red edge at waistline can be tucked under the blue and secured, and the red sleeve brought over and tucked into the pocket. Now apply Willum's hair and his cheeks, and finish up with his blue muffler. Add his yarn lips, now, if you wish, or wait till everything else is done—but don't forget them.

If you make Katji next she will be soon done. Put her cap in place first, then her arms, next her dress, then her face (no, it does not tuck under her cap anywhere) so that her chin overlaps the neck of her frock. Now add her cheeks and her mouth, and conclude with her apron. Remember that she has single-stitch nostrils which can be added now.

Geertje is a bit more complicated. Start at her shoe, and overlap that with her skirt-hem, adding next the yellow band and green top. Now apply her hands, putting a tulip into one of them, her thumb overlapping the stem which must be applied before the flower. Slip the handle of her basket over her arm, and apply her arm and neck-sections, and the basket. Now put on her red bodice, and finish with her apron. Now for her head-cap first, face, cheeks, mouth, and single-stitch nostrils.

All that remains are the tulips. For the most part these require the leaves and stems, cut in one, to be applied first, then the blossoms. In one—the orange tulip below the boy's heel—a leaf is left detached till it can be brought over the blossom and sewed down.

The hanging may be left as it is with ring stitched at the back by which to hang it, or it can be 'framed' in gray felt band with mitered corners, using tiny overlapped seams, and rings at the back. ""

Crib Cover

These instructions are adapted from a set first published over seventy years ago. Use a solid-color fabric.

" Here is an adorable crib-cover which everybody will enjoy, so appealing are pretty things for the wee ones. White and pink sateen are used for it—which may be white and blue, of course, if the crib it is to cover affords a resting-place for a tiny son, and one wishes to change the color. Pink is very lovely, however; and when the white are blocks embroidered with matching pink cotton, using three strands in the needle, the little quilt seems all that can be desired. The squares are cut seven inches, the panels are of the same width, and the bands, or border, of pink, are five and one-

Fig. 74. Holland Hanging

quarter inches wide before applying; a plain white lining extends to the band. The cunning little cavorting animals and birds and bugs are all worked in the regular outline-stitch, care being taken to keep the corners sharp and the curves rounded by using neat stitchery. There is a wonder 'go' to each one of the little pictures; just study them a minute and see if you do not discover it. Yet there is very little work in them; one can easily be completed in an hour, or less. The panels, in their nice conventional pattern, are done in running stitch, with the same pink needle; and all the embroidery is completed before the blocks are sewed together.

As some materials shrink a little more one way than the other, when laundered, it is well to take care in keeping all the block with the lengthwise thread running in the same direction when putting them together. There will be no difficulty in doing this if, when cutting, a few basting stitches are run lengthwise in each block. Sew the squares together in strips with quarter-inch seams, press the seams open, sew the strips together, matching the block accurately, and again press the seams. Sew the side panels, then the end-panels and corners, and press all seams open; a great deal depends on careful pressing.

Cut the lining the same size as the patchwork, lay the two parts together, back to back, on a large table or the floor, then pin and baste very carefully, so the work will be absolutely smooth. Sew one edge of the sidebands in place, beginning at the middle of the sides, fold the bands through the middle, after turning in a narrow edge, and whip down on the wrong side, mitering the corners neatly.

To insure the seams staying flat and to give a quilted appearance, run a row of fine stitches parallel with and close to each seam on both sides, using sewing-cotton and a fine needle. If one wishes to make the cover for warmth, a layer of flannel may be placed between the top and the lining; be sure, however, that the flannel has been shrunk. If this interlining is used, the running stitch designs in the panels may be considered as actual quilting patterns, and worked after the spread is made up, the stitches being taken through all thicknesses. In either case, the dainty cover is sure to be a 'thing of beauty and a joy forever.'

The outline stitch used for the embroidery is made by working toward the right, and always keeping the needle pointed to the left. Do not tie a knot in the thread, but take two or three short running-stitches on the dotted line, which will be worked over. Put the needle down on the same line, and bring it up on the last line at the end of the last stitch, always holding the thread on the same side. It is easy to let the thread fall below or on the right side of the line, as in the detail, and this gives a more twisted effect than if the thread is held on the other side; either way is correct, depending upon the effect desired. In making abrupt short turns, the stitches should be very short; otherwise they should be of the same length throughout, this being determined by the quality of the materials used.   **,,**

Fig. 75. Crib Cover Designs

Fig. 75. Crib Cover Designs *(cont.)*

Appliqué Pictures or Hangings

These are fun to do, and any fabric can be used. Collect as wide a range of scraps as possible, and then choose pieces whose pattern or texture suggests the object you wish to represent. Cut out all the shapes in paper first, carefully marking the way they should go. This is most important, as all the pieces applied should run the same way as the background material. Next use these pieces of paper as patterns to cut out the fabric. Place the fabric pieces in position on the background, juggle them around until you have an arrangement which satisfies you, then pin them in place. Tack them along the edges, which can be fastened by using the zigzag attachment on the sewing machine, or fastened down with embroidery stitches, such as blanket stitch, herringbone, or Rumanian stitch. For a picture that is later to be covered with glass, the raw edges need not be turned in. Lines of embroidery can then be worked to link the main shapes, or around the outlines.

In a lake scene there might be flowers on a hill in the foreground, faint light lines on the lake surface. The texture of the material plays an important part in the effect that the picture will give.

Should the picture include children, have them dressed in gingham, milkmaids in sprigged muslin, ladies in brocades, or animals in fur or felt.

Quilted Cushions

The following instructions were given to women who lived at the turn of the century. The material which is used for the cushions is no longer used and therefore it is suggested that you use a smooth thin fabric. Fill the pillows with foam rubber so that the shape of the cushion never varies and the cushion remains firm.

" While sateen can be recommended for these cushions it is by no means taboo to use taffeta or any preferred fabric. All the designs, however, are intended for the ordinary and not the stuffed Italian method of quilting. The work is done with self-color sewing-cotton, using fine running-stitches just as our grandmothers used to do.

The quilting method used should be no problem for the novice. Any worker who will give as much care to her quilting as to her finest embroidery will achieve gratifying results. There is no mystery about the process; one just cuts out a back of self-fabric as big as the muslin design on which the quilting lines appear, and a front the same size and a layer of cotton wadding to match. Then one lays the piece intended for the front, or top, of the cushion, glossy side down, on a flat surface, places the wadding carefully and evenly on top of it, and lays the muslin design, with the design uppermost, on top of the wadding. Then one bastes from corner to corner diagonally, from edge to edge vertically and horizontally, and anywhere else one deems advisable. This prevents the wadding from slipping.

Quilting may, of course, be done in a frame, but with pieces as small as these it may as readily be done 'in the hand.' Run the lines of the design with tiny stitches, being sure to take them through all three thicknesses of the fabric, and working, of course, from the muslin side. Draw the quilting-thread a bit tightly—not so taut as to break it, however—enough to give the work a very slight but very desirable puffiness. This will make the design show up in relief on the fabric background.

With the quilting done and basting removed, all that remains is to add the fabric back. The method by which this is done depends on the style of the cushion.

Boxed cushions can be easily finished in a very workmanlike fashion if one follows the mode of the upholsterer. For the 'box' cut a strip of fabric, perfectly straight, two and a half inches wide, and long enough to go around the cushion, allowing for a seam. Cut also a bias strip, about three-fourths of an inch wide, and long enough to go twice around the cushion, allowing a little extra for 'take-up.'

Of course, one may cut two strips, each long enough to go around the cushions once. Piece the bias strips no oftener than you must. Supply yourself with some medium-weight padding-cord, fold the bias fabric over it, and baste close to the cord. Sew one cord to the top of the cushion and the other to the bottom of the boxing band, stitching close to the cord.

Finishing 'pillow' type cushions is still another matter. They are finished with a double row of cording (not piping, however) all around. Provide yourself with enough medium-weight or fine padding-cord to go twice around the cushion, and cut it in halves. Quilt the inside line of the edge, slip the cord well up against the quilted line, between the muslin and the wadding, and quilt the line below. Slip in the second cord well up against this quilted line, and quilt or baste below it. Then seam the back to the top, leaving most of the bottom open for stuffing. With the pillow in place, turn in the open edges and whip them together.

If the pillow used does not adequately fill the scalloped corners, as may conceivably happen, just tuck some cotton wadding into each one before inserting the pillow, to keep it trim and shapely.

Sateen pillows and cushions may be laundered when their 'innards' have been removed. It is a wise idea to prevent any possible packing or lumping of the wadding in laundering by basting as you did for quilting. This is particularly advantageous when the designs show much 'open' or unquilted surface, as in some of the design pictures.
"

Today's Uses of Patchwork, Appliqué, and Quilting

Crazy patchwork can be used for tablecloths or place mats lined with vinyl so that they can easily be washed. Skirts, blouses, vests, jackets are made in true patchwork. The easiest way to do this is to make up large pieces of crazy patchwork without the third layer, which can then be cut and sewn into the items desired.

A quilted handbag can be made by cutting a paper pattern of the size and shape of the handbag you wish to make. You can buy a plastic or wooden handle at the department store, but you should purchase the handle first and then cut the pattern to fit.

You can also make cushions of crazy-quilt design for informal room, bedspreads and drapes for young people's rooms, and throws and curtains for dens.

Of course, you can also make tablecloths, napkins, and place mats.

Patchwork

Two twelve-inch patches of any design can be used for a place mat when a thin layer of washable foam is placed between. These can be washed easily in a washing machine. A number of squares put together will form a beautiful cloth.

Large patches can be used for various types of handbags and tote bags.

Skirts can be made of patches. It would be very effective to make a skirt with large squares on the bottom and smaller squares as the skirt gradually tapers off to the waist.

Practically any type of pillow, throw, or drape can be made with small squares or any large square, or even squares of various sizes.

Patchwork can be used as a picture, circle skirt for a table, oven mitt, laundry bag, picture frame, tennis racquet cover, napkins, and even dolls.

Clothing and decorations can be made too for a doll family and a doll house.

Appliqué

Many items of clothing or things for the home would be made more attractive if an appliqué or patchwork motif were added to them.

Quilting

Quilting if used judiciously on clothing or on items used in the home makes very unusual pieces.

A Patchwork of Memories

How a New Kind of Quilt Provided A Unique and Treasured Wedding Present for a Bride-to-Be

This article first appeared in the May 1973 issue of Lady's Circle. *Through the gracious permission of the author of the article, Mary Jo Davis, we have been able to reprint it. The author has been kind in supplying additional photographs.*

" 'That's my old doll blanket!' said the bride-to-be as she opened the last of her shower gifts. The 'gift' was a piece of faded flannel scarcely fit for a dustcloth, but a week later it would take its place in a colorful, imaginative patchwork comforter that the young couple would treasure all their lives and pass on to their children with pride.

The making and giving of a memory patchwork combines the modern search for roots and heritage with a love of what is unique and personal. In this case, the shower guests had undergone a treasure hunt for the fabrics which had meant the most to the young people in their growing-up years. They had made tiny patchworks of some, embroidered or appliquéd others; and, with no attention at all paid to color combinations, the result was strikingly beautiful. The squares included part of a football jersey, ballet slipper insoles and ties (carefully appliquéd onto a square of tutu), bits of Scout uniform, a baby bonnet, gym shorts, and an embroidered version of the groom's first car. There were scraps of a prom dress, a patched T-shirt, a freshman beanie, an iron-on patch of a five-year-old's handprint, and many other treasured memories.

At the shower, the guest of honor arranged the gift squares as she wanted them, laying them out on an available floor with help from the guests. A week later, the completed comforter was presented as the shower hostess's wedding gift to the bride.

And it was easy! Here's how:

The memory squares should be checkerboarded with solid-color squares, preferably in black or a very dark shade of green or blue, to set off the various shades of the other patches and give a blending, 'stained-glass' effect. If the same fabric is used for the backing, a matching border will result.

You will need, for a full-sized comforter, 82″ x 97″:

9½ yards of dark, solid-color (but color-fast) no-iron percale, 42″ to 45″ wide
Matching thread
One 90″ x 108″ Polyester comforter batting
Color-fast yarn (synthetic is best) in a contrasting or matching shade
A large-eyed needle
Fifteen 16″ memory squares, to finish to 15″.

Allow half-inch seams throughout. Cut a 3-yard length off the percale. From the remaining 6½ yards, cut lengthwise a 16″ strip and set aside. Cut two 3-yard lengths from the wide strip remaining. Pin and sew the three 3-yard lengths together along selvedges so that the full-width piece is in the center of the three. Press seams open. Trim the side edges so that you have a backing measuring 92″ wide and 108″ long. Press under one half inch on all outside edges.

From the 16″ strip, cut fourteen 16″ squares; cut the fifteenth one from the small remaining scrap. The 'layout' is five squares wide and six squares long. Machine-piece the top together, all five lengthwise strips first, alternating memory squares with solid squares as it was laid out. Press seams open, then join the strips in order, matching all corners. Press these four seams open.

Lay the percale backing out flat, wrong side up, and center the batting on it, smoothing wrinkles. Lay the patchwork on top, right side up. Make sure that the edges are parallel with, and an equal distance from, the backing edges. Trim the batting so that it extends 5″ beyond the quilt top on all sides. Tack the batting edges to the backing with tiny stitches every few inches. Fold the back over the top, turning under the pressed edge, and pin. At the corners, clip for hand mitering and pin.

Now, if you're working on the floor, take off your shoes to work in the middle of the comforter! Pin two pins, crossed, through all three layers at every block corner, starting in the center and working out. These are the tying points. If you feel that more ties are necessary, pin the centers of each of the block edges as well.

When the comforter is completely pinned, you can pick it up, check for unwanted wrinkles on the back, put it on a bed, and admire it. The size can still be changed if you want it narrower or shorter, simply by changing the border width.

All the rest is fun handwork. Have friends come in to help, if you like. The needle must go through all three layers, and all the knots must be square knots. Leave yarn ends at least 1″ long. The hem should be blindstitched by hand, and after it's done, don't forget to tie the block corners that are next to it.

It's a good idea to mention in your shower invitations that the quilt block materials must be washable and color-fast. Sometime in the comforter's long life, someone is going to wash it, even if dry cleaning is thought to be best to begin with.

And if your favorite bride and groom are still part of the bubble-gum set, clip this article and store it away in a hope chest, along with the patches that you save from the special fabrics of their lives.   "

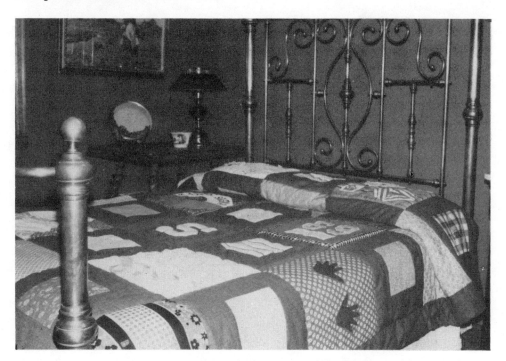

Fig. 76. Memory Patchwork Quilt as Spread on Bed

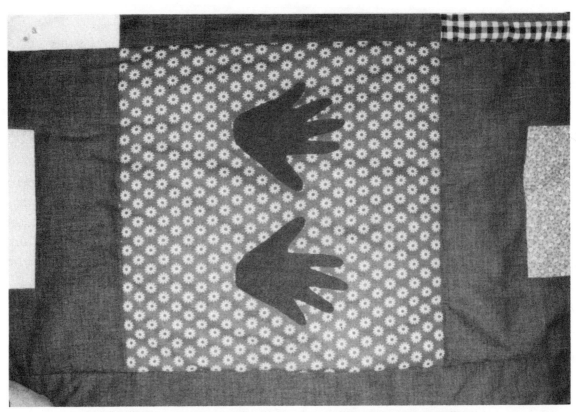

Fig. 77. The Groom's Handprints at Age Five Duplicated in Iron-on Tape

Fig. 78. A Mended T-Shirt, Paint-stained Blue Jeans, and a Friend's Bandanna as Mementoes of College Life

Fig. 79. The Bride's Favorite Doll Clothes Appliquéd onto a Square of the Uniform She Wore on Her First Job

Fig. 80. The Couple's First Car in Appliqué and Embroidery

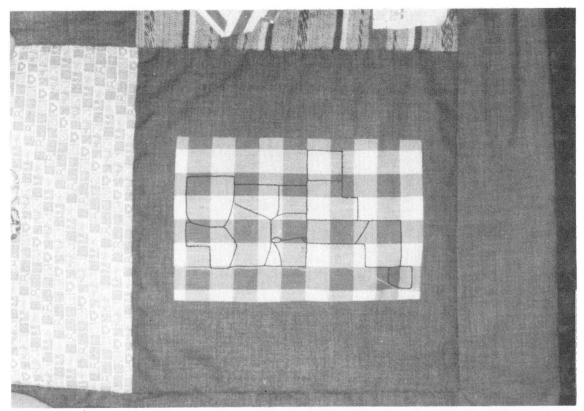

Fig. 81. The Map of the Ranch on Which the Young Couple Will Begin Their Married Life
Embroidered onto Gingham

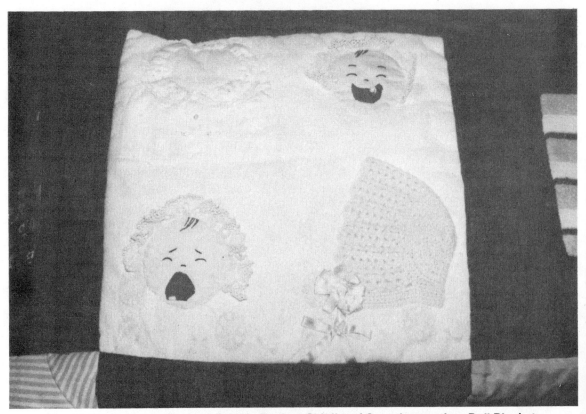

Fig. 82. Handwork Dating from Bride's Earliest Childhood Superimposed on Doll Blanket

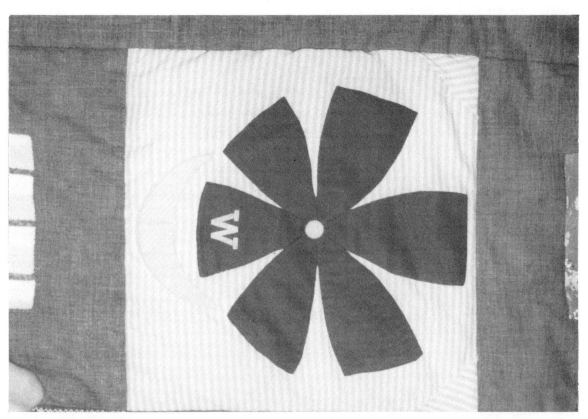

Fig. 83. A Freshman Beanie Expanded to Form a Pretty Pattern on a Special Skirt

Fig. 84. High School and College Athletic Memories Preserved on Fabric from Early Teen Pajamas

Patchwork Tote Bag

You will need fifty 4"-square fabric patches for this 12" x 15" tote bag. Rummage through your drawers, sewing boxes, and other hideaways for scraps, or ask friends and neighbors. The more varied the scraps, the nicer will be the tote bag.

Sew ten separate strips of five patches each together, using ½" seam allowances throughout. Press all the seams. Then sew eight of these strips together to make a rectangle five squares by eight squares and press again.

To make the handles, fold the long edges of each of the two remaining strips ½" toward the center, wrong side in; press, fold in half lengthwise, and stitch the folded edges together on the right side. Sew three more rows of stitches for reinforcement along each handle.

Now split a piece of batting, 25" x 16", into two pieces of the same dimensions but half the original thickness. Pin the batting, smooth side out, to the wrong side of the patchwork piece. Sew around all four sides. Then sew along all the seams of the patches, first the horizontal and then the vertical.

Fold the patchwork piece crosswise, right side in, and sew up the two sides. Turn down the unfinished top edges ½" and stitch all around.

Pin handles to wrong side, lined up with the inside seam of the end squares on each side and extending 1½" down from the top edge. Stitch handles to top edges and around extension as reinforcement.

Fold lining crosswise (you need a piece 17" x 25"), right side in, and sew up the two sides, leaving the end open. Turn and press. Fold under raw edge ½" and press. Fit lining, right side out, over patchwork bag, wrong side out, and stitch top edges together. Turn the whole thing right side out, or you can use the bag reversed with the lining outside and the patchwork inside.

Patchwork Place Mats and Napkins

For each mat sew four 8" x 8" squares of gingham together and add 3" x 15" solid-color rectangles along two sides, using ½" seams. With right sides together, stitch this to a 13" x 19" backing, leaving one side open. Clip seams, turn right side out. Press; top stitch ½" all around.

For napkins cut 18" squares of gingham and fringe edges all around.

Use four colors of gingham for each mat and then use the various colors of the gingham for the napkins.

Basic Patchwork

A 5" square is a good size for anything you wish to make. Just remember that the size depends on what you wish to do with the patchwork.

Basic construction is as follows:

1. Cut all squares at 5″. This will allow you to have a ½″ seam allowance on all sides, and the finished square will measure 4″ x 4″.

2. Lay out the patches so that the overall pattern is pleasing. The more of a variety you have in the patches, the more colorful will be the finished product.

3. Pin the patches in rows, left to right. Then pick up each row in its proper sequence.

4. Sew all patches together, using the ½″ allotted seam allowance.

5. Iron all seams open (flat). You are now ready to cut any shape you wish.

6. Use this basic patchwork for the following items.

Oven Mitt

Make the patchwork and then cut out the shape of an oven mitt by tracing the one you now have in your kitchen.

Next cut from the same pattern one terry-cloth mitt, two felt insulators, and two linings.

Construct by sewing all layers together, making certain that the terry cloth is the bottom layer and the patchwork the top layer. After you have it all put together, use a bias tape of a contrasting color completely around all the seams and top.

Laundry Bag

1. Construct two patchwork sides, each five squares by seven squares.

2. At the top of each side fold in the patchwork ¾″ and hem either by hand or machine. This will give space for the drawstring.

3. Stitch two pieces together on the remaining three sides.

4. Thread a ribbon or cord around the top and you have a very colorful laundry bag.

Patchwork Pillow

These directions are for a 16″-square pillow.

1. Make two sides of patchwork, each four squares by four squares.

2. Put a zipper in one of the four sides and stitch around the other three. You now have a pillow.

Patchwork Tablecloth

For a 52″ x 52″ tablecloth:

1. Make one large square of patches, thirteen patches by thirteen patches of the 4″ patch.

2. Now buy a vinyl plastic 52″ x 52″ tablecloth in a solid color or any print.

3. Sew the top and the vinyl bottom together at the edges and then finish off by using a bias tape around the four sides.

The tablecloth will be reversible and washable.

Picture Frame

1. Make patchwork strips 1″ wider than the exact dimensions of sides of picture frame. This gives a ½″ seam allowance on each side of the strip.

2. Glue the two vertical strips down; then glue the horizontal pieces in place. Overlap material at corners, or, if you can successfully miter the corners, do so.

3. Trim the corners with rick rack or braid to hide the seams.

If you wish a more sophisticated frame, use materials such as silk, velvets, gold braid for the basis.

Reversible Baby Quilt

A most interesting quilt for a newborn is one that is made blue on one side and pink on the other. You can use any sort of washable material in solids, prints, or ginghams. Since you are probably going to make it before the baby is born, you cannot miss with this reversible quilt.

From both the pink and blue, cut a piece measuring 38″ x 54″. With the right sides together, lay the two pieces on a table and place the batting on top. Pin and stitch through all three layers, ½″ from edges around three sides and four corners. Trim corners.

Turn inside out. Fold in seam allowance of open section and stitch. Use a 2″ grosgrain ribbon to cover the side seams so that one half of the width of the ribbon is sewn on the pink and the other half of the ribbon is sewn on the blue. You can use either pink or blue ribbon unless you can find a pink-and-blue checked ribbon, found in some stores.

Quilt the cover in old-fashioned "tacking." With heavy thread, take small stitches through all three quilt layers about 5″ apart and then fasten 3½″ pieces of ribbon in the center of the ribbon onto the quilt. Knot the ribbon to form bows. Do this to both sides of the quilt, using pink ribbon on the blue and blue ribbon on the pink as a contrast.

Contemporary Quilts

Are you interested in making a truly contemporary quilt? Here are the photographs of two of them developed by Contemporary Quilts, of Memphis, Tennessee.

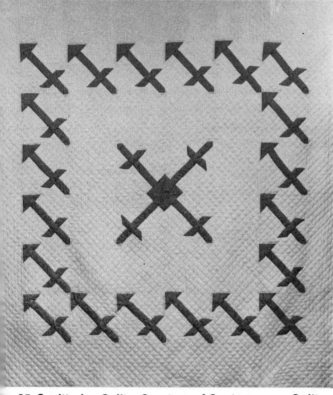

g. 85. Sagittarius Quilt—*Courtesy of Contemporary Quilts*

Fig. 86. Libra Quilt—*Courtesy of Contemporary Quilts*

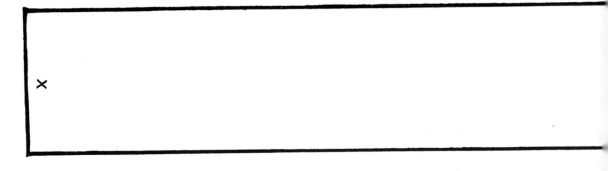

SAGITTARIUS
(Born Nov. 23—Dec. 21)

A pieced and appliqued quilt. Approximately 88" x 88". Designed and copyrighted by *Marilyn Califf, 1971.*

MATERIALS: 45" width
6 yds. yellow
1 yd. medium blue or aqua
1 Dacron batt, 90" x 108"
6 yds. lining material
3 pkgs. commercial binding, or make your own from excess yellow
2 spools yellow thread (500 yds.)
1 spool blue or aqua (500 yds.) thread

DIRECTIONS:
Cut yellow material into 64 blocks 11" square.
Cut blue or aqua material into pattern pieces as follows:
  24 triangles for arrow heads
  24 strips for arrow shanks
  48 small pieces for cross sections on arrow shanks

Trace pattern of Sagittarius sign from this sheet. Paste tracing on smooth side of fine sandpaper or cardboard. Cut out and use pattern to cut listed number of pieces.

Place blue pattern pieces on 24 yellow blocks, pinning in place as you go. See diagram for position of pieces. Us blue thread, overcast with narrow open zig-zag stitch for machine applique. If appliquing by hand, turn edges of 1/8th inch under and baste in place with contrasting color thread. Applique by machine with close zig-zag or by with decorative stitch.

Assemble top by joining 4 appliqued blocks together with points of arrows meeting. See diagram. Make ¼" se Extreme care must be taken to see that the arrows meet correctly. You may sew blocks together into strips foll order as in diagram. Then sew strips together as in diagram. An alternate method would be to add blocks to the four and work from the center to the outer edge.

Divide lining material equally and seam together to make a lining 108" x 90". Trim to 88" x 88". Stretch lin in frame and tack tightly. Spread Dacron batt over lining, smooth out wrinkles, trim. Stretch top over batt and frame. With a yardstick and hard lead pencil draw quilting lines 1" apart diagonally across the top in two direc Do now mark across the Sagittarius pattern of arrows. If machine quilting is to be done, baste quilt securely an remove from frame. To quilt by hand, no basting is necessary, and leave quilt in frame. Quilt around Sagittarius design first, then quilt along marked lines starting at the center and work outward.

When quilting is finished, bind with commercial binding or some you have cut from excess yellow material.

Your sunny Sagittarian will welcome this quilt. You have made him an heirloom!

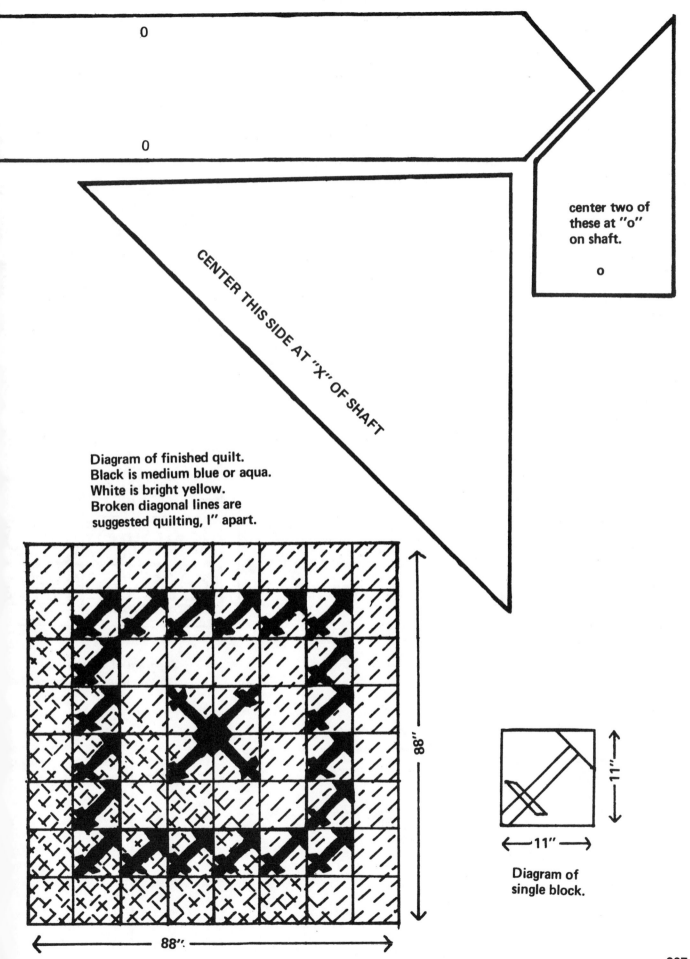

o

o

center two of
these at "o"
on shaft.

o

CENTER THIS SIDE AT "X" OF SHAFT

Diagram of finished quilt.
Black is medium blue or aqua.
White is bright yellow.
Broken diagonal lines are
suggested quilting, l" apart.

88"

88"

11"

11"

Diagram of
single block.

Fig. 87. Pattern for Sagittarius Quilt—*Courtesy of Contemporary Quilts*

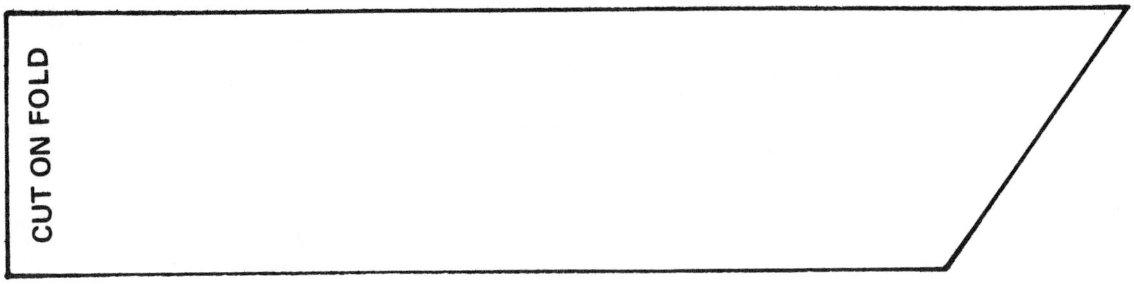

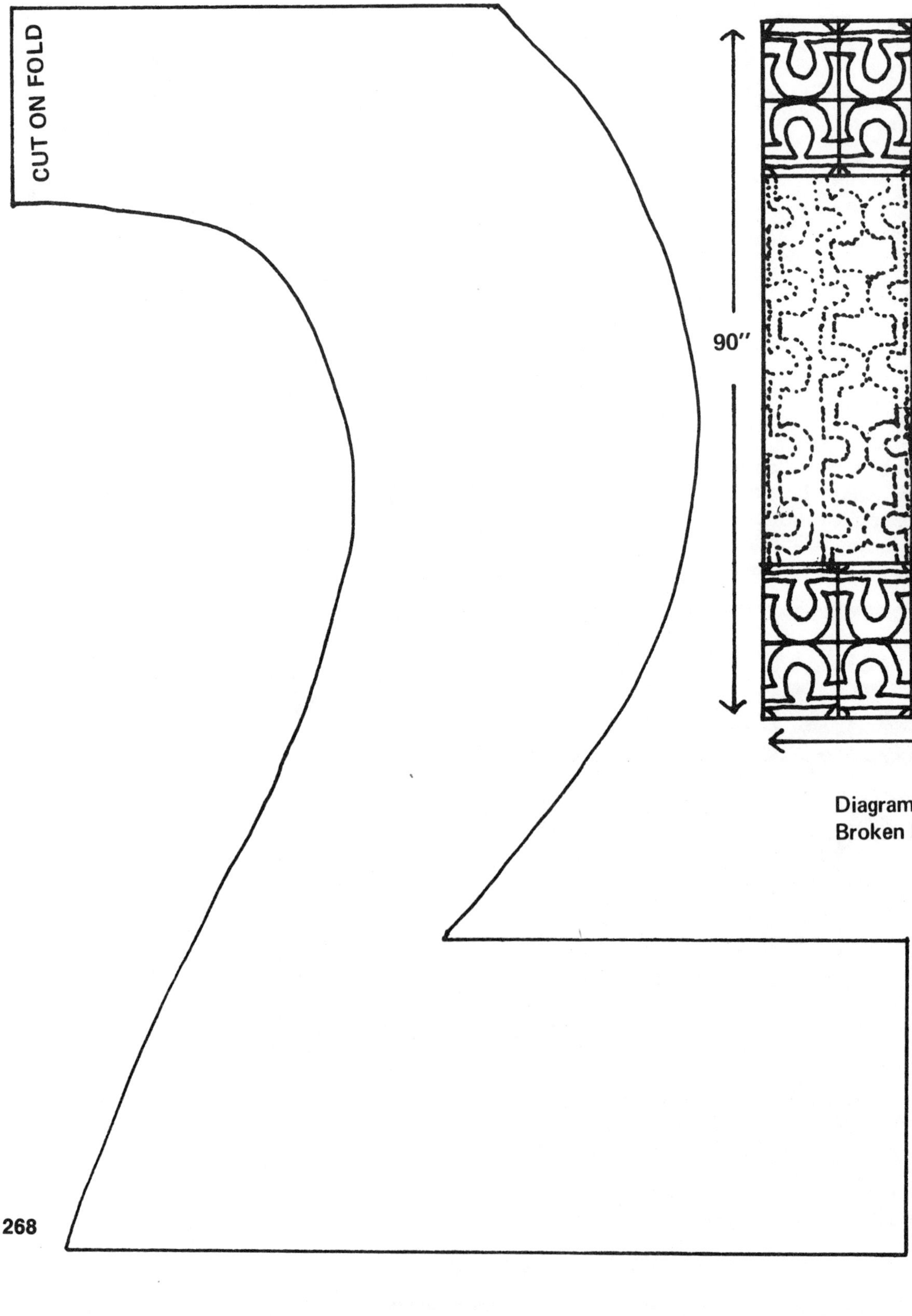

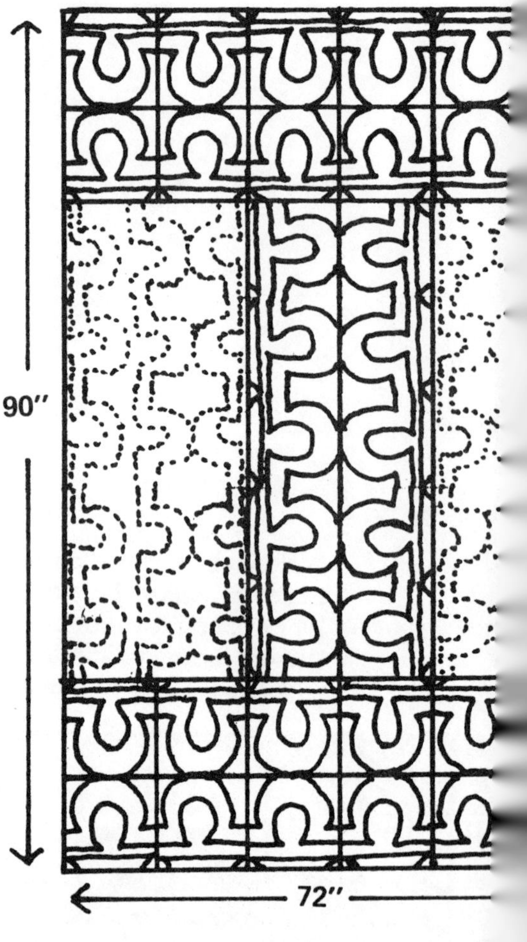

90"

72"

Diagram of finished quilt.
Broken lines are suggested q

LIBRA

Born Sept. 24—Oct. 23
(approximately 72" x 90")
A pieced and Appliqued quilt, designed and copyrighted
by Marilyn Califf, 1971

MATERIALS: 45" width

3 yds. black
3 yds. coral or shell pink
1 Dacron batt, 90" x 108"
6 yds. lining material
3 pkgs. bias binding or make binding from black material
4 spools coral, 500 yds. each (if appliquing with 3/16ths inch
zig-zag on machine, if appliquing by hand, only 1 spool is needed.)
2 spools black, 500 yds. each, for quilting.

DIRECTIONS:

Trace pattern of Libra sign from this sheet. Paste tracing on smooth side of fine sandpaper or cardboard. Cut out and use pattern to cut 34 Libra signs from Coral fabric. From black material cut 34 blocks 10" x 12". This includes ¼" seam allowance. Be sure to place Libra pattern on fold.

Position the top of the rounded part of the Libra sign even with a 12" edge of a block and pin in place. Place the rectangular piece with the pointed ends even with the other 12" edge of the block and pin. See diagram. If appliquing by machine, use coral thread and overcast edges of pattern. Then applique with wide (3/16ths) zig-zag stitch. If applique is to be done by hand turn under edges of Libra about 1/8th inch and baste in place with contrasting color thread. Applique with coral thread and then remove basting.

Join blocks as shown in diagram. There will be 3 sections. The end sections contain 2 strips of 12 blocks. The center section contains 2 strips of 10 blocks. Join strips to form sections. But do not join sections to form main body of top, yet. Extreme caution must be used at this point. Cut from the remaining black material 2 pieces 28" x 60". This includes ¼" seam allowance. Sew a black piece to each side of the center section with symbols. To join the two end sections to this center section, match center seam of center section with center seams (between 3rd and 4th blocks) of end sections and pin in place. Sew together. If necessary, trim edges of black fabric to even with end sections.

Divide 6 yds. lining equally in two and seam two pieces together. Trim to get lining 72" x 90". Stretch lining on frame tightly. Spread filler over lining, smooth out wrinkles, trim. Stretch top over filler and tack to frame. At this point take the pattern used for cutting the Libra sign and a pencil with white lead or any color that will show up on black and starting next to the center appliqued section, outline the pattern for quilting lines. There will be 3 lines of outlined patterns on each large black section.

If quilting is to be done by machine, baste the three layers securely and remove from frame. If quilting is done by hand, no basting is necessary. Quilt in frame. Quilt around the Libra sign both of which is appliqued and marked with pencil.

Bind with commercial binding or cut your own from black fabric. All Libras will appreciate this balanced, harmonious design.

Congratulations, you've got a family heirloom!

Fig. 88. Pattern for Libra Quilt—*Courtesy of Contemporary Quilts*

Potholders

The potholders in Figures 90, 92, and 94 were designed by Betty James, who is well-known for her original designs. She will be happy to supply you with information on her designs if you write to Betty James, 105 Cedar Road, Severna Park, Maryland 21146.

Betty James suggests many uses for potholders:

"Besides using your quilted patchwork and/or appliqué potholder in the kitchen to grab a hot pan, you can display one or more of them near the stove for mere decoration. Or you can piece several blocks together and finish as a chair pad or bench pad.

"Several of them sewed together, either the same pattern or a gay hodgepodge of patterns, can be made into a tote bag complete with crochet or macramé handle.

"A number of them can be arranged artistically as an antique picture frame of huge dimensions to hang in a family room of colonial decor. You can hang some of them around the room from beams. This forms an interesting collection of patterns which will never be complete, as the combination of colors and arrangements is endless."

Lela's Choice block: There is a story behind the name of this pattern. Betty James tells us that her grandmother made and sent her a patchwork pillow (see photo) when she was in her early nineties and just before her eyesight failed com-

Fig. 89. Patchwork Pillow Made by Lela Duvall, Grandmother of Betty James—*Courtesy of Betty James*

pletely. A daughter of pioneers, who lived in Indian Territory and then in Oklahoma for most of her life, she had made many quilts. She followed a pattern for cutting, but in putting it together, she often ignored the pattern because of the necessity of using whatever materials were at hand.

Betty James named the quilt pattern Lela's Choice since her grandmother's maiden name was Lela Dameron. Her grandmother is now close to one hundred years of age.

Allow ¼″ for seams on each piece.

Block finishes to 7½″ square.

Cut 8 B from light plain color; 8 B-1 from dark print #1; 4 A-1 from light print; 1 A from dark print #2 (see pattern on p. 272).

Piece the block.

Cut back from plain color or white same size as block, for backing.

Cut double thickness of batting same size as block.

Place batting between block and backing and baste around edges, from corner to corner and from side to side.

Quilt through all thicknesses around pattern pieces.

Trim edges even.

Bind with 1″ bias of one of the materials and make hanging loop attached at one corner.

Fig. 90. Lela's Choice Potholder—*Courtesy of Betty James*

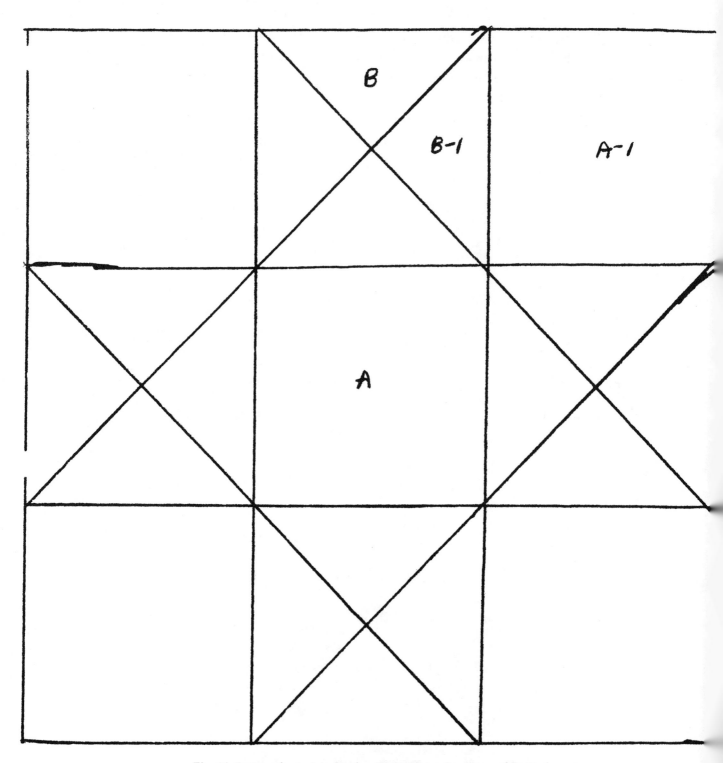

Fig. 91. Pattern for Lela's Choice Potholder—_Courtesy of Betty James_

Job's Trouble block made into potholder:

Finishes to 8″ square block, allowing ½″ seam allowance on all pieces.

Cut 4 A from white of unbleached muslin; 2 B from light print or plain; 2 C from dark print or plain (see pattern on p. 274).

Follow instructions for Lela's Choice quilt block.

Fig. 92. Job's Trouble Potholder—*Courtesy of Betty James*

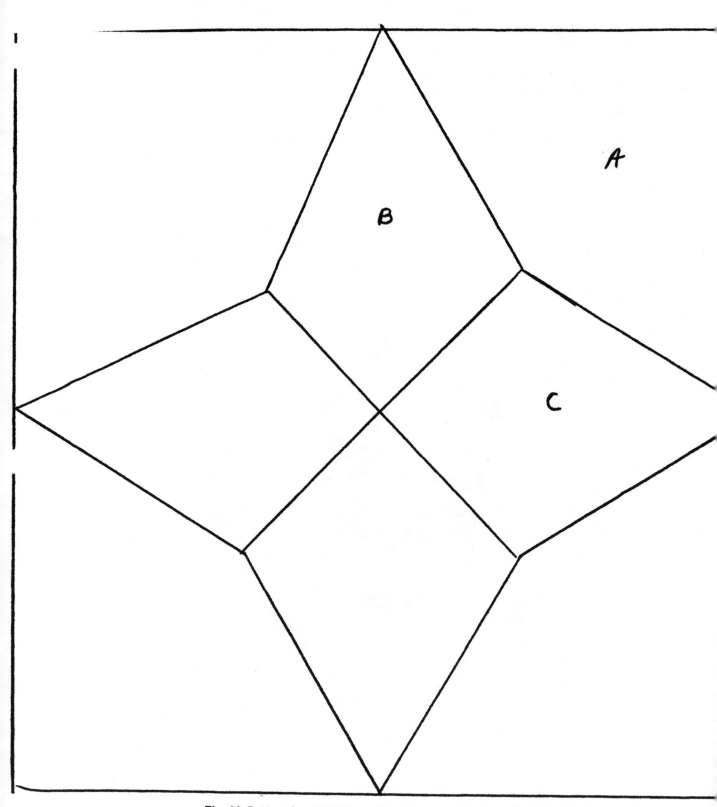

Fig. 93. Pattern for Job's Trouble Potholder—*Courtesy of Betty James*

274

Shoo Fly block made into potholder:

Finishes to 7½" square block allowing ½" seams on all pieces.

Cut 4 A from white or unbleached muslin; 1 B from dark or light print; 4 A-1 from white or unbleached muslin; 4 B-1 from dark or light print (see pattern on p. 276).

Follow instructions for Lela's Choice quilt block.

Fig. 94. Shoo Fly Potholder—*Courtesy of Betty James*

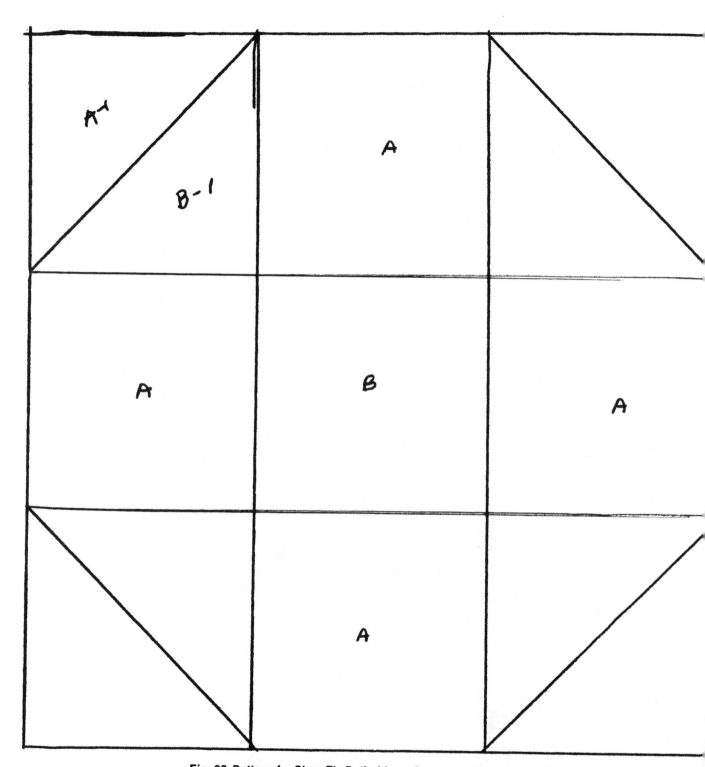

Fig. 95. Pattern for Shoo Fly Potholder—*Courtesy of Betty James*

McCall's Needlework

McCall's Needlework & Craft Publications have been kind enough to supply us with the three following photographs, all of which illustrate various types of patchwork. If you are interested in obtaining information and directions for any of the items, write to *McCall's Needlework & Crafts Magazine,* 230 Park Avenue, New York, N.Y. 10017.

Figure 96: Patchwork Quilt
Figure 97: Patchwork Animals
Figure 98: Patchwork Tablecloth, Cushion, and Wall Hanging.

Fig. 96. Patchwork Quilt—*Courtesy of* McCall's Needlework & Crafts Magazine

Fig. 97. Patchwork Animals—*Courtesy of* McCall's Needlework & Crafts Magazine

Fig. 98. Patchwork Tablecloth, Cushion, and Wall Hanging—*Courtesy of* McCall's Needlework & Crafts Magazine

Two More Designs

Mrs. Eloise Brittingham, of Plainfield, Indiana, is another quilter who has been very kind and helped us by giving permission to use two of her designs and patterns.

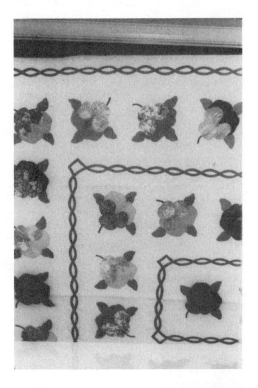
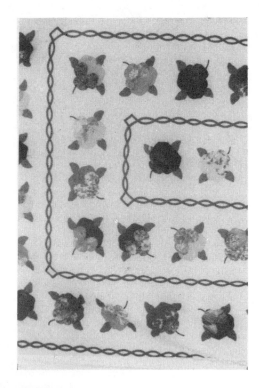

Fig. 99. Pansy Quilt—*Courtesy of Eloise Brittingham*

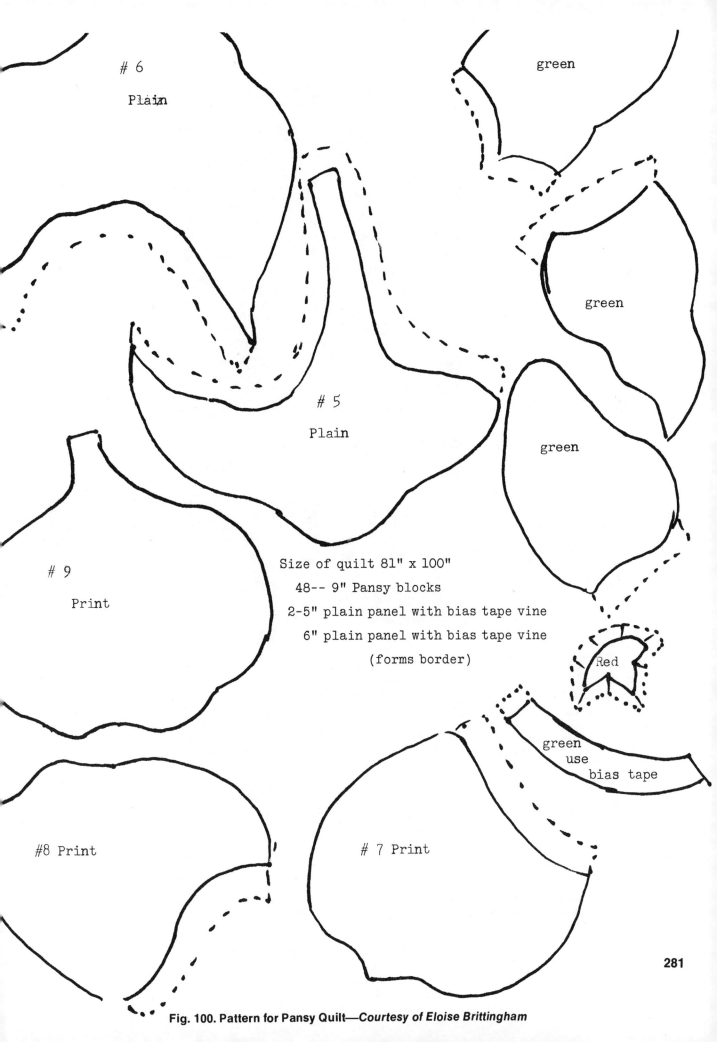

6
Plain

green

green

green

5
Plain

green

9
Print

Size of quilt 81" x 100"
48-- 9" Pansy blocks
2-5" plain panel with bias tape vine
6" plain panel with bias tape vine
(forms border)

Red

green
use
bias tape

#8 Print

7 Print

Fig. 100. Pattern for Pansy Quilt—*Courtesy of Eloise Brittingham*

Fig. 101. Expanded Star Quilt—*Courtesy of Eloise Brittingham*

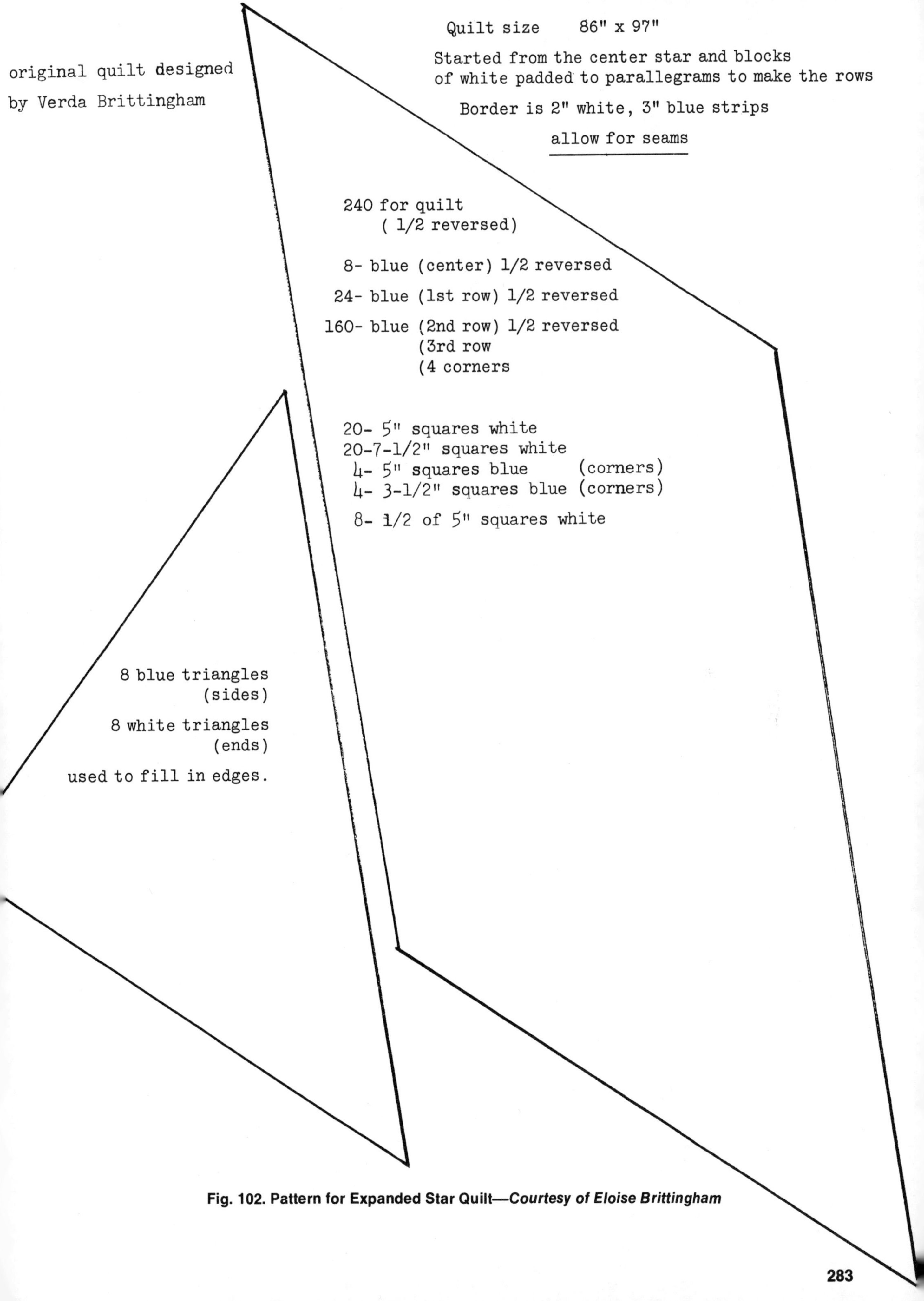

original quilt designed
by Verda Brittingham

Quilt size   86" x 97"

Started from the center star and blocks
of white padded to parallegrams to make the rows

Border is 2" white, 3" blue strips

allow for seams

240 for quilt
   (1/2 reversed)

8- blue (center) 1/2 reversed

24- blue (1st row) 1/2 reversed

160- blue (2nd row) 1/2 reversed
       (3rd row
       (4 corners

20- 5" squares white
20-7-1/2" squares white
 4- 5" squares blue   (corners)
 4- 3-1/2" squares blue (corners)

8- 1/2 of 5" squares white

8 blue triangles
   (sides)

8 white triangles
   (ends)

used to fill in edges.

Fig. 102. Pattern for Expanded Star Quilt—*Courtesy of Eloise Brittingham*

283

Part IV
Quilts on Display

Chapter 14

Collecting Quilts

OLD QUILTS ARE being collected as examples of a practical art that lives on. You can do much with a quilt today. It can be draped on a wall or over a railing or put to its original use on a bed.

Not long ago many dealers did not stock quilts, but today dealers are buying from owners, fairs, and other dealers. Auction galleries, large and small, and traveling auctioneers are careful to include quilts in their listings. Even tops are eagerly bought just for their own beauty, although there are some who use these tops for skirts or dresses, which is truly a great waste of an exciting art. There also are well-done antique single blocks to be found.

With the increase in demand has come a sharp increase in price especially in the last year or two. Time was when a quilt at a country auction would bring in $5.00 to $25.00 if the quilt was an outstanding piece of work. Now some of the older quilts command hundreds of dollars.

A true collector of quilts looks for exciting graphic design as well as elegant needlework. The quilt that has both is the prize. Value is measured by uniqueness of design, quality of stitchery, condition (many old quilts have never been used or washed), interesting fabrics or an extraordinary border. While the immediate charm of a quilt comes from its color, its design, and its fabric, that appeal is augmented by its history, which may be personal in its association but which also may recollect important aspects of our national history.

One can date an appliqué quilt back to early days before the Civil War if it is found down South. Few appliqué quilts were made in the North until after 1870 except by those women who were affluent and had both the time and money. Appliqué quilts in the South were made for show and not utility.

The pieced quilt, however, had more charm even at the time that it was not yet considered an antique and was used as a bed covering in the family. Children enjoyed having pieced quilts for covers because there were so many stories that could be told to them about each piece of material when it was part of someone's clothing and about what happened to the person when he wore that outfit.

When one is looking at an antique quilt, one sees that the very early colors tend to be muted or soft or else to become so with age. A bright color usually means that the quilt was made recently with aniline dyes and when mechanized printing was available. Prints of more than fifty years ago were also muted. They were not bright and harsh. The tones are not the same if you try to duplicate a piece of calico of fifty or more years ago.

One can establish the age of the quilt by establishing the date of the cloth used in the quilt. During the colonial period cloth used in quilts were either homespun or imported. Homespun is easily recognizable since handspun thread shows irregularities which recur at random and the weaving is not even, with some places being woven tighter or looser than others. Thus any quilt of homespun would be prior to 1820 with certainty.

If the quilt were made of other materials a clue to the age of the quilt can be found by reading the advertisements of dry goods stores. The various types of materials were usually listed in the advertisements and therefore you could date the quilt if you were to find the period in which that particular type of material was sold. After all, the quilts were made of remnants left over from dressmaking or else from worn-out clothing.

The Victorian quilt was usually a fancy one made of silk, velvet, or satin. However, it would be wise to examine one of these quilts very carefully since the silks of that period were often saturated with shellac to make them stiff enough for the ladies' demands for stiff skirts and sleeves in the fashion of the day. If one handles that type of material a little too hard, the entire cloth can disintegrate.

If one looks at the quilting, it might help. Quilting patterns usually followed patterns found on other articles of the period, such as those on furniture, cotton-print piece goods. For example, fruit was very popular in designs from 1820 to 1860 and it would be found on practically anything that needed a decorative touch at that time. Look at various books of decorations and you may find the period of the quilting.

Quilting is also significant in determining the quality of the quilt. On a plain background having for ornamentation only the quilting, the patterning becomes very important, as well as the stitching and padding if the Italian-style or trapunto quilting is done.

The quilting designs of pieced and appliquéd quilts are likely to be less obvious, but nonetheless important in quality. In the simplest procedure the quilting follows the pattern or elements of it; but, especially where there are sizable plain or open areas, additional patterning adds to the beauty and the value. At all times the quilting should be fine and even, with as many as twelve to fifteen stitches per inch. A truly fine quilting might have stitches only ⅛″ to ¼″ apart.

The stitches can be a help in dating the quilt. Tiny regular stitches will place the quilt before 1820, since in colonial days the young girl was taught to sew as part of her formal education. She spent several hours a day at it, both at home and in school. Her sewing was perfect, each stitch the same size.

Before the middle 1800's quilts were often made eight to ten feet square because the beds were larger and concealed a trundle bed slid under them in the daytime. Beds also were higher; therefore, to cover the bed meant that large-size quilts had to be made. As the fashion in beds changed, the quilts became smaller in the late 1800's. Today these old quilts are needed for king-sized beds.

If one looks at the filler of cotton and finds seeds left in, the quilts was made prior to the time that Eli Whitney perfected his cotton gin in 1793. After that quilts made in the South had fewer seeds and often none because of the gin removing the seeds. On the other hand, those quilts made in the North contained fillers with seeds, since the housewife in the North had no time to remove them and the gin was not in use there. After 1830 or so it is not easy to date the quilt because of its filler, since both sections of the country had cotton that was comparatively free of seeds.

If one is really interested in collecting antique quilts, remember that stains or wear should not destroy the value of a quilt if the color and workmanship is perfect. Look at some of the quilt exhibitions that are now to be found in various art museums throughout the country, and you will see that this is true.

Chapter 15

Premium and Museum Quilts

ALTHOUGH FEW PERSONS know it, at one stage of the quilting boom in the late 1800's and early 1900's, women were making quilts from premiums that they collected. With each purchase of flour, sugar, or tea, the housewife collected a small square, which was either a flag or a banner. At the same time small flags were given with each purchase of tobacco.

Although the feminine smoker was then in a very small minority, the tobacco people appealed to her at that time as they do now. They distributed these silk premiums to use as decorations on pillow tops, table covers, quilts, et cetera. Literature was circulated to illustrate and encourage such use.

Mrs. Robert Reed, of Harvard, Massachusetts, found one such quilt in her mother's attic (see p. 232). It was made by her great-grandmother, Mrs. Simon Foster Cooley, born in 1824 and died in 1918.

The quilt is six feet square. The light areas are unbleached cotton. The center section depicts the main buildings of the 1876 Centennial International Exhibition in Philadelphia. In the circles are the Main Exhibition Building, Machinery Hall, Agricultural Hall, and Horticultural Hall. These circles surround the Memorial Art Gallery. Strolling in front of this gallery are elegant ladies and gentlemen of the era, the ladies in long skirts and carrying parasols; there are a few horses and carriages of various sorts. The eagle at the top of this center section has its individual feathers all outlined with quilting stitches. Surrounding this center square are eight other squares, two plain, two with a narrow flag border, and four containing American flags of thirty-nine stars (see p. 232).

Around the entire edge, and also around the four corner flags, are rows of little (2 x 3-inch) flags of nations of the world as they existed in 1876. Some of these are Germany, Austria, China, Persia, and Russia. Each little flag is named.

The blue and red colors are still bright, but the green has turned a sort of khaki shade.

There might be a few quilts around that were made from the premiums collected with various purchases, but then each one of the quilts would be different since no two women made the quilt in a similar manner. Each woman who tackled the project no doubt had her own ideas.

Quilts are now to be found in the various museums and historical society exhibits throughout the country. There are hundreds of quilts to be seen but the author has reproduced just a few of them here. What follows is a sampling of the various types of quilts that have been described in this book.

Fig. 103. Log Cabin Quilt—*Courtesy of Hennepin County Historical Society, Minneapolis, Minn.*

The Log Cabin design uses contrasting rectangular pieces of light and dark patches of wool and cotton throughout the quilt. Each block is built around a center square and four strips and sewn around the square overlapping the previous strip, then folded over and pressed down. These narrow pieces represent the logs of the early settlers. The contrast of light and dark material must be very evident; otherwise the design will not stand out. Dark patches are used on one diagonal side of the square and lighter are used on the opposite side. Patterns can be varied by placing the light and dark material at different angles. Traditionally, no border is used on this quilt.

This quilt is 88 inches by 72 inches in measurement; ten squares long and eight squares wide. It has a red cotton lining; at the intersections of the squares and in the center of each square it is tied with red yarn. The material used is checkered, flowered, striped, and plain, and the colors used include red, blue, black, green, beige, and brown.

Fig. 104. Hexagonal Quilt—*Courtesy of Hennepin County Historical Society, Minneapolis, Minn.*

Note the color contrast. Hexagon blocks of light- and dark-colored wools are pieced together in a diamond shape. The whole work is carried out with one shape—the hexagon, the six-sided figure. Each complete diamond pattern is composed of 25 hexagons which are sewed to the next 25-hexagon grouping. The hexagon offers a very wide field of design and, when used *en masse,* gives a very rich effect.

Fig. 105. Churn Dash—*Courtesy of Hennepin County Historical Society, Minneapolis, Minn.*

This pattern is also known as Monkey Wrench. Each square is 8½ inches square and is composed of 4 square pieces and 4 triangular pieces having a 3-inch base and 2½-inch sides. Latticed strips of dark orange calico 2¼ inches wide separate the squares, but also serve to tie the whole design together. Each square has a light background. The complete quilt, measuring 80 inches long and 66 inches wide, is beautifully made. The cotton materials are as fresh as if they were new. The lining is of unbleached muslin. The delight of this work of art is the perfect quilting that is evident on the underside.

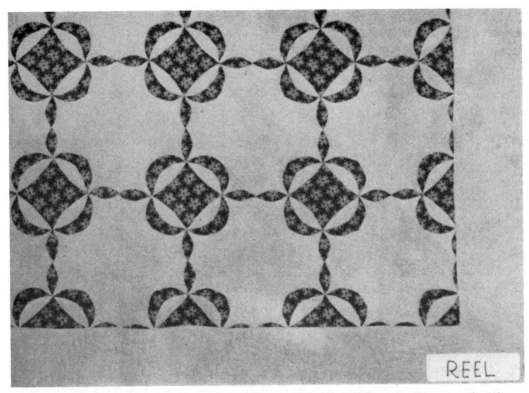

Fig. 106. Reel Quilt—*Courtesy of Hennepin County Historical Society, Minneapolis, Minn.*

This quilt measures 84 inches by 92 inches, with 4 complete designs one way and 5 complete designs the other way. The 9-inch border is elaborately hand-quilted with undulating vines. The quilting is puffed out on the top by pushing pieces of cotton in through the threads underneath, then carefully rearranging the disturbed threads so no evidence of this work is seen.

The reel pattern is pieced on a square and joined together with plain white squares. The center is diamond-quilted, and the border is quilted to follow the meandering vines.

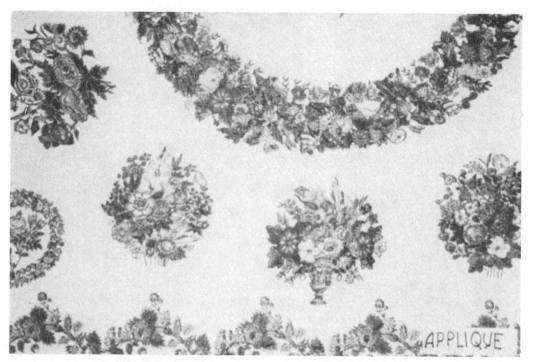

Fig. 107. Appliqué Quilt—*Courtesy of Hennepin County Historical Society, Minneapolis, Minn.*

This quilt is a flowered chintz appliquéd pattern, 108 inches square. Often these were made very large to be thrown over the high featherbeds, not for warmth, but for the elegant look. The center appliqué is a wreath 50 inches in diameter; its center has a 19-inch solid flower motif stitched on the material. Many different flowers are used, including roses, pansies, and daisies in the colors of yellow, red, blue, and green on the white background. The motifs used include three urns, one large wreath, two medium wreaths, and three smaller wreaths scattered on the quilt in a very definite pattern. The colors are very bright and the finish on the chintz is very new and shiny. The white lining is made up of 24 6-inch strips plus a 4-inch strip, and the quilt top is three strips of 30 inches and one of 18 inches. The edges are hand-turned.

The entire quilt is diamond-quilted ⅜ inch apart, which means that diagonal lines of quilting intersect in the shape of a diamond. The decoration is of two kinds: the appliqué and the quilting. The charm of perfect appliqué is to keep it free from puckers. It is the delicate and accurate appliquéing of the patches that makes such a distinguished piece.

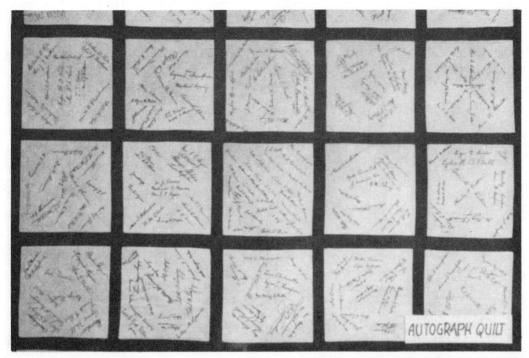

Fig. 108. Autograph Quilt—*Courtesy of Hennepin County Historical Society, Minneapolis, Minn.*

The 1850s and 1860s were the years of the sentimental quilts. In this category fall the Friendship Quilt, the Presentation Quilt, and the Autograph Quilt.

Six hundred and twenty-five people signed the cover of this quilt in ink, and one maker very carefully embroidered each name in red embroidery floss on the white squares, which total forty-two. It is six squares wide and seven squares long, with a width of 67 inches and a length of 80 inches. The 10-inch squares are separated by 1½-inch strips of red cotton. The backing or lining of this quilt is a red-and-white plaid material edged with a red binding.

Evidently this quilt was not made to be used, as it is not interlined for warmth, and the white material must be handled very carefully to prevent it from becoming soiled.

Fig. 109. Victorian Crazy Quilt—*Courtesy of Hennepin County Historical Society, Minneapolis, Minn.*

This quilt is truly unique. The cover of the quilt contains beautifully embroidered sayings, poems, tributes, name badges, objects, memories, relatives, and dates. It measures approximately 76 inches by 78 inches and is finished the edge with a 2½-inch moss green ruffle around the entire quilt. It is composed of six squares lengthwise and squares crosswise, each one measuring 12 to 13 inches square. It is a heterogeneous collection of irregularly shap pieces of silk, wool, velvet, and ribbon joined together with elaborate stitchery. Usually each piece was stitched or square of plain material, which often was cotton flannel. This flannel base would then eliminate the need of a filli before the backing or lining was added. The first piece was placed on the square in the center or the corner ri side up and basted; then the subsequent pieces were placed face down and stitched, and then turned right side ready for the addition of another piece.

The exceptionally fine stitching on this work is composed of feather stitching, outline, buttonholing, the sa stitch, and the chevron stitch. One of the difficulties of this type of work was to keep the surface flat, because of numerous types of material used and the various sizes and shapes to be fastened down to make it ready for the namental stitches which were used to unify the entire top surface.

Each square must have been given to a different family to do with as they wished and then returned to the mak to have her put them all together as a unit. One square has ribbons from Abraham Lincoln, General U. S. Grant, a the American flag; another square commemorates Labor Day of 1894; a poem says, "Work for the Good, Pray Success, Wait for the Result"; one square contains the baby's first cloak, with the date June 11, 1860; and one compl square is dedicated to the pets of one family: "Crippled Jack, our blackbird; Poor Old Shep; the lost kitty."

This quilt is an outstanding example of the artistry, labor, and thriftiness that our ancestors lovingly applied quiltmaking.

Fig. 110. Patchwork Quilt—*Courtesy of Louisiana State Museum, New Orleans*

This is a primitive patchwork with embroidered or appliquéd designs of flowers, insects, birds, animals, and people.

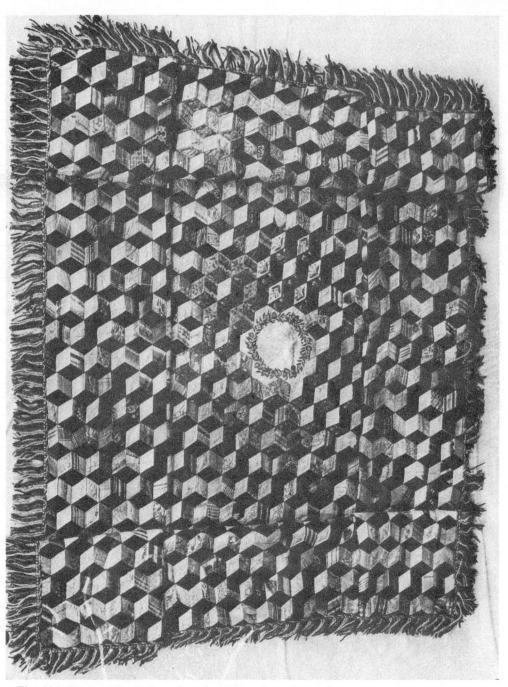

Fig. 111. Zachary Taylor's Quilt—*Courtesy of Louisiana State Museum, New Orleans*
The quilt was presented to Taylor by the women of Danville, Virginia. In the center is the inscription "General Zachary Taylor presented by the Ladies of the Danville Working Society as a Slight Testimony of their Admiration for one not less distinguished for his clemency and forebearance than for his valor and patriotism 1848." Scattered throughout the quilt are the signatures of the various ladies making the presentation.

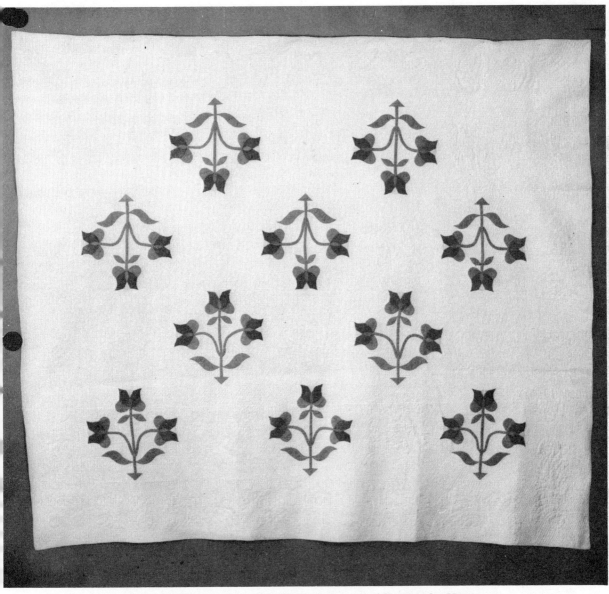

Fig. 112. Single Tulip, 1825-1850—*Courtesy of Denver Art Museum*

This version of the tulip pattern has the simplicity and grace which characterize many of the quilts from the first half of the nineteenth century. Plain red-and-yellow cotton combine with a quaint and unusual yellow-green fabric printed with feathery fern sprays. The quilting has diagonal lines only a half-inch apart. Measures 74 by 89 inches.

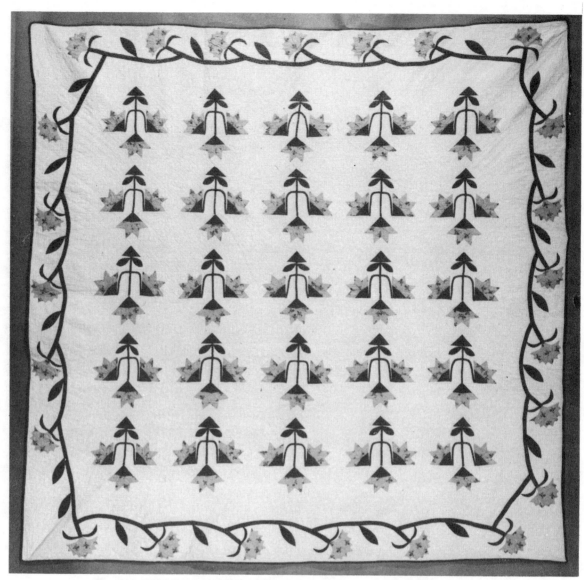

Fig. 113. Virginia or North Carolina Lily—*Courtesy of Denver Art Museum*

A pattern of many names, this basic lily form can be a flower, crown, or footprint. The names run through varieties of lilies to Cross-and-Crown, Bear Tracks, Duck Tracks, and Duck-in-the-Mud. A combination of piecing and appliqué, the pattern in whatever form is always crisp and elegant. In this instance the choice of calicoes for the lily and leaf are most appropriate; the lily is a tawny yellow, printed with a red-and-brown spray, and the leaves and stems are in green calico resembling the dogtooth violet leaf, flecked with brown. It is closely quilted in the older style, and bound with the green print. Measures 78 by 81 inches.

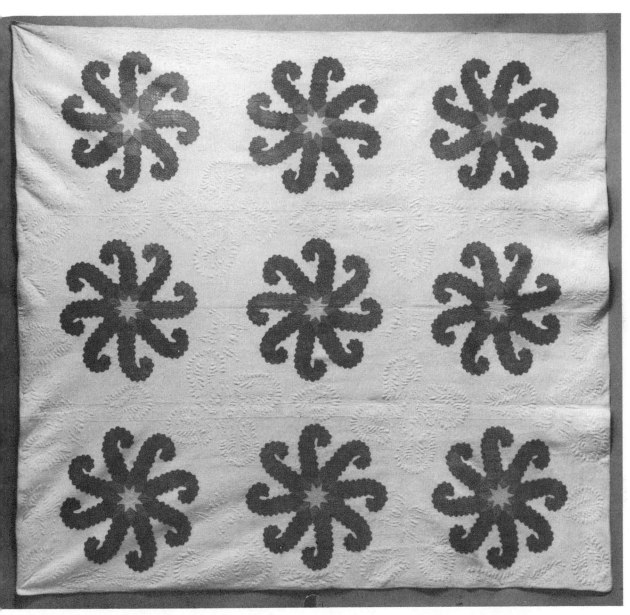

Fig. 114. Ben Hur's Chariot Wheels, 1825-1850—*Courtesy of Denver Art Museum*

Though faded and mellowed with time, this large spread from the early nineteenth century remains amazingly beautiful. The red and green calico of the wheels and the yellow of the hub have softened with age so that against the ivoried ground they have a special richness. It is an outstanding example of closeness of quilting. Between the padded leaf forms and even across the appliqué there are lines and lines of running stitch, often a mere eighth of an inch apart: Measures 82 by 100 inches.

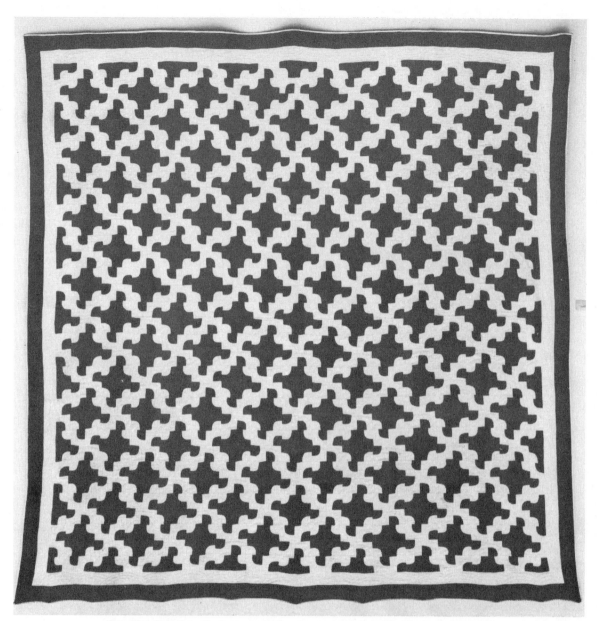

Fig. 115. Drunkard's Path, 1825-1850—*Courtesy of Denver Art Museum*

This pattern is formed by transposing cut pieces alternately from square to square. This pieced quilt in "Turkey red" is an excellent example of this technique. As interpreted in red and white, the resulting chain effect is most decorative. The quilting follows simple lines which a housewife might have been able to accomplish in her spare time. Measures 86 inches square.

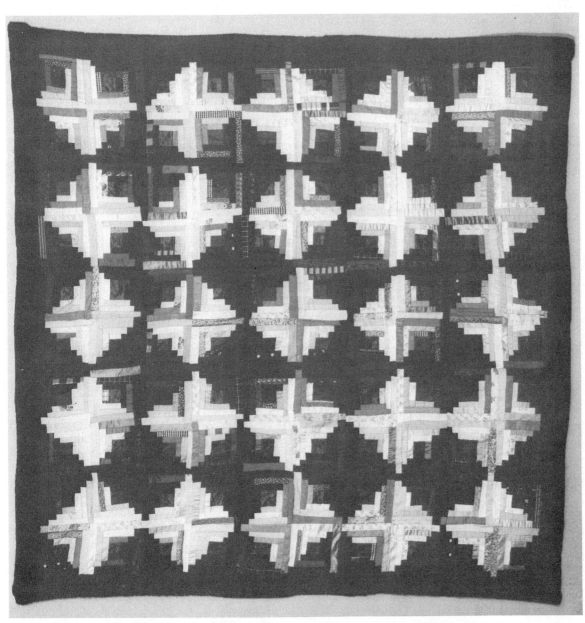

Fig. 116. Log Cabin, 1890—*Courtesy of Denver Art Museum*

One of the oldest designs for a pieced quilt, usually seen without a border, is here firmly outlined with a band of black plush. In contrast with early colonial days when sturdier materials would probably have been used, only silk occurs in this one, emphasized with a deep garnet satin in each center square. Measures 69 inches square.

Fig. 117. Flower Basket, 1825-1850—*Courtesy of Denver Art Museum*

A definite effort was made to obtain slanting lines across the basket by quilting across the grain. A form of Whig Rose occurs in the center. There is a vine border which has not come out evenly. Blanket stitch outlines the flowers, among which it would be difficult to select a favorite since all have charms; there are no repeats. Measures 77 inches square.

Fig. 118. Quilt with English Wood Block Border, 1806—*Courtesy of Denver Art Museum*

This quilt was made in New York. The wood block border, probably with some hand painting added, was directly influenced by the printed cottons of India. Apparently, the quilt was washed many times, judging by the center section, where the original vine design that wound among the small bouquets has almost completely vanished. Yet the border colors remain as clean and fresh as ever. Interlocking fan shapes are minutely quilted in the center, and diamond patterns in the border. The spread is lined with cotton; in its center embroidered in black thread are the initials "M. L." for Maria Lush, married in Albany, New York, in 1806. Measures 83 by 90 inches.

Fig. 119. English Wood Block and Copper Plate Prints—*Courtesy of Denver Art Museum*

Beautiful old English fabrics are preserved in a quilt which was in the Biddle Reeves family for 150 years. An example of the European type of spread, it is composed of large sections of rare old prints and toiles. The Shakespearean scene in the center could be from the hand of the designer of the better-known eighteenth-century print *Penn's Treaty with the Indians*. The farm scenes are close to the style of a printer known as John Collins of Woolmers, Hertfordshire, who dated his work 1765. Above the center still another copper plate design is of seashells and garlands reminiscent of the tapestries of like extravagance. Though the remainder of the center band with its striped block prints seems to have been pieced in strips, actual joining of fragments occurs only in the floral-patterned frames which surround the trees. The spread is lined with hand-woven linen and lightly quilted in diamond squares. Measures 75 by 95 inches.

Fig. 120. Pieced Quilt, 1865—*Courtesy of Denver Art Museum*

Double X, Anvil, and Jacob's Ladder all are suggested by this design, though none is actually reproduced. Very quaint old calicoes—red leaves on black, soft grays with paisley-type patterns, dark blue with white scrolled leaves—combined with dark blue print for the alternate squares, are used in the piecing. The quilting was done at home with the Hanging Diamond pattern. Measures 74 by 74 inches.

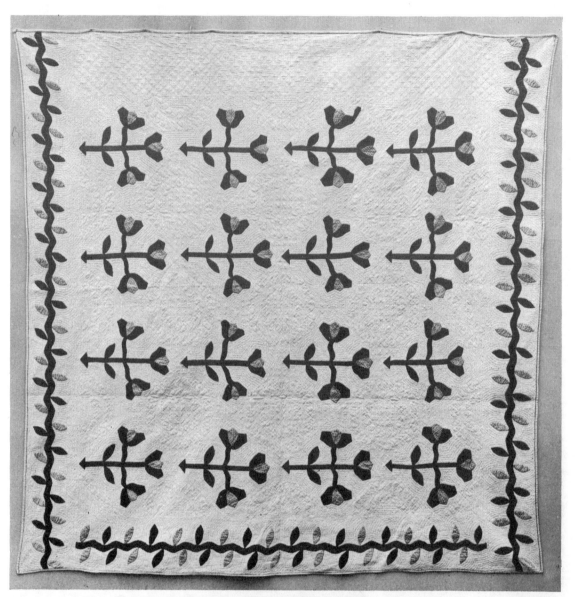

Fig. 121. Tulip Design, 1862—*Courtesy of Denver Art Museum*

Quaintly placed tulip sprays, all crossing from left to right across the bed, characterize this old quilt from the middle of the nineteenth century. The favored oil calico forms the leaves and border vine, combined with one rose-colored print. Many of the older spreads left the top border undecorated, a practice rarely seen in the later quilts. Closely followed outlines of leaf and flower forms, interspersed with feather circle, comprise the quilting. Measures 82 by 86 inches.

Fig. 122. Peony, 1863—*Courtesy of Denver Art Museum*

The embroidered label claims that Mrs. Cline rode twenty miles on horseback to obtain what was called in those days "oil calico"—a cotton noted for its fast dye. In this quilt the red, green, orange, and yellow are all of this fabric and the colors after many washings are still brilliant. The peony, like the tulip, was the inspiration for countless patterns and reappears under different names in many parts of the country. In this version the flowers are clipped from a pattern formed of a double diamond. Measures 70 by 77 inches.

Fig. 123. An Indian Pattern, 1855—*Courtesy of Denver Art Museum*

Over 115 years have passed since Mrs. Cline made this copy of Mary Jane Maxwell's quilt in Knightstown, Indiana. It is an old colonial pattern similar to the Whig Rose, but unusual in that the roses are placed on stems joined to the border, causing it to seem an integral part of the design. The materials in the roses—red and green calico and red gingham—probably were saved from the first half of the nineteenth century. The outer heavy looped design is in green calico with rose-print bow-knots. Measures 73 by 82 inches.

Fig. 124. Crazy Quilt—*Courtesy of Denver Art Museum*

The fabrics in this quilt may date from 1850 or even earlier, for they were given to Mrs. Whitehill (the maker of the quilt) by her grandmother, who died in 1882. Many pieces hold special memories for her; the red-and-white polka dot is part of a favorite dress which she wore as a child, and a flowered brown is from her grandmother's cape. Lined with pieced squares of curious old woolen materials, this quilt probably comes very close in type to those made by the early settlers from their cloth scraps. Using textile designs characteristic of the nineteenth century, the top surface combines silk and velvet, wool and cotton, with feather stitching neatly covering most of the seams. Measures 72 by 92 inches.

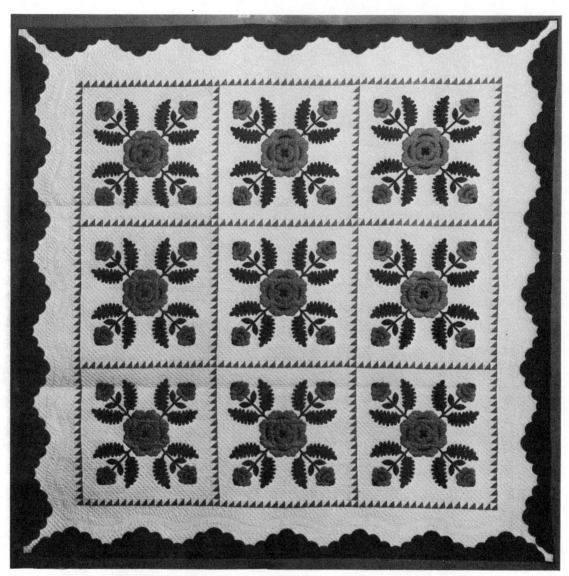

Fig. 125. Oriental Poppy, 1937—*Courtesy of Denver Art Museum*

A fragment of this pattern was found in a hope chest in a partly burned house in Chicago after the fire of 1871. It is a wonderfully stylized rendering of a poppy design, made even stronger by the addition of the massive blue-green frame. Rose calico forms the poppies, sharpened by dark red in the slashings. Piece saw-tooth lines in rose calico separate the squares, and a trim line of the same rose tone edges the inner scallop of the frame. Close quilting of diamond squares covers the entire quilt with the exception of the feather band in the border. Measures 85 inches square.

Fig. 126. Autumn Leaf, 1934—*Courtesy of Denver Art Museum*

An exact copy of a quilt exhibited at the Chicago World's Fair in 1893, except that where pink was its basic color, this example has yellow. Leaf shapes cut from calico were donated by friends, so that in the 115 leaves in the center, no printed cotton repeats. Padded quilting is worked into the bands of yellow, and folds of fabric form a saw-tooth border. It is a complicated design, gay and busy, far removed from the earlier patterns of the same name. Measures 89 inches square.

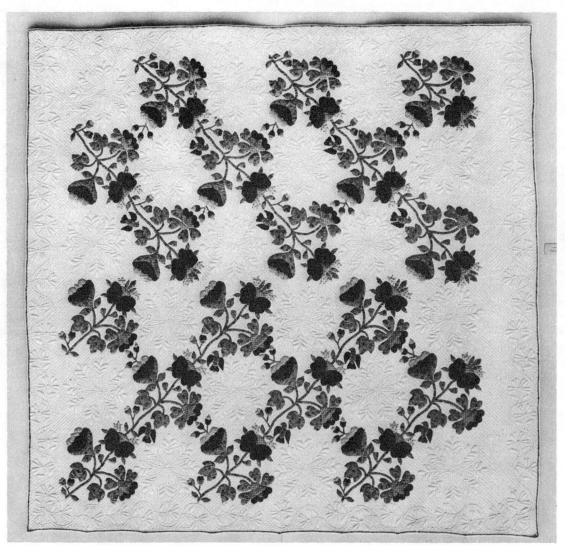

Fig. 127. Martindale Pattern, 1933—*Courtesy of Denver Art Museum*

An embroidered label on the back of the quilt says: "An old pattern from Aunt Martha Shaw, Carlyle, Ohio, about 1840. Pattern owned by the Martindale family." It is a pattern of great verve. The gray-green percale was ordered from Canada, since the Ohio stores could provide none that would serve. It was a happy choice, contributing much gaiety as combined with the bright red and yellow calico of the flowers, and the lavender print and rose gingham of the buds. The printed fabric is offset by added attention to the quilting, padded after the completion of the running stitch. Measures 84 inches square.

Fig. 128. Flower Basket, 1932—*Courtesy of Denver Art Museum*

The original of this version of the Flower Basket was made in 1857 by Mrs. Clara Weaver, mother of the Ida Irwin who lent the family quilt for copying. As in many of the older quilts, beautiful use is made of the background spaces. The blocks holding the four baskets are set diagonally, and, as if to maintain these forms in space, the small squares of the quilted lines establish a firm lattice behind them. Though green calico was one of the most difficult to obtain, the two chosen for this design are most fortunate. The basket print has a yellow stripe on the green, which suggests texture and gives lightness. The border scallop is in a yellow-green percale, very old in feeling, helping to place the pattern back in time. Every dark red cherry of the border was carefully padded before appliquéing. The quilt measures 90 inches square.

Fig. 129. Steeple Chase, 1865—*Courtesy Denver Art Museum*

Twenty different dark blue-and-white percales and calicoes are used in the piecing of this quilt, and almost as many variations of white materials. Three of the blue prints hold special interest and may have been saved from many years past—one with a twisted lace motif, another of a curling leaf, and a third with a shadowy flower spray—all with the quality of resist printing. The Steeple Chase pattern is based on simple transposition of quarter-circle from square to square. Measures 69 by 81 inches.

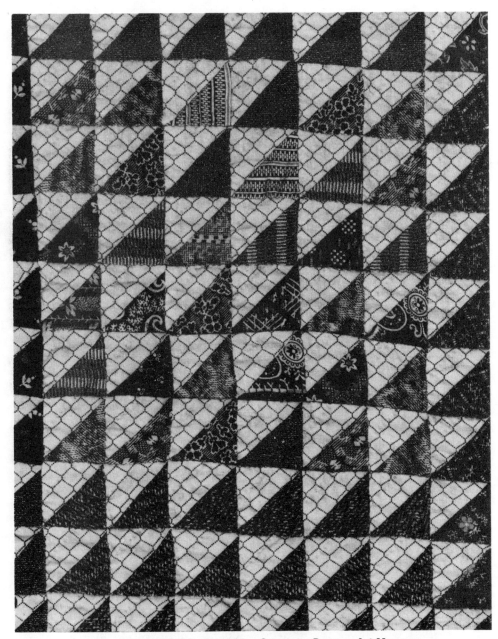

Fig. 130. Pieced Quilt, 1883—*Courtesy Denver Art Museum*

This quilt contains 17,424 pieces. Squares an inch in size, cut diagonally and set in blocks of related tone, achieve the surface texture of a modern painting. Some of the triangles catch the light in recessed pockets; others project forward with the solidity of chiseled stone. Calicoes saved from Civil War days recall the wide-skirted cotton gowns of the fifties and the sixties. The entire underlining and the border, both of lavender calico, appear to contain the top surface as though it were inlaid mosaic. Measures 76 inches square.

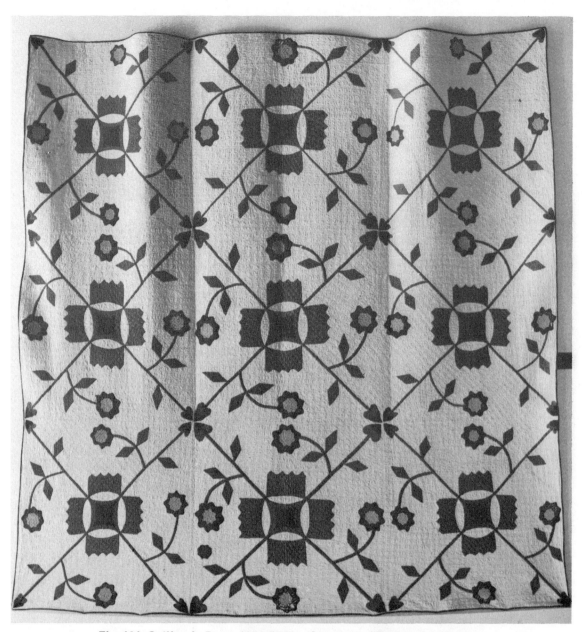

Fig. 131. California Rose, 1825-1850—*Courtesy of Denver Art Museum*

Whig Rose, Democrat Rose, Tea Rose—the name depends on the section of the country where the quilt was made. Since this comes from Fayette County in Pennsylvania, where the name Democrat Rose was favored, possibly it bore that name. It is a smaller quilt, made to fit the three-quarter-width bed introduced in the early part of the nineteenth century. The red, blue, and yellow fabrics are as fresh and bright as the day the quilt was made. A spool was used for the quilting markings, resulting in hundreds of little interlocking circles. Measures 72 inches square.

**Fig. 132. Friendship Quilt, 1848—*Courtesy of the St. Louis Art Museum,
gift of Mrs. Stratford Lee Morton***

It is cotton, appliquéd and quilted. It also employs embroidery and sepia ink. Measures 100 by 99 inches.

Fig. 133. Coverlet, 1807-1809—*Courtesy of the St. Louis Art Museum*

This coverlet was made by John Hewson, printer who worked in Philadelphia ca. 1773-1822. It is printed and quilted cotton. Measures 116⅓ by 112¼ inches.

Fig. 134. Appliqué Quilt—*Courtesy of Museum of Fine Arts, Boston*
This quilt was made in Georgia ca. 1900.

Fig. 135. Patchwork and Embroidered Bed Quilt—*Courtesy of Museum of Fine Arts, Boston*

This quilt is said to have been made by Miss Celestine Bacheller, of Wyoma, Massachusetts, sometime between 1850 and 1900.

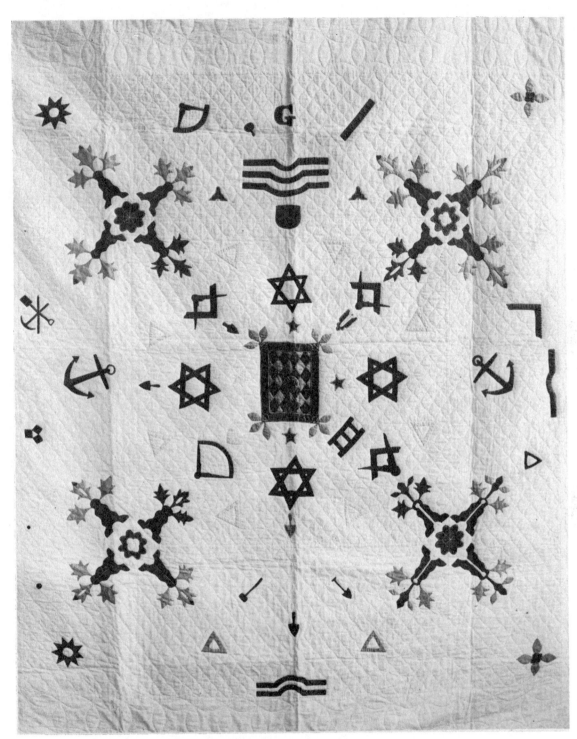

Fig. 136. Masonic Quilt, 1856—*Courtesy of Newark Museum*
The quilt is calico on a muslin ground and measures 68 by 76 inches.

Fig. 137. Friendship Quilt, 1876—*Courtesy of Newark Museum*

Fig. 138. Hawaiian Quilt—*Courtesy of Honolulu Academy of Arts, gift of Mr. Damon Giffard*

This breadfruit design quilt dates from the late nineteenth or early twentieth century. The design is appliquéd in yellow on red cotton ground. Back is cream-colored cotton. Measures 78 by 83 inches.

Fig. 139. Patchwork Quilt, 1876-1883—*Courtesy of Cincinnati Art Museum*

This is an American quilt, measuring approximately 64 by 62 inches. It is all silk with varicolored floss feather stitching around each piece. The wide border is dark red satin with meandering ribbon flowers and chenille leaves. There is a square of the same in the center; also some gathered satin flowers. Nettie Milan started the quilt when she was fifteen years of age in 1876 and finished it when she married Dr. Marshall Beaty in 1883. It is the gift of Mrs. V. M. Kunkel, niece of the maker.

Fig. 140. American Quilt, 1850—*Courtesy of Cincinnati Art Museum,*
gift of Misses Alice and Kate Neave

The quilt is approximately 101 inches long and 110 inches wide, including the 4-inch fringe. The material is all-white cotton with white linen backing. The quilting is stuffed and corded in a pattern of grapes, pineapples, palms, etc. There is a knotted cotton fringe on three sides.

Fig. 141. Patchwork Quilt for a Large Bed—*Courtesy of Baltimore County Historical Society, Inc.*
The quilt was pieced together with no design in mind. It is not quilted.

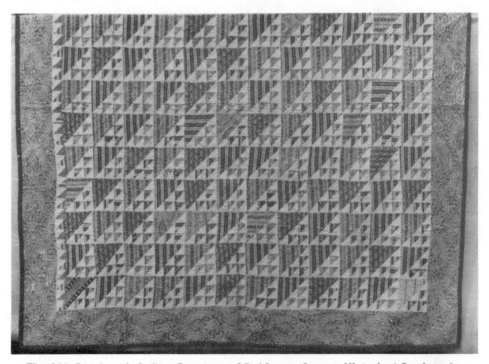

Fig. 142. Patchwork Quilt—*Courtesy of Baltimore County Historical Society, Inc.*
Quilted paisley cotton material was used for the border and some of the squares. The pattern seems to be an original one based on Old Maid. Measures 77 by 69 inches.

Fig. 143. Nine-Square Patchwork Quilt for Child's Bed—
Courtesy of Baltimore County Historical Society, Inc.

This quilt has a white background with an orange border. Measures 64 by 50 inches.

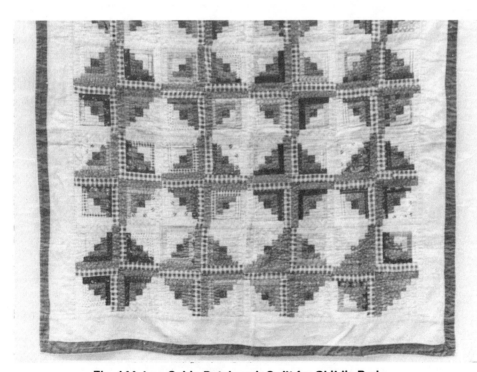

Fig. 144. Log Cabin Patchwork Quilt for Child's Bed—
Courtesy of Baltimore County Historical Society, Inc.

The quilt is 43 inches square, has a narrow red border, and dates from ca. 1890.

Fig. 145. Crazy Quilt or Parlor Throw—*Courtesy of Baltimore County Historical Society, Inc.*

This appliqué and patchwork quilt, measuring 5 feet by 5 feet, was made by Mina Antoinette Barrington Chew in 1888. She lived in Baltimore until her marriage to Mr. Chew. The dark red velvet border is 5 inches wide. Velvet, silk, calico, and wool were used. They were sewed together in a crazy fashion, usually on an inner lining as a help in holding the pieces together while they were being sewed. Mrs. Chew used different types of embroidery. The quilt contains some hand-painted blocks, some with names and the date embroidered on them. It was not quilted but tacked with bows of ribbon on the underside.

Fig. 146. Jacquard Double Weave Coverlet, ca. 1843—
Courtesy of Baltimore County Historical Society, Inc.

The design is a double rose with bird border. Colors are blue, red, and tan on dark natural. The inscription "Middletown Frederick County Maryland Joshua Corick" appears in two corners. Measures about 94 by 80 inches.

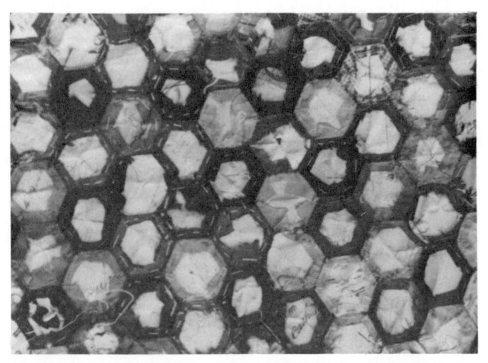

Fig. 147. Hexagon or Honeycomb Quilt—*Courtesy of Baltimore County Historical Society, Inc.*

The entire quilt cover is composed of hexagonal patches, pieced together. It is all silk and measures 75 by 52 inches. Each piece is based on a hexagonal piece of brown paper, and old letters and even some bits of old stamps show. The bottom picture shows the underside magnified so you can see how the material was attached to the paper pieces.

Fig. 148. Baltimore Bride's Quilt, 1846—*Courtesy of the Peale Museum, Baltimore*

Fig. 149. Patchwork Quilt—*Courtesy of the Cleveland Museum of Art, gift of Vera Esther La Dow*

This quilt has squares of calico patchwork with appliqué on a ground of white cotton. It was made in the United States ca. 1857. The colors are greens, pinks, red, and buff on white. Measures 84½ by 82 inches.

Fig. 150. Variation of Lily or Tulip Design—*Courtesy of Detroit Historical Museum*

The design consists of appliquéd orange and red flowers on green stems in green pots. Green crescents joined with red bows comprise the border.

Fig. 150. Variation of Lily or Tulip Design *(cont.)*

Fig. 151. Political Campaign Crazy Quilt—*Courtesy of Detroit Historical Museum*

Fig. 151. Political Campaign Crazy Quilt *(cont.)*

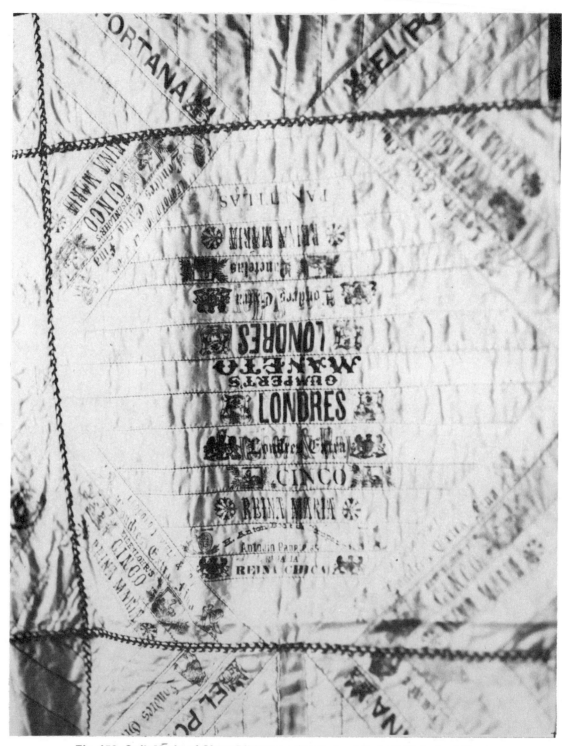

Fig. 152. Quilt Made of Cigar Ribbons—*Courtesy of Detroit Historical Museum*

This quilt, measuring 54 by 65 inches, was made ca. 1904.

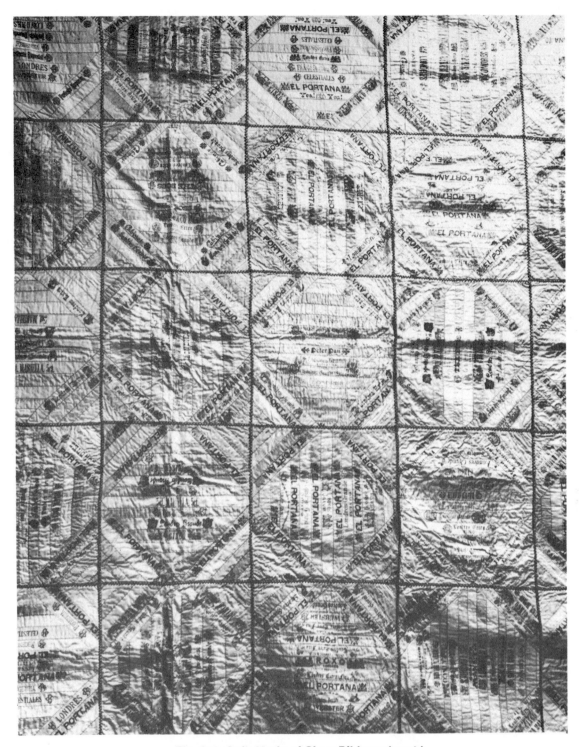

Fig. 152. Quilt Made of Cigar Ribbons *(cont.)*

341

Acknowledgments

The author would like to thank the following persons who gave me permission to use material that they had developed for their own purposes:

Patricia Almy
Nimble Needle Treasures
Almy Publications

Betty James
Betty James Originals

Bonnie Leman
Leman Publications
Heirloom Plastics

Eleanor Spencer
McCall's Needlework & Crafts Magazine

Marilyn Califf
Contemporary Quilts

Dennis B. Schmidt
Taylor Bedding Mfg. Co.

Peg Zercher
Kutztown Folk Festival

The author would also like to thank those persons who responded so generously to my request for photographs of quilts that they had made or that were in their museums.

Resource Material

SUPPLIERS

Aunt Martha's Studios, Inc.
North Kansas City, Missouri 64116
Patterns

Contemporary Quilts
5305 Denwood
Memphis, Tennessee 38117
Kits and patterns

Mrs. Danner's Quilts
P.O. Box 650
Emporia, Kansas 66801
Patterns

House of Patterns
726 Benton
Valley Park, Missouri 63088
Patterns

Huckabone Tops
Box 273
North Troy, Vermont 05859
Quilt tops

Quality Quilting
Stover, Missouri 65078
Quilting

Mrs. Bobbie Morton
P.O. Box 184
Virgil, Kansas 66870
Patterns

Quilts of Appalachia
1021 Carolina
Bristol, Tennessee 37620
Patterns

Stearns & Foster Company
Box 960
Rosemount, Minnesota 55068
Kits, batting, hoops

Sue's Custom Quilting
3010 East Harry
Wichita, Kansas 67211
Custom quilting

Taylor Bedding Mfg. Co.
Taylor, Texas 76574
Supplies

Use "M" Up Co.
4411 Elston Avenue
Chicago, Illinois 60630

McCall's Needlework & Crafts Magazine
230 Park Avenue
New York, New York 10017
Patterns

Pursenalities, Inc.
1619 Grand Avenue
Baldwin, New York 11510
Patterns and handles for handbags

Betty James Originals
P.O. Box 774
Severna Park, Maryland 21146
Potholders and other supplies

Heirloom Plastics
Leman Publications
Box 394
Wheat Ridge, Colorado 80033
Patterns, designs, templates

PUBLICATIONS

Nimble Needle Treasures
Almy Publications
Box 1082
Sapulpa, Oklahoma 74066

Quilters' Newsletter
Leman Publications
Box 394
Wheat Ridge, Colorado 80033

Tower Press, Inc.
Box 428
Seabrook, New Hampshire 03874

Aunt Martha's Studios, Inc.
North Kansas City, Missouri 64116

McCall's Needlework & Crafts Magazine
230 Park Avenue
New York, New York 10017

PLACES TO PURCHASE QUILTS

American Hurrah Antiques
316 East 70th Street
New York, New York 10021

American Quilts
136 East 64th Street
New York, New York 10021

Cabin Creek
P.O. Box 295
Oakvale, West Virginia 24739

Margaret Cavigga
18065 Sunburst Street
Northridge, California 91324

Elder Craftsmen Showcase
850 Lexington Avenue
New York, New York 10021

Fox and Geese Quilt Shop
Lemasters, Pennsylvania 17231

The Freedom Quilting Bee
Rt. 1, Box 72
Alberta, Alabama 36720

The Gazebo
14th East 57th Street
New York, New York 10022

Hands All Around
Wharam Wharf
Mystic, Connecticut 06355

Kelter-Malce
361 Bleecker Street
New York, New York 10014

Kilkenny Shop
900 North Point
San Francisco, California 94109

Leman's Quilts
5315 W. 38th Avenue
Denver, Colorado 80212

Measures Workshop
703 N. Midkiff
Midland, Texas 79701

Mountain Artisans, Inc.
147 Summers Street
Charleston, West Virginia 25301

Mountain Cabin Quilts
Effingham, Illinois 62401

Needle in the Haystack Country Things
P.O. Box 351
Grand Island, Illinois

New York Exchange for Woman's Work
541 Madison Avenue
New York, New York 10022

Nonesuch, Ltd.
1023 Lexington Avenue
New York, New York 10021

Patch-works
770 Madison Avenue
New York, New York 10021

Peaceable Kingdom
390 Bleecker Street
New York, New York 10014

Porthault Linens
55 East 57th Street
New York, New York 10022

Powers Crossroads Country Fair
Franklin Road, Rt. 1
Newman, Georgia

Quilt Gallery
55 East 86th Street
New York, New York 10028

Real Tinsel
137 Ludlow Street
New York, New York 10002

Josephine Rogers
32 West 82nd Street
New York, New York 10024

Ryther House Gallery
Bernardston, Massachusetts 01337

George E. Schoellkopf
1065 Madison Avenue
New York, New York 10028

Lynne Spiegel
151 Raymond Street
Cambridge, Massachusetts 02140

Sunshine Lane
Box 262
Millersburg, Ohio 44654

Taylor and Ng
651 Howard Street
San Francisco, California 94105

West of the Moon
3464 Sacramento Street
San Francisco, California 94118

QUILTS ON DISPLAY

Abby Aldrich Rockefeller Folk Art
Collection
Williamsburg, Virginia

Antiquarian and Landmarks Society, Inc.
Hartford, Connecticut

Baltimore County Historical Society, Inc.
Cockeysville, Maryland

Bedford Historical Society
Bedford, New York

Brooklyn Museum
Brooklyn, New York

Bostonian Society
Boston, Massachusetts

Bucks County Historical Society
Doylestown, Pennsylvania

Charleston Museum
Charleston, South Carolina

Cincinnati Art Museum
Cincinnati, Ohio

Cleveland Museum of Art
Cleveland, Ohio

Colonial Williamsburg
Williamsburg, Virginia

Connecticut Historical Society
Hartford, Connecticut

Cortland County Historical Society
Cortland, New York

Daughters of the American Revolution
Museum
Washington, District of Columbia

Denver Art Museum
Denver, Colorado

Detroit Historical Museum
Detroit, Michigan

Erie County Historical Federation
Cheektowaga, New York

Essex Institute
Salem, Massachusetts

Genesee County Museum
Mumford, New York

Greenfield Village and Henry Ford Museum
Dearborn, Michigan

Gunston Hall
Lorton, Virginia

Hennepin County Historical Society
Minneapolis, Minnesota

Henry Francis du Pont Winterthur Museum
Winterthur, Delaware

Historical Deerfield, Inc.
Deerfield, Massachusetts

Historical Society of Delaware
Wilmington, Delaware

Honolulu Academy of Arts
Honolulu, Hawaii

Hudson River Museum
Yonkers, New York

Kentucky Historical Society
Frankfort, Kentucky

Ladies' Hermitage Association
Hermitage, Tennessee

Litchfield Historical Society
Litchfield, Connecticut

Louisiana State Museum
New Orleans, Louisiana

Lyman Allyn Museum
New London, Connecticut

Massillon Museum
Massillon, Ohio

Metropolitan Museum of Art
American Wing
New York, New York

Mount Vernon Ladies' Association
    of the Union
Mount Vernon, Virginia

Museum of Fine Arts
Boston, Massachusetts

Newark Museum
Newark, New Jersey

New Hampshire Historical Society
Concord, New Hampshire

New Jersey Historical Society
Newark, New Jersey

New York Historical Society
New York, New York

Oaklands Associations, Inc.
Murfreesboro, Tennessee

Oklahoma Historical Society
Oklahoma City, Oklahoma

Old Economy Village
Ambridge, Pennsylvania

Old Gaol Museum
York, Maine

Old Salem
Winston-Salem, North Carolina

Old Slave-Mart Museum
Charleston, South Carolina

Old Sturbridge Village
Sturbridge, Massachusetts

Peale Museum
Baltimore, Maryland

Pennsylvania Farm Museum of
    Landis Valley
Lancaster, Pennsylvania

Philadelphia Museum of Art
Philadelphia, Pennsylvania

St. Louis Art Museum
St. Louis, Missouri

Shelburne Museum, Inc.
Shelburne, Massachusetts

Stamford History Society, Inc.
Stamford, Connecticut

Valentine Museum
Richmond, Virginia

Wadsworth Atheneum
Hartford, Connecticut

Western Reserve Historical Society
Cleveland, Ohio

Witte Memorial Museum
San Antonio, Texas

Yale University Art Gallery
New Haven, Connecticut

Index

(*Note:* Page numbers in italics refer to illustrations.)